construction arbitration:
selected readings

MARGARET GIBBONS &
LINDA M. MILLER,
EDITORS

1981

**AMERICAN
ARBITRATION
ASSOCIATION**

Price: $10, AAA dues-paying members
$15, nonmembers

Library of Congress Catalog Card Number:
81-67636

ORDER FROM:
American Arbitration Association
140 West 51st Street
New York, New York 10020

CONTENTS

PREFACE

Arbitration of construction disputes is not a new concept in the United States. As early as the 1800s, arbitration provisions appeared in construction contracts. Builders had, even then, begun to recognize that courts were overcrowded and not too knowledgeable about construction problems.

The American Institute of Architects' (AIA) "General Conditions of the Contract for the Construction of Buildings" provided for the resolution of construction disputes through arbitration. The parties selected either an ad hoc, party-appointed system or administration under the Commercial Arbitration Rules of the American Arbitration Association (AAA). This AIA provision seemed ideal because it gave the parties an option, but in practice it was a Hobson's choice: neither alternative was good. The need to decide between AIA's party-appointed system or AAA-administered arbitration sometimes created delay in initiating a claim. In addition, the party-appointed system could be stalled, and the AAA had not yet recruited enough construction experts. Neither procedure was perfect.

In 1964, an AIA-AGC (Associated General Contractors) liaison committee initiated a survey as to the effectiveness of arbitration procedures. After reviewing their members' experience under both systems, a recommendation was made to designate the AAA as the sole administrator of an arbitration procedure to be custom tailored for the construction industry. A National Construction Industry Arbitration Committee (NCIAC) was formed representing the following organizations: American Consulting Engineers Council (then the Consulting Engineers Council); American Institute of Architects; Associated General Contractors; Associated Specialty Contractors, Inc. (then Council of Mechanical Specialty Contracting Industries); and National Society of Professional Engineers.

After a thorough study by the NCIAC, the Construction Industry Arbitration Rules were adopted, with the AAA as administrator, providing a uniform, nationwide set of procedures for the industry. A specialized panel, made up of construction practitioners and professionals, was recruited and approved by local advisory committees. Today more than 18,000 arbitrators, drawn from all segments of the construction industry, serve on the AAA's national construction panel. More than 100 categories of expertise are represented.

The NCIAC serves as an advisory body to the AAA, meeting regularly to ensure that the Construction Industry Arbitration Rules remain responsive to the needs of the construction community. With the expansion of the NCIAC membership to include the American Society of Civil Engineers, American Society of Landscape Architects, American Subcontractors Association, Construction Specifications Institute, and the National Utility Contractors Association, Inc., ten national construction associations actively monitor this arbitration system.

American companies in the construction industry continue to discover that it is good business to arbitrate. In 1966, the first year of the AAA Construction Industry Arbitration Rules, 460 construction arbitrations were administered by the AAA. By 1980, the AAA's construction caseload had grown to 2,831.

The use of arbitration is also increasing in the international arena. As American companies expand their market to other jurisdictions, they find that the uncertainties of foreign law tip the scales in favor of arbitration. This is particularly true when projects must be carried out in foreign countries.

Arbitration provides a practical alternative to litigation in the courts. Since construction industry professionals routinely try to settle their disputes by negotiation, it is helpful to have a fallback mechanism. Arbitration allows parties to submit unresolved issues to an impartial member of their own industry for a final and binding decision. Arbitration is an industry forum. The outcome is determined by someone who has a practical understanding of the controversy, including the customs of the trade, the contractual relationships between the parties, and the ever-increasing technological background. There is less need in arbitration to "educate the bench," which is so frequently necessary with a judge or jury.

Arbitration can be a speedy way to resolve construction industry disputes, although the pace may depend upon the parties. Whether they include an arbitration clause in their contract documents or file a case under a submission agreement once a dispute occurs, arbitration is a consensual process, and the proceedings are private. The active participation of the parties governs how smoothly their arbitration proceeds from its initiation to the decision. Arbitration results in awards that are final and binding.

A major service of the AAA, in addition to case administration, is to educate the people involved in the arbitration process. In cooperation with the member organizations of the NCIAC, the AAA's Department of Education and Training provides seminars and arbitrator training sessions. Literature and films that update construction industry professionals on the dispute settlement procedures are available through the Association's Publications Department.

This book is a collection of professional journal articles, conference papers, and AAA educational materials on dispute resolution in the construction industry. It offers a realistic look at arbitration and at mediation, another settlement process available through the AAA. Certain aspects of the process are noted that require special attention. The articles offer a wide range of viewpoints about how to make arbitration work for you.

Not all of the opinions expressed are necessarily shared by the AAA. But many valuable points are made, presenting a well-rounded look at factors that should be considered. It is our hope that the reader will gain a better understanding of the important role that arbitration plays in the construction industry.

ROBERT COULSON
President
American Arbitration Association

Arbitration and Mediation: The Modern Approach to Resolving Construction Disputes

MICHAEL F. HOELLERING

The need for effective machinery for the resolution of contract disputes is of importance to every participant in a new construction project. Experience has shown that with large projects, changing conditions on the construction site, advancing technology, and the complicated interrelationships between owner, architect, engineer, contractor, subcontractor, and supplier, disputes over contract performance are almost inevitable. How quickly and effectively they can be resolved between the parties often determine the ability to successfully complete the work required by the contract documents, meet established time schedules, and receive payment for the work performed.

Since 1880, when early owner-contractor agreements first provided for disputes to be resolved by a panel of three disinterested arbitrators, the use of arbitration has grown throughout the industry. By 1966, arbitration had become the preferred mode of settlement, and all major segments of the building community had provided for arbitration between owners, architects, engineers, general contractors, and subcontractors. The standard form contracts of the American Institute of Architects, the Associated General Contractors, and the National Society of Professional Engineers now contain the following arbitration clause:

> All claims, disputes and other matters in question between the contractor and the owner arising out of, or relating to, the contract documents or the breach thereof . . . shall be decided by arbitration in accordance with the Construction Industry Arbitration Rules of the American Arbitration Association then obtaining unless the parties mutually agree otherwise. [AIA document 201 (1976), para. 7.9]

Construction Caseload

How frequently contractors are engaged in arbitration is reflected by the AAA's caseload. During 1979 a total of 2,648 construction disputes, with claims totaling $175,314,945, were filed for arbitration pursuant to the Construction Industry Arbitration Rules.[1] In 2,345 of these cases, the contractor was a party to the proceeding. In 1,626, the dispute was with the owner; 489 were between contractors and subcontractors; and the remainder involved a combination of owners, subcontractors, architects, and engineers.

Geographically, the largest number of disputes was handled in Los Angeles (330), followed by Boston (187), San Francisco (175), Philadelphia (165), New Jersey (150), and Seattle (146). The remaining cases were distributed throughout the AAA's national network of regional offices. In 16 of the cases the parties were also in disagreement over where the arbitration was to be held and the Association had to determine the appropriate locale. The AAA's conclusive authority in that regard has been consistently upheld by the courts.

In terms of size, 872 of the cases involved claims of less than $10,000; 838 were in the $10,000–$50,000 range; 222 were between $50,000 and $100,000; 247 between $100,000 and $500,000; 35 between $500,000 and $1,000,000; and 10 were claims for more than $1,000,000. A total of 424 cases were undetermined at the time of filing, subject to subsequent disclosures as to the exact amount claimed.

Advantages

There are a number of reasons for the use of arbitration by the construction industry. Primary is that construction disputes often involve technical questions that can best be understood and decided by construction experts. Arbitration is also generally faster than litigation in resolving claims. While the largest construction cases often require extensive and protracted hearings, the vast majority of AAA construction cases are resolved within six to nine months. This is of particular importance to contractors seeking to collect money owed since the passing of time can significantly reduce the chances of a successful recovery. The costs of arbitration are usually reasonable and moderate compared to the cost of litigation. The proceeding is simpler, arbitrators may schedule hearings at the parties' convenience, and the entire process gives all participants greater flexibility in time, place of hearing, choice of decision makers, and with regard to special locale requirements.

The AAA construction tribunal is supervised by the National Construction Industry Arbitration Committee (NCIAC), which consists of representatives of the various industry and professional associations, and by regional advisory committees in 35 metropolitan areas across the country.[2]

The participating NCIAC organizations are the American Institute of Architects, the American Society of Civil Engineers, the American Society of Landscape Architects, the American Subcontractors Association, Associated Specialty Contractors, Construction Specifications Institute, American Consulting Engineers Council, Associated General Contractors of America, the National Society of Professional Engineers, and the National Utility Contractors Association.

Legal Enforcement

Both the existing legal framework and attitude of the courts reflect a strong public policy in favor of arbitration and the enforcement of arbitration agreements and awards. The Federal Arbitration Act and modern state arbitration laws in many jurisdictions[3] (see appendix), coupled with the AAA's Construction Industry Arbitration Rules,[4] serve to provide a cohesive, nationwide arbitral approach to the settlement of construction disputes. Since most construction contracts involve labor and materials crossing state lines, the benefits of the Federal Arbitration Act extend even to those few remaining jurisdictions which do not as yet enforce agreements to arbitrate future disputes. The following quotation from a recent federal court opinion in a complex construction case illustrates how judges tend to view construction arbitration:

> This court entertains grave doubts as to whether courts should monitor major construction contracts and should involve themselves in the multiplicity of disputes which might arise under such contracts . . . The court shares the view that it might be initiating a dangerous precedent if it involves itself in construction disputes when . . . there are ample provisions in the contract for arbitrating all of the various disputes . . . This is not the first construction contract in which the nerves of the owner and contractor have become taut, and certainly will not be the last, but the arbitration provisions of the contract are especially designed to alleviate this condition when disputes similar to those in this case arise, and the court cannot urge too strongly that the use of arbitration for future disputes should be compelled.[5]

Expert Arbitrators

There are presently more than 17,000 arbitrators on the AAA's construction panel, without whose dedication and specialized knowledge of the industry the system could not function. Their backgrounds are representative of all segments of the industry and include attorneys specializing in construction and related fields. Every effort is being made by the AAA to provide to the parties the most up-to-date information about these arbitrators so that they can select the most qualified individuals for their cases.

Since most construction arbitrators are not full-time adjudicators, annual arbitrator training programs, designed to supplement the information regularly provided to panelists, are conducted by the Association. Twenty-two such construction arbitrator development programs were held in 1979 in different parts of the country. Seasoned arbitrators and AAA staff discussed the causes of construction disputes, the arbitrator's powers, duties, and responsibilities, the conduct of hearings, and related subjects bearing on the arbitrator's role in construction arbitration.

The number of arbitrators assigned to a case is usually determined by the size of the claim. If the arbitration clause does not specify the number of arbitrators and the amount of claim is less than $50,000, the AAA generally designates a single arbitrator. Sometimes, of course, the parties stipulate that three arbitrators hear the case.

Pre-Arbitration Conferences

As indicated by the statistics, about 10 percent of the caseload is made up of large, complicated disputes involving substantial sums of money, a multitude of claims and counterclaims, and often issues of great complexity. In order to expedite the arbitration of these "heavy" cases, experienced AAA staff conduct pre-arbitration conferences with the parties and their counsel prior to the commencement of hearings in order to arrange for the exchange of bills of particulars, the stipulation of uncontested facts, and, whenever appropriate, the resolution for collateral issues by mediation.[6] Experience has shown that such conferences, when approached with a spirit of cooperation by the parties and their counsel, can be of great value in shortening what would otherwise be lengthy, protracted proceedings.

For example, in a case handled by the AAA's Los Angeles office, where it seemed at the outset that the hearings would require 15 full days, a pre-arbitration conference resulted in various stipulations as to the authenticity of documents that eliminated the need for the testimony of numerous witnesses, thereby reducing the actual hearing time to 5 days.

In another case in New York, which the parties estimated would take at least 37 days of hearings, the matter was disposed of in 6½ days of conferences and hearings. We urge the parties to request a pre-arbitration conference whenever they believe that it would serve to expedite a particular matter.

Consolidation of Proceedings

One of the questions that has been considered extensively by NCIAC is whether the construction rules should be amended to provide for the consolidation of multiple-party construction claims, where the same construction project but separate agreements between the parties are involved. The conclusion of NCIAC, based upon surveys which have shown that consolidation might be appropriate in some instances but not in others, was that the parties themselves should continue to regulate—either in their arbitration agreement or at the time of arbitration—the question of whether multiple claims involving the same construction project but separate construction agreements should be arbitrated jointly or separately.

At the present time, the AIA's Owner-Architect Agreement prohibits consolidation or joinder of additional parties without the written consent of all concerned parties. On the other hand, many agreements between owners and contractors expressly provide the right to implead separate contractors having contractual relationships with the owner, who in any manner may be involved in any arbitrable claim of the owner or contractor. Some of these agreements also contain provisions permitting consolidation of two or more related controversies involving the contractor, subcontractor, or other persons having contractual relations with the contractor.

AAA administrative policy on consolidation and joinder is to initiate the arbitration—be it the claim, counterclaim, or request to join additional parties—as filed by the moving party, even though separate contracts may be involved, thereby providing parties with an opportunity to proceed jointly if they so desire. Should one or more parties object to such a procedure, the cases will be separated and individually processed unless a court orders otherwise. Separately instituted cases may be consolidated whenever all parties mutually agree or consolidation is ordered by the courts.

A review of court decisions indicates that, in the absence of specific contractual provisions, some courts, such as those in California,[7] New York,[8] Massachusetts,[9] and Minnesota,[10] are liberal in granting consolidation where the court feels that common issues are involved. In other states, such as Michigan[11] and New Jersey,[12] the decisions have been in favor of separate arbitrations when separate contracts are involved.

Public Construction

With increasing frequency, governmental entities as large construction owners are arbitrating public construction disputes. In several states arbitration is expressly provided for by statute. For example, highway and bridge disputes in Connecticut are referred to the AAA for purposes of arbitration. Public works disputes in Nevada are arbitrated pursuant to the Construction Industry Arbitration Rules of the AAA. Other states with express provisions for the arbitration of public construction disputes include California, Michigan, Minnesota, and Rhode Island.[13]

One of the largest federally funded construction projects to date is the Metropolitan Atlanta Rapid Transit Authority (MARTA). To assure federal officials that the project would proceed without incident and reduce the frequency of conflict over contract disputes, the authority agreed to assume part of the risk of performance and took measures to have the project proceed while disputes were being resolved. These steps, however, could not prevent all potential disagreements about differing interpretations of the contract. After considering a number of alternative dispute settlement procedures, MARTA executives settled on the use of arbitration under the Construction Industry Arbitration Rules.[14] One of the important objectives of arbitration was to assure contractors that conflicts involving interpretations of the contract and change-order problems would not be delayed or arbitrarily handled by the owner so as to require increased contract bids to guard against such eventuality.

Mediation

Despite arbitration's acknowledged success, the NCIAC has recently concluded that it would be desirable to provide an additional supplementary procedure that will serve the parties by resolving disputes in their early stages. This alternative—mediation—seeks to obviate the kind of preparations necessary for an arbitration or court proceedings which, being adversary in nature, tend to polarize the parties and harden them in their respective positions.

Mediation consists of the effort of an individual, or several individuals, to assist the parties in reaching the settlement of a controversy or claim by direct negotiation between and among themselves. The mediator participates impartially in the negotiations, advising and consulting the various parties involved. The result of the mediation should be an agreement that the parties find acceptable. The mediator cannot impose a settlement but can only seek to guide the parties to the achievement of their own settlement.

To implement this program, the NCIAC on February 1, 1980, published specially designed Construction Industry Mediation Rules.[15] The AAA's role is to administer the mediation process, teach mediation skills to selected members of the industry, and collect data on the results of mediation efforts and the costs involved.

The administrative fee for instituting mediation is $200 per party. Mediators are compensated at a reasonable daily rate agreeable to the parties. To preserve the privacy of the mediation proceeding, the rules expressly provide that nothing that transpires during mediation is intended in any way to affect the rights, or prejudice the position, of any of the parties in a subsequent arbitration or litigation.

Particular disputes may be submitted by the parties to mediation under AAA auspices by means of the following agreement:

> The parties hereby submit the following dispute to mediation under the Voluntary Construction Mediation Rules of the American Arbitration Association. The requirement of filing a notice of claim with respect to the dispute submitted to mediation shall be suspended until the conclusion of the mediation process.

The clause can also provide for the number of mediators, their compensation, method of payment, locale of meetings, and any other item of concern to the parties.

A very similar mediation program for roofing failures was also recently instituted under AAA auspices by the National Roofing Contractors Association and the Asphalt Roofing Manufacturers Association.[16] Resort to the time-tested technique of mediation to settle construction disputes is based on the belief that the potential for a mutually arrived at, less costly, and less time-consuming resolution will be welcome by owners, design professionals, general contractors, material suppliers, and contractors. The AAA's mediation services are available to parties regardless of whether arbitration is provided for in their basic construction documents.

Underground Disputes

Another significant development is the publication by the U.S. National Committee on Tunneling and Technology of "Recommended Procedures for Settlement of Underground Construction Disputes."[17] These procedures give parties, for the first time, the opportunity to experiment with a number of different dispute settlement techniques. Patterned on the AAA's Construction Industry Arbitration Rules and relying on AAA administration, they provide parties with a choice of five different techniques—the use of impartial or advisory committees for emerging problems, mediation, mediation-arbitration, final and binding arbitration, and nonbinding arbitration.

The use of nonbinding arbitration is recommended because it has been successfully employed by the construction industry in Europe with the provision that, while the determinations of the arbitrators are not binding, they are admissible in any subsequent proceedings between the parties. The European experience suggests that the parties do their best in the presentation of their cases and that, while the findings and conclusions of the arbitrator are not binding, they are usually accepted by the parties because of their admissibility in future court proceedings. The experience was the same when advisory arbitration was first introduced in the United States to deal with public sector labor-management impasses.

Especially unique among the proposed techniques is mediation-arbitration. As its name implies, it is a procedure that combines in a single individual the functions of a mediator and arbitrator. If the parties cannot resolve their dispute, the mediator-arbitrator is authorized to (1) meet with anyone connected with the dispute to investigate, inspect, or discover relevant facts, (2) call together all interested persons or parties for negotiating sessions, (3) retain engineers, attorneys, and technical experts for the purpose of obtaining independent advice concerning the dispute, (4) engage in mediation with the parties, either separately or together, (5) determine that certain issues are appropriate for arbitration, and (6) hold evidentiary hearings and issue a final and binding award on the remaining issues. Since the neutral would at times be deciding matters that have been dealt with in the give-and-take of settlement discussions, often in separate meetings without the presence of the other party, it would seem to be of critical importance that the chosen mediator-arbitrator be someone in whom all of the parties have the utmost confidence—not only to help them achieve settlement, but also to make final decisions on those issues that cannot be resolved during the mediation efforts.

Appendix

MODERN ARBITRATION STATUTES IN THE UNITED STATES
(as of June 1, 1981)

United States Arbitration Act 9, U.S.C.A. §1 *et seq.*

Alaska Stat. §09.43.010 *et seq.** (4).
Ariz. Rev. Stat. §12-1501 *et seq.** (4).

---

* Referred to as Uniform Arbitration Act. Numbers following the asterisk indicate statute exclusions as to: (1) Construction, (2) Insurance, (3) Leases, (4) Labor Contracts, (5) Loans, (6) Sales, (7) Torts, (8) Uninsured Motorists, (9) Doctors, Lawyers.

Ark. Stat. Ann. §34-511 *et seq.** (2, 4, 7).
Cal. Code Civ. Proc. §1280 *et seq.*
Colo. Rev. Stat. §13-22-201 *et seq.**
Conn. Gen. Stat. Ann. §52-408 *et seq.*
Del. Code Ann. Title 10, §5701 *et seq.** (4).
D.C. Law 1-117.*
Fla. Stat. Ann. §682.01 *et seq.*
Ga. Code Ann. §7-301 *et seq.*
Hawaii Rev. Stat. §658-1 *et seq.*
Idaho Code §7-901 *et seq.** (4).
Ill. Rev. Stat. Chap. 10, §101 *et seq.**
Ind. Code Ann. §34-4-2-1 *et seq.** (3, 5, 6).
Kan. Stat. §5-401 *et seq.** (2, 4, 7).
La. Rev. Stat. §9:4201 *et seq.** (4).
Me. Rev. Stat. Ann. Title 14, §5927 *et seq.** (8).
Md. Cts. & Jud. Proc. Code Ann. §3-201 *et seq.** (4).
Mass. Ann. Laws Chap. 251, §1 *et seq.** (4).
Mich. Comp. Laws §600.5001 *et seq.*
Minn. Stat. Ann. §572.08 *et seq.**
Miss. S.B. 2036, Chap. 495, Laws of 1981.
Mo. Ann. Stat. §435.350 *et seq.**
Mo. Ann. Stat. §435.350 *et seq.**
Nev. Rev. Stat. §38.015 *et seq.**
N.H. Rev. Stat. Ann. §542:1 *et seq.*
N.J. Stat. Ann. §2A:24-1 *et seq.*
N.M. Stat. Ann. §22-3-9 *et seq.**
N.Y. Civ. Prac. Law §7501 *et seq.*
N.C. Gen. Stat. §1-567.1 *et seq.** (4).
Ohio Rev. Code Ann. §2711.01 *et seq.*
Okla. Stat. Ann. Title 15, §801 *et seq.** (2, 4).
Or. Rev. Stat. §33.210 *et seq.*
Pa. Stat. Ann. Title 5, §161 *et seq.*
R.I. Gen. Laws §10-3-1 *et seq.*
S.C. Code §15-48-10 *et seq.** (2, 4, 7, 9).
S.D. Codified Laws §21-25A-1 *et seq.** (2).
Tex. Rev. Civ. Stat. Ann. Title 10, Art. 224 *et seq.** (1, 2, 4).
Utah Code Ann. §78-31-1 *et seq.*
Va. Code Ann. §8.01-577 *et seq.*
Wash. Rev. Code Ann. §7.04.010 *et seq.*
Wis. Stat. Ann. §298.01 *et seq.*
Wyo. Stat. §1-36-101 *et seq.**
See also Laws of Puerto Rico Ann. Title 32, §3201 *et seq.*

Notes

[1] These statistics are regularly kept by the American Arbitration Association.

[2] American Arbitration Association. "Construction Contract Disputes: How They May Be Resolved." New York: AAA, 1980.

[3] Modern statutes are those enforcing agreements to arbitrate existing controversies and any arising in the future. Other state arbitration statutes (for example, Alabama) apply to existing controversies only. (Code of Alabama, Chap. 19.)

⁴ American Arbitration Association. "Construction Industry Arbitration Rules (Effective January 1, 1981)." New York: AAA, 1981. These rules appear on pages 199–206 of this book.
⁵ Paul A. Lawrence Co. v. Metropolitan Waste Control Commission & Toltz, King, Duvall, Anderson & Associates, Inc., U.S. District Court, 2d Judicial District, File No. 440829.
⁶ See section 10 of the Construction Industry Arbitration Rules.
⁷ Cal. Code Civ. Proc. §1281.3.
⁸ In the Matter of Raisler v. N.Y.C. Housing Authority, 32 N.Y.2d 274, 344 N.Y.S.2d 917, 290 N.E.2d 91 (1973); Mtr. Chariot Textiles Corp. (Wannalancit Textile Co.), 18 N.Y.2d 793, 275 N.Y.S.2d 382.
⁹ Chapter 252, section 2.
¹⁰ In the Matter of Groves Diamond Associates v. AAA et al., 211 N.W.2d 787 (Minn. 1973).
¹¹ In the Matter of J. Brodie & Sons, Inc. v. George A. Fuller Co., 16 Mich. App. 137, 167 N.W.2d 886 (1969).
¹² In the Matter of William C. Blanchard v. Beach Concrete Co., Inc., 297 A.2d (N.J. 1972).
¹³ Connecticut Public Act 78-333; Nevada Revised Statutes §338.150(2); Cal. Civ. Code 1670; Michigan MCLA 252.153; Minnesota, State of Minnesota v. McGuire Architects & Planners, 245 N.W.2d 218 (Minn. 1976); Rhode Island Gen. Laws 37-16-2 (1977).
¹⁴ See Robert T. Golembiewski, Jeffrey B. Trattner, and Gerald J. Miller, "Designing an Arbitration System for a Mass Transportation Construction Project," The Arbitration Journal. vol. 34 (Sept. 1979). This article appears on pages 79–102 of this book.
¹⁵ American Arbitration Association. "Construction Industry Mediation Rules (Effective February 1, 1980)." New York: AAA, 1980. These rules appear on pages 207–208 of this book.
¹⁶ Roofing Industry Mediation, effective February 1, 1980, is a service administered by the American Arbitration Association. A set of applicable rules has been published by the AAA.
¹⁷ This report appears on pages 11–30 of this book.

Recommended Procedures for Settlement of Underground Construction Disputes[1]

Preface

In 1973 and 1974 the Subcommittee on Contracting Practices of the U.S. National Committee on Tunneling Technology conducted an intensive study of practices in contracting for underground construction in the United States and in seven other countries. The results of that study were set forth in a report, *Better Contracting for Underground Construction.*

One of the most important objectives of the subcommittee that conducted the study was to recommend actions that would minimize the adversary relationship between the owner and contractor that has developed on most underground construction projects in the United States. The subcommittee observed in the course of its study that the adversary relationship had caused great losses of time and increases in cost. It also diverted the attention of the owner and contracting personnel from management of the job to management of disputes.

Among the subcommittee's recommendations to abate the widespread adversary relationship was the development of a system of arbitration, for use throughout the United States, that would achieve prompt and equitable settlement of disputes. The recommendation for establishing an arbitration system and panels of full-time arbitrators was discussed in the report *Better Contracting for Underground Construction.* (The discussion, excerpted from the report, is attached as an appendix.)

Following the 1973–74 study, a Task Group on Arbitration was appointed within the Subcommittee on Contracting Practices to study the settlement of disputes and to prepare recommendations for the organization and procedures for the prompt and efficient resolution of disputes arising in underground construction projects. This report discusses only the settlement of disputes. In it, the subcommittee has emphasized the urgent need for reducing the frequency and the magnitude of disputes. The subcommittee has observed that the majority of the recommendations found in the previous report, *Better Contracting for Underground Construction,* if implemented, will go far toward eliminating disputes entirely. These recommendations are therefore not covered in this report.

The subcommittee gratefully acknowledges the contributions of many owners, engineers, geologists, contractors, lawyers, and others who gave their views on the settlement of disputes by means of questionnaires, interviews, and workshop discussions in the 1973–74 study, and those who discussed and reviewed the task group's proposals during the course of preparing this report.

Objectives

Because serious losses of time and money have resulted from the adversary relations between owners, contractors, and engineers engaged in underground construction projects in the United States, the Subcommittee on Contracting Practices is making an effort to improve the relationships among management personnel. While doing this, the subcommittee also seeks to improve the quality of decisions related to the settlement of disputes—and the speed with which they are made—through the use of specifically qualified adjudicators and simplified procedures rather than through the current system of adjudication and procedures connected with court litigation.

To achieve the above objectives, the subcommittee recommends the procedures proposed by its Task Group on Arbitration and presented in this report.

Methodology

The task group reviewed methods other than court litigation currently used for the settlement of disputes in the United States, particularly in the construction industry. None of the methods currently available in the dispute settlement process seemed suitable for settling underground construction disputes because they do not provide for participation of individuals skilled in the geotechnical issues that often cause underground construction disputes. Therefore, the task group considered it important to prepare recommended procedures for settlement of disputes and an organizational arrangement under which such procedures could be administered effectively.

In drafting the procedures, the task group decided that the Construction Industry Arbitration Rules established by the American Arbitration Association would be a suitable model on which to base a set of similar procedures for the settlement of underground construction disputes. Initiated in 1964, these rules have stood the test of time throughout the construction industry and have served well in the settlement of disputes. Accordingly, the president of the American Arbitration Association was invited to serve on the subcommittee and the task group and to assist in drafting the procedures that are recommended in this report.

In its work the task group also was assisted by other members of the subcommittee, who provided technical expertise and legal knowledge. Based on such knowledge and experience, the proposed rules have been adapted from the time-tested rules of the construction industry to accommodate the special conditions and circumstances of underground projects.

The task group decided that for the proposed procedures to be effective, some organization would have to provide administrative services. Such services would include arranging for competent people to serve as arbitrators, helping interested parties to prepare contracts with provisions for settlement of disputes, and providing the educational services needed to make the procedures known to the underground construction community. The task group observed that the American Arbitration Association is organized to provide the required administrative services. The Association is permanent, national in scope, service oriented, and nonprofit—all prerequisites of the desired type of administrative organization. The American Arbitration Association would, however, need some assistance from professional and technical organizations in selecting experts.[2]

In attempting to determine how the American Arbitration Association could obtain this assistance in identifying capable people to serve as experts, the task group considered it necessary that the Association consult with professional and technical organizations in the fields of mining, civil engineering, engineering geology, and contracting. Organizations in these fields include the American Institute of Mining, Metallurgical and Petroleum Engineers, American Society of Civil Engineers, Geological Society of America, Association of Engineering Geologists, and Associated General Contractors of America. The task group recommends that procedures be developed to provide for such assistance to the Association from organizations such as those listed, when requested by the Association.

Recommendations

The procedures recommended in this section should be administered by a permanent, nonprofit organization, experienced in the handling of such matters and not susceptible to a charge of bias toward any segment of the underground construction community. Because the American Arbitration Association is such an organization, the Task Group on Arbitration recommends that the Association assume this task.

Manner of Implementation

Assuming that the above recommendation is acceptable, the subcommittee proposes that the procedures be implemented by the following steps:

1. A panel of highly qualified experts should be established, from which impartial advisors, mediators, and arbitrators are selected. The panel roster should be established and maintained by the Association and should be composed of experts suggested or approved by professional and technical organizations in the fields of mining, civil engineering, engineering geology, and contracting as such suggestions and approvals are requested by the Association. Those selected should be experts in the fields of construction contracting practices or of underground construction technology and should have demonstrated characteristics of integrity and a sense of justice. If the nominee is not an expert in both fields of construction contracting and underground construction technology, he should have a good working knowledge of the field in which he is not an expert. The experts should be used as needed and should be required to commit themselves to the Association in one or the other of the following categories[3]:

Category #1

Each expert in this category must be in a position to commit himself to a long-term assignment whenever such an assignment is offered and accepted by him. He shall commence, conduct, and conclude the matter involved, whether it be an advisory function, mediation of a dispute, or arbitration with or without previous efforts at mediation. All of the above functions are to be performed expeditiously and with consecutive hearings, except as desired by all parties involved or as determined by the expert for good cause. A written decision shall be promptly issued. At the request of either or both of the parties it shall be accompanied by a written opinion setting forth in concise detail the issues in dispute, the pertinent facts relating thereto, the finding or findings, and the reasoning in support thereof. In consideration of such commitment the expert shall be paid on a per diem basis for actual time spent in preparing for and handling the matter, and for the time spent in preparing a written opinion or decision.

Category #2

Each expert in this category must commit himself to perform in the same manner as a category #1 expert, except that such commitment may be only for short-term assignments. Such times are to be agreed on between the expert and the Association when the assignment is made. When serving, however, an expert in this category shall be paid on the same basis as above indicated for an expert in category #1.

2. When the services of an expert or experts are desired, the Association should provide the services on the basis requested, viz., as impartial advisor,

mediator, mediator-arbitrator. If an arbitrator is specified, his services should be provided either for a final and binding arbitration or for a nonbinding arbitration, as agreed on by the parties involved or as agreed by such parties at the time of request.

3. The Association should publish a set of rules, to be called the Underground Construction Dispute Settlement Rules. A preliminary draft of these rules, with suggested provisions whereby contracting parties could avail themselves of the various settlement procedures, is included in this section.[4]

4. The Association should, without further compensation, supplement its administrative role, described above, by ensuring a clear understanding and successful implementation of the parties' chosen procedure. Specifically, it should perform the following tasks:

- Help explain the general principles and specific procedures outlined in the Underground Construction Dispute Settlement Rules to the underground construction community.
- Conduct training programs to familiarize impartial advisors, mediators, and arbitrators with the duties and responsibilities of the particular role involved.
- Make available manuals, training films, and explanatory publications concerning the techniques peculiar to the particular role involved.
- Provide speakers at national and local meetings to explain the various procedures and to encourage their use.
- If necessary, testify concerning the operation of these procedures and serve in negotiations with the insurance industry and with financial institutions.

The Functions of the American Arbitration Association

The procedures recommended by the subcommittee, adapted from the American Arbitration Association's Construction Industry Arbitration Rules, are given in the following section. The functions of the Association are first described to demonstrate the manner in which it can administer the procedures.

With the assistance of the Association, an emerging problem or existing claim or controversy may be settled by voluntary submission to a disinterested competent person or persons having a demonstrated sense of justice. To make possible an orderly, economical, and expeditious settlement in accordance with federal and state laws, the Association provides a mechanism to resolve potential disputes and to administer appropriate procedures under various specialized rules. When an agreement to use such rules is written into a construction contract, it may expedite a peaceful settlement without the necessity of submitting to arbitration or going to court.

The Association maintains a national panel of experts in underground construction practices and construction technology who are available to serve as arbitrators-mediators throughout the United States. By arranging for settlements under the Underground Construction Dispute Settlement Rules, the parties in a dispute may obtain the service of experts familiar with underground construction.

The Association does not act as an expert. Its function is to administer a settlement procedure in accordance with the agreement of the parties and to maintain panels from which experts may be chosen by parties. Once designated, the expert advises, mediates, or arbitrates the issues.

Recommended Procedures

Section 1. AGREEMENT OF PARTIES—The parties shall deem to have made these rules a part of their agreement covering settlement of emerging problems or existing claims or controversies (hereinafter called "settlement procedures") whenever they have provided for such settlement under the Association's Underground Construction Dispute Settlement Rules. These rules and any amendment thereof shall apply in the form obtaining at the time a settlement procedure is agreed upon.

Either in their original contract or by submission, the parties may agree to use any one or more of the optional settlement procedures hereinafter described.

Section 2. NAME OF TRIBUNAL—Any expert or experts selected for a settlement procedure under these rules shall be called the Underground Construction Dispute Settlement Tribunal (hereinafter "tribunal").

Section 3. ADMINISTRATOR—When parties agree to implement a settlement procedure under these rules, they thereby designate the American Arbitration Association (hereinafter "AAA") as the administrator of the procedure. The authority and duties of the administrator are prescribed in the agreement of the parties and in these rules.

Section 4. DELEGATION OF DUTIES—The duties of the AAA under these rules may be carried out through tribunal administrators or other such officers or committees as the AAA may direct.

Section 5. NATIONAL PANEL OF EXPERTS AND OPTIONAL SETTLEMENT PROCEDURES—

A. Experts

The AAA shall establish and maintain a National Panel of Underground Construction Experts, in two categories as described in paragraph 1, "Manner of Implementation" (above). An expert or experts shall be appointed from the national panel. A neutral expert selected unilaterally by one party is hereinafter called the "party-appointed expert." The term "expert" may hereinafter be used to refer to one expert or to a tribunal of more than one expert.

B. Optional Settlement Procedures

Impartial or Advisory Committee for Emerging Problems

Exceptionally large or complicated projects as well as those having unprecedented features are almost certain to encounter unexpected problems during their execution. These problems emerge slowly, with the job-level management of both the owner and the contractor failing to immediately appreciate their gravity. By the time their full implications become apparent, both parties may have made mistakes and assumed positions that are difficult to reconcile.

It is fairly common practice for the owner or the engineer to engage a standing board of consultants to review the technical aspects of the work from time to time. Such a board can make a significant contribution to the technical success of the project, but it seldom becomes involved in contractual problems. Moreover, because it is the creation only of the owner or his engineer, its advice on both technical and contractual problems is understandably not as well received as advice from a board jointly selected by both contracting parties.

On many projects an impartial advisor or advisory committee representing various disciplines could not only provide technical assistance but could promote cooperation between the contractor and the owner/engineer in the solution of contractual problems before they become unmanageable at job level. By anticipating problems and proposing both technical and contractual solutions before the problems become serious, the use of such a committee could, in the long run, prove much less expensive than other methods of dispute adjudication.

The AAA will, if desired, appoint impartial advisors from either category #1 or #2, as desired by the parties, and assist in the administration of the advisory program. When the parties wish to incorporate provisions for an impartial advisor or advisors in their agreement, the following clause, or a clause to like effect, should be inserted therein:

> Any potential controversies or claims arising under or relating to the terms and conditions of this contract, or the breach thereof, shall, upon written request of either party, be submitted to an Impartial Advisor or Impartial Advisory Committee to be appointed by the American Arbitration Association under the Underground Construction Dispute Settlement Rules. Such appointment shall be made promptly following execution of the contract. The advice of such Advisor or Committee shall be nonbinding on the parties involved.

Mediation

Mediation constitutes the effort of an individual or individuals to assist the parties in reaching a settlement of a controversy or claim by direct negotiations between or among themselves. A mediator participates in the negotiations and acts as an impartial advisor and consultant to the various parties involved. He cannot impose a settlement and can only seek to guide the parties to direct settlement between or among themselves.

Where parties wish to use mediation, the following clause, or a clause to like effect, should be inserted in the agreement:

> Any controversy or claim arising out of or relating to this contract, or the breach thereof, shall be submitted to mediation in accordance with the Underground Construction Dispute Settlement Rules of the American Arbitration Association.

Mediation-Arbitration

This method of resolving disputes involves the designation of an impartial expert, called a mediator-arbitrator, either in the original contract, through mutual agreement of all parties at the beginning of the contractual relation, or by selection by the AAA. As agreed to by the parties or incorporated in the original contract, the mediator-arbitrator may be given specific powers such as the following:

(a) In the event that the parties are unable to resolve a dispute, he may meet at any time with anyone connected with the matter in dispute to investigate, inspect, or discover facts relevant to the controversy.

(b) Thereafter, he may call together all interested persons or parties for negotiating sessions.

(c) He may retain engineers, attorneys, and technical experts for the purpose of obtaining independent advice concerning the issues in dispute.

(d) He may engage in mediation with the parties, either separately or together.

(e) He may determine that certain issues are appropriate for arbitration, hold hearings concerning such issues under the Underground Construction Dispute Settlement Rules, and determine such issues and incorporate such determinations in an award that is final and binding on the parties involved.

Where parties desire to use mediation-arbitration, the following clause, or a clause to like effect, should be inserted in the agreement:

> Any controversy or claim arising out of or relating to[5] this contract, or the breach thereof, shall be settled by a mediator-arbitrator in accordance with the Underground Construction Dispute Settlement Rules of the American Arbitration Association. The mediator-arbitrator shall endeavor to secure settlement of the controversy or claim by and between the parties themselves, with the aid and advice of the mediator. In the event that the mediator-arbitrator deems it appropriate, or upon demand of any party to such controversy or claim made to the American Arbitration Association, the matter shall be settled by final and binding arbitration conducted by the mediator-arbitrator in accordance with the rules hereinabove referred to, and judgment upon the award rendered by the arbitrator may be entered in any court having jurisdiction thereof.

Final and Binding Arbitration

Under final and binding arbitration, the award of the tribunal will settle all controversies or claims arising under or relating to the contract or the breach thereof, pursuant to the terms and provisions of applicable arbitration law.

Where parties wish to use final and binding arbitration, the following clause, or a clause to like effect, should be inserted in the agreement:

Any controversy or claim arising out of or relating to[6] this contract, or the breach thereof, shall be settled by arbitration in accordance with the Underground Construction Dispute Settlement Rules of the American Arbitration Association, and judgment upon the award rendered by the arbitrator(s) may be entered in any court having jurisdiction thereof.

Nonbinding Arbitration

Under nonbinding arbitration, the award of the arbitrator does not legally bind the parties but may be introduced as evidence as a matter of right in any subsequent proceeding.

Where parties wish to use nonbinding arbitration, the following clause, or a clause to like effect, should be inserted in the agreement:

Any controversy or claim arising out of or relating to this contract, or the breach thereof, shall be submitted to nonbinding arbitration in accordance with the Underground Construction Dispute Settlement Rules of the American Arbitration Association. The award of the arbitrator shall not legally bind the parties but may be introduced as a matter of right in any subsequent proceeding.

Section 6. OFFICE OF TRIBUNAL—The general office of a tribunal is the headquarters of the AAA which may, however, assign the administration of a settlement procedure to any of its regional offices.

Section 7. INITIATION UNDER A SETTLEMENT PROCEDURE PROVISION IN A CONTRACT—A dispute settlement procedure under a provision in a contract providing for recourse under these rules shall be initiated in the following manner:

The initiating party shall, within the time specified by the contract, if any, file with the other party a notice of intention to initiate a specified procedure (demand). This notice shall contain a statement setting forth the nature of the dispute, the amount involved, if any, and the remedy sought. The initiating party shall file two copies of said notice with any regional office of the AAA, together with two copies of the dispute settlement provisions of the contract and the appropriate filing fee as provided in section 47 hereunder.

The AAA shall give notice of such filing to the other party. If desired, the party upon whom the demand is made may file an answering statement in duplicate with the AAA within ten days after notice from the AAA, in which event a copy shall be simultaneously sent to the other party. If a monetary claim is made in the answer, the appropriate administrative fee provided in the fee schedule shall be forwarded to the AAA with the answer. If no answer is filed within the stated time, it will be treated as a denial of the claim. Failure to file an answer shall not delay the proceeding.

Section 8. CHANGE OF CLAIM—After filing of the claim, if either party desires to make any new or different claim such claim shall be made in writing and filed with the AAA and a copy thereof shall be mailed to the other party, who shall have a period of ten days from the date of such mailing within which to file an answer with the AAA. After the expert is appointed, however, no new or different claim may be submitted, except with his consent.

Section 9. INITIATION UNDER A SUBMISSION—Parties to any existing dispute may commence a settlement proceeding under these rules by filing at any regional office two copies of a written agreement under these rules (submission), signed by the parties. The written agreement shall contain a statement of the matter in dispute, the amount of money involved, if any, and the remedy sought, together with the appropriate filing fee as provided in the fee schedule.

Section 10. FIXING OF LOCALE—The parties may mutually agree on the locale where the proceeding shall be conducted. If any party requests a specific locale and the other party files no objection within ten days after notice of the request is mailed to such party, the locale shall be the one requested. If a party objects to the locale requested by the other party, the AAA shall have power to determine the locale and its decision shall be final and binding.

Section 11. QUALIFICATIONS OF EXPERT—No person appointed as a neutral shall serve if he has any financial or personal interest in the result of the proceeding unless the parties, in writing, waive such disqualification.

Section 12. APPOINTMENT FROM PANEL—If the parties have not appointed an expert and have not provided any other method of appointment, the expert shall be appointed in the following manner: Immediately after the filing of the demand or submission, the AAA shall simultaneously submit to each party to the dispute an identical list of names of persons chosen from the panel. Each party to the dispute shall have ten days from the mailing date in which to cross off any names to which he objects, number the remaining names indicating the order of preference, and return the list to the AAA. If a party does not return the list within the time specified, all persons named therein shall be deemed acceptable. From among the persons who have been approved on both lists, and in accordance with the designated order of mutual preference, the AAA shall invite the acceptance of an expert to serve. If the parties fail to agree on any of the persons named, or if acceptable experts are unable to act, or if for any other reason the appointment cannot be made from the submitted lists, the AAA shall have the power to make the appointment from other members of the panel without the submission of any additional lists.

Section 13. DIRECT APPOINTMENT BY PARTIES—If the agreement of the parties names an expert or specifies a method of appointing an expert, that designation or method shall be followed. The notice of appointment, with name and address of such expert, shall be filed with the AAA by the appointing party. Upon the request of any such appointing party, the AAA shall submit a list of members from the panel from which the party may, if he desires, make the appointment.

If the agreement specifies a period of time within which an expert shall be appointed and any party fails to make such appointment within the period, the AAA shall make the appointment.

If no period of time is specified in the agreement, the AAA shall notify the parties to make the appointment. If within ten days after mailing of such notice the expert has not been so appointed, the AAA shall make the appointment.

Section 14. APPOINTMENT OF EXPERT BY PARTY-APPOINTED EXPERTS—If the parties have appointed their party-appointed experts, or if either or both have been appointed as provided in section 13 and have authorized such experts to appoint an additional expert within a specified time but no appointment is made within such time or any agreed extension thereof, the AAA shall appoint the expert who shall act as chairman.

If no period of time is specified for appointment of the third expert and the party-appointed experts do not make the appointment within ten days from the date of the appointment of the last party-appointed expert, the AAA shall appoint the expert who shall act as chairman.

If the parties have agreed that their party-appointed experts shall appoint the expert from the panel, the AAA shall furnish to the party-appointed experts, in the manner prescribed in section 12, a list selected from the panel, and the appointment of the expert shall be made as prescribed in such section.

Section 15. NATIONALITY OF ARBITRATOR IN INTERNATIONAL ARBITRATION—If one of the parties is a national or resident of a country other than the United States, the expert shall, upon request of either party, be appointed from among the nationals of a country other than that of any of the parties.

Section 16. NUMBER OF EXPERTS—If the dispute settlement agreement does not specify or if the parties are unable to agree upon the number of experts, the proceeding concerning the dispute shall be conducted by three experts unless the AAA, in its discretion, directs that a single expert or a greater number of experts be appointed.

Section 17. NOTICE TO EXPERT OF HIS APPOINTMENT—Notice of the appointment of the expert, whether mutually appointed by the parties or by the AAA, shall be mailed to the expert by the AAA, together with a copy of these rules, and the signed acceptance of the expert shall be filed prior to the commencement of the proceeding.

Section 18. DISCLOSURE AND CHALLENGE PROCEDURE—A person appointed as a neutral expert shall disclose any circumstances likely to create a presumption of bias or that might disqualify him as a neutral expert, including any past or present relationship with the parties or their counsel. Upon receipt of such information from any source, the AAA shall immediately communicate it to the parties. If a party challenges a neutral expert he shall be replaced unless the AAA determines that the circumstances do not disqualify the expert from serving as a neutral.

Section 19. VACANCIES—If any expert should resign, die, withdraw, refuse, be disqualified, or be unable to perform the duties of his office, the AAA shall, on proof satisfactory to it, declare the office vacant. Vacancies shall be filled in accordance with the applicable provisions of these rules and the proceeding shall be recommenced unless the parties shall agree otherwise.

Section 20. TIME AND PLACE—The expert shall fix the time and place for each meeting he conducts. The AAA shall mail to each party notice thereof at least five days in advance unless the parties by mutual agreement waive such notice or modify the terms thereof.

Section 21. REPRESENTATION BY COUNSEL—Any party may be represented by counsel. A party intending to be so represented shall notify the other party and the AAA of the name and address of counsel at least three days prior to the date set for meeting at which counsel is first to appear. When a proceeding is initiated by counsel, or where an attorney replies for the other party, such notice is deemed to have been given.

Section 22. STENOGRAPHIC RECORD—The AAA shall make the necessary arrangements for taking a stenographic record whenever such record is requested by a party. The requesting party or parties shall pay the cost of such record as provided in section 49.

Section 23. INTERPRETER—The AAA shall make the necessary arrangements for the services of an interpreter upon the request of one or both parties, who shall assume the cost of such service.

Section 24. ATTENDANCE AT HEARINGS—Persons having a direct interest in an arbitration matter are entitled to attend hearings. The expert shall otherwise have the power to require the retirement of any witness or witnesses during the testimony of other witnesses. It shall be discretionary with the expert to determine the propriety of the attendance of any other persons.

Section 25. ADJOURNMENTS—The expert may take adjournments upon the request of a party or upon his own initiative and shall take such adjournment when all of the parties agree thereto.

Section 26. OATHS—Before proceeding with the first hearing, if the procedure is an arbitration, or with the examination of the file, each expert may take an oath of office and, if required by law, shall do so. The expert may, at his discretion, require witnesses to testify under oath administered by any duly qualified person or, if required by law or demanded by either party, shall do so.

Section 27. MAJORITY DECISION—Whenever there is more than one expert, all decisions of the experts must be by at least a majority. The award must also be made by at least a majority unless the concurrence of all is expressly required by the agreement or by law.

Section 28. ORDER OF PROCEEDINGS—An arbitration hearing shall be opened by the filing of the oath of the arbitrator, where required, and by the recording of the place, time, and date of the hearing, the presence of the arbitrator and parties, and counsel, if any, and by the receipt by the arbitrator of the statement of the claim and answer, if any.

The arbitrator may, at the beginning of the hearing, ask for statements clarifying the issues involved.

The complaining party shall then present his claim and proofs and his witnesses, who shall submit to questions or other examination. The defending party shall then present his defense and proofs and his witnesses, who shall submit to questions or other examination. The arbitrator may, at his discretion, vary this procedure, but he shall afford full and equal opportunity to the parties for the presentation of any material or relevant proofs.

Exhibits, when offered by either party, may be received in evidence by the arbitrator.

The names and addresses of all witnesses and exhibits in order received shall be made a part of the record.

Section 29. ARBITRATION IN THE ABSENCE OF A PARTY—Unless the law provides to the contrary, an arbitration may proceed in the absence of any party who, after due notice, fails to be present or fails to obtain an adjournment. An award shall not be made solely on the default of a party. The arbitrator shall require the party who is present to submit such evidence as he may require for the making of an award.

Section 30. ARBITRATION PROCEEDING EVIDENCE—The parties may offer such evidence as they desire and shall produce such additional evidence as the arbitrator may deem necessary to an understanding and determination of the dispute. When the arbitrator is authorized by law to subpoena witnesses or documents, he may do so upon his own initiative or upon the request of any party. The arbitrator shall be the judge of the admissibility of the evidence offered and conformity to legal rules of evidence shall not be necessary. All evidence shall be taken in the presence of all of the arbitrators and all of the parties, except where any of the parties is absent in default or has waived his right to be present.

Section 31. EVIDENCE BY AFFIDAVIT AND FILING OF DOCUMENTS— An arbitrator may receive and consider the evidence of witnesses by affidavit but shall give it only such weight to which he deems it is entitled after consideration of any objections made to its admission.

All documents not filed with the arbitrator at the hearing but arranged for at the hearing or subsequently by agreement of the parties shall be filed with the AAA for transmission to the arbitrator. All parties shall be afforded an opportunity to examine such documents.

Section 32. INSPECTION OR INVESTIGATION—Whenever an arbitrator deems it necessary to make an inspection or investigation in connection with the arbitration, he shall direct the AAA to advise the parties of his intention. The arbitrator shall set the time, and the AAA shall notify the parties thereof. Any party who so desires may be present at such inspection or investigation. In the event that one or both parties are not present at the inspection or investigation, the arbitrator shall make a verbal or written report to the parties and afford them an opportunity to comment.

Section 33. CONSERVATION OF PROPERTY—An arbitrator may issue such orders as may be deemed necessary to safeguard the property that is the subject matter of the arbitration without prejudice to the rights of the parties or to the final determination of the dispute.

Section 34. CLOSING OF HEARINGS—An arbitrator shall specifically inquire of the parties whether they have any further proofs to offer or witnesses to be heard. Upon receiving negative replies, the arbitrator shall declare the hearings closed, and a minute thereof shall be recorded. If briefs are to be filed, the hearings shall be declared closed as of the final date set by the arbitrator for the receipt of briefs. If documents are to be filed as provided for in section 31 and the date set for their receipt is later than that set for the receipt of briefs, the later date shall be the date of closing the hearing. The time limit within which the arbitrator is required to make his award shall commence to run, in the absence of other agreements by the parties, upon the closing of the hearings.

Section 35. REOPENING OF HEARINGS—Arbitration hearings may be reopened by the arbitrator on his own motion or upon application of a party at any time before the award is made. If the reopening of the hearing would prevent the making of the award within the specific time agreed upon by the parties in the contract out of which the controversy has arisen, the matter may not be reopened unless the parties agree upon the extension of such time limit. When no specific date is fixed in the contract, the arbitrator may reopen the hearings, and the arbitrator shall have 30 days from the closing of the reopened hearings within which to make an award.

Section 36. WAIVER OF ORAL ARBITRATION HEARING—The parties may provide, by written agreement; for the waiver of an oral arbitration hearing. If the parties are unable to agree on the procedure, the AAA shall specify a fair and equitable procedure.

Section 37. WAIVER OF RULES—Any party who proceeds with an arbitration after knowledge that any provision or requirement of these rules has not been complied with and who fails to state his objection thereto in writing shall be deemed to have waived his right to object.

Section 38. EXTENSIONS OF TIME—The parties may modify any period of time by mutual agreement. The AAA for good cause may extend any period of time established by these rules, except the time for making the award. The AAA shall notify the parties of any such extension of time and its reason therefor.

Section 39. COMMUNICATION WITH ARBITRATOR AND SERVING OF NOTICES—There shall be no communication between the parties and an arbitrator other than at oral hearings. Any other oral or written communications from the parties to the arbitrator shall be directed to the AAA for transmittal to the arbitrator.

Each party to an agreement that provides for a settlement procedure under these rules shall be deemed to have agreed that any papers, notices, or process necessary or proper for the initiation or continuation of the procedure, and for any court action in connection therewith, or for the entry of judgment, if provided for in such procedure, on any award made thereunder may be served on such party by mail addressed to such party or his attorney at his last known address or by personal service, within or without the state wherein the proceeding is to be held (whether such party be within or without the United States), provided that reasonable opportunity to be heard with regard thereto has been granted such party.

Section 40. TIME OF AWARD—Award shall be made promptly by the expert and, unless otherwise agreed by the parties or specified by law, not later than 30 days from the date of closing the proceeding.

Section 41. FORM OF AWARD—The award shall be in writing and shall be signed either by the sole expert or by at least a majority if there be more than one. It shall be executed in the manner required by law.

Section 42. SCOPE OF AWARD—The expert may grant any remedy or relief which he deems just and equitable and within the terms of the agreement of the parties. The expert, in his award, shall assess fees and expenses as provided in sections 47 and 49, equally or in favor of any party, and in the event any administrative fees or expenses are due the AAA, in favor of the AAA.

Section 43. AWARD UPON SETTLEMENT—If the parties settle their dispute during the course of proceeding, the expert, upon their request, may set forth the terms of the agreed settlement in an award.

Section 44. DELIVERY AND AWARD TO PARTIES—Parties shall accept as legal delivery of the award the placing of the award or a true copy thereof in the mail by the AAA, addressed to such party at his last known address or to his attorney, or personal service of the award, or the filing of the award in any manner that may be prescribed by law.

Section 45. RELEASE OF DOCUMENTS FOR JUDICIAL PROCEEDINGS— The AAA shall, upon written request of a party, furnish to such party at his expense certified facsimiles of any papers in the AAA's possession that may be required in judicial proceedings relating to the proceeding.

Section 46. APPLICATIONS TO COURT—No judicial proceedings by a party relating to the subject matter of the proceeding shall be deemed a waiver of the party's right to a proceeding under these laws.

The AAA is not a necessary party in judicial proceedings relating to a proceeding under these rules.

Parties to these rules shall be deemed to have consented that judgment upon the award rendered by the arbitrator(s) under a final and binding arbitration proceeding may be entered in any federal or state court having jurisdiction thereof.

Section 47. ADMINISTRATIVE FEES—As a nonprofit organization, the AAA shall prescribe an administrative fee schedule and a refund schedule to compensate it for the cost of providing administrative services. The schedule in effect at the time of filing or the time of refund shall be applicable.

The administrative fees shall be advanced by the initiating party or parties in accordance with the administrative fee schedule, subject to final apportionment by the expert in his award.

When a matter is withdrawn or settled, the refund shall be made in accordance with the refund schedule.

The AAA, in the event of extreme hardship on the part of any party, may defer or reduce the administrative fee.

Section 48. FEE WHEN ORAL HEARINGS ARE WAIVED—Where all oral hearings are waived under section 36, the administrative fee schedule shall apply.

Section 49. EXPENSES—The expenses of witnesses for either side shall be paid by the party producing such witnesses.

The cost of the stenographic record, if any is made, and all transcripts thereof, shall be prorated equally between the parties ordering copies unless they shall otherwise agree and shall be paid for by the responsible parties directly to the reporting agency.

All other expenses of the proceeding, including required traveling and other expenses of the expert and of AAA representatives and the expenses of any witness or the cost of any proofs produced at the direct request of the expert, shall be borne equally by the parties unless they agree otherwise or unless the expert in his award assesses such expenses or any part thereof against any specified party or parties.

Section 50. EXPERT'S FEE—Each expert shall, regardless of the type of settlement procedure upon which engaged, be paid $____ for each day of service. Partial days of service shall be paid for pro rata.

Section 51. DEPOSITS—The AAA may require the parties to deposit in advance such sums of money as it deems necessary to defray the expense of the proceeding, including the expert's fee, and shall render an accounting to the parties and return any unexpended balance.

Section 52. INTERPRETATION AND APPLICATION OF RULES—The expert shall interpret and apply these rules insofar as they relate to his powers and duties. When there is more than one expert and a difference arises among them concerning the meaning or application of any such rules, it shall be decided by a majority vote. If that is unobtainable, either an expert or a party may refer the question to the AAA for final decision. All other rules shall be interpreted and applied by the AAA.

Administrative Fee Schedule

Administrative fee schedules may be established by the AAA for arbitration cases and for advisory and mediation services based on the AAA's experience in administering similar services in other fields.

Arbitration Cases

A filing fee of $100 will be paid at the time the proceeding is initiated.

The balance of the administrative fee of the AAA is based on the amount of each claim as disclosed when the claim is filed and is due and payable prior to the notice of appointment of the neutral expert or experts.

In those controversies and claims that are not for a monetary amount, an appropriate administrative fee will be fixed by the AAA, payable prior to such notice of appointment.

Amount of Claim	Fee
Up to $10,000	3% (minimum $100.00)
$10,000 to $25,000	$300, plus 2% of excess over $10,000
$25,000 to $100,000	$600, plus 1% of excess over $25,000
$100,000 to $200,000	$1,350, plus ½% of excess over $100,000
$200,000 to $1,000,000	$1,850, plus ⅕% of excess over $200,000
$1,000,000 to $5,000,000	$3,450, plus $\frac{1}{10}$% of excess over $1,000,000
$5,000,000 to $10,000,000	$7,450, plus $\frac{1}{20}$% of excess over $5,000,000

Where the controversy or claim exceeds $10,000,000, an appropriate fee will be fixed by the AAA.

If more than two parties are represented in the proceeding, an additional 10 percent of the administrative fee will be due for each additional represented party.

Other Service Charges

A party causing an adjournment of any scheduled hearing shall pay a $50 fee.

Each party shall pay a fee of $25 for each second and subsequent hearing that is either clerked by the AAA or held in a hearing room provided by the AAA.

Refund Schedule

If the AAA is notified that a dispute has been settled or withdrawn before it mails a notice of appointment to a neutral expert or experts, all of the fee in excess of $100 will be refunded.

If the AAA is notified that a dispute is settled or withdrawn thereafter but at least 48 hours before the date and time set for the first meeting or hearing, one-half of the fee in excess of $100 will be refunded.

Advisory Expert and Mediation Services

An administrative fee of $____ per calendar year will be charged by the AAA for support of services performed by one or more impartial advisory experts or mediators appointed by the AAA. The fee for a partial calendar year will be assessed on a pro rata basis. The AAA will, in addition to making appointments, provide meeting rooms and clerical assistance, to the extent that they are reasonably available, for the duration of such services. Such charge will be in addition to any fee charged with respect to administrative services performed by the AAA in connection with an arbitration case.

Appendix

EXCERPT: *BETTER CONTRACTING FOR UNDERGROUND CONSTRUCTION*[7]

Arbitration

One of the most important objectives of this study is to minimize the adversary relationship between owner and contractor that is causing so much loss of time, particularly of top management personnel, and increasing the cost of projects. All entities involved know that too much time and money is spent in disputation and litigation.

All should accept a share of the responsibility for the situation that exists today. Owners are not spending sufficient money or providing sufficient time for the procurement of adequate subsurface information, and engineers are making insufficient use of the information received. Complete information covering subsurface data, interpretative opinions, and the effect of geological investigations on design are not being provided to prospective contractors. Subsurface information, when provided, is often accompanied by exculpatory language, even in cases where relief under a changed-conditions clause is promised. Owners and their engineers are not giving objective consideration to claims received concerning changed conditions or inadequacy or errors in design. Contractors are prosecuting claims that far exceed the amount of their actual additional costs, particularly when they have a losing job or have at least contributed to the problems complained of, and lawyers often engage in delaying tactics, with consequent loss and expense to both sides.

Although everyone agrees that problems should be resolved at the lowest level in the entities involved and although everyone realizes the great expense involved in the event that this does not happen, personalities intrude, with the result that some matters develop into lengthy, costly disputes and court litigation. The extent of contribution to the situation that exists in the United States today is not important—what is important is that there is too much of an adversary relationship, and steps must be taken to minimize it.

As an alternative to court litigation, it is considered that a significant reduction in the cost and time expended in disputes and litigation can be achieved by the use of binding arbitration before an arbitrator or panel of qualified persons familiar with construction practices and costs in the industry, who would be empowered to develop an improved arbitration practice. Courts, with certain exceptions, have exhibited limited experience in the handling of construction litigation, and their decisions, based on conflicting testimony or evidence concerning construction practices and problems, are often unsatisfactory to both owner and contractor.

The difficulty that arises with arbitration proceedings as they are now conducted is that controversy over construction matters usually requires an extended time for submission of the evidence required. The best-qualified and knowledgeable arbitrators are too busy to give extensive and continuous time to the required hearings; consequently, those arbitrators who are able to sit for extended periods too often are less experienced. Even when qualified arbitrators are obtained, they cannot sit continuously through the hearings because they cannot absent themselves from their businesses or professions for too long. Accordingly, hearings are held on one or two days in the week, then postponed for a week, a month, or even more. Hearings are therefore held sporadically, extending over a period of a year or longer; when hearings are resumed, it is necessary to review the facts and problems to understand the evidence about to be presented. In sum, a construction arbitration proceeding, as now conducted, is time consuming and costly, particularly in an involved controversy.

It is suggested that arbitration proceedings are preferable to court litigation. Such proceedings would be improved by an organization of competent, adequately paid, full-time arbitrators, appointed to serve for a term of several years, who could sit on consecutive days during the entire course of a hearing. Their specialized knowledge would unquestionably be reflected in quicker and better decisions.

Funding for such an organization and selection of the membership could be arranged between interested contractor associations and owner organizations. One suggestion is that a small percentage of the contract price might be paid into the fund. Another suggestion might be that mass-transit authorities, for example, could join together in the creation of such a fund. Provisions requiring reference to the special group of full-time arbitrators would then be incorporated into their contracts. To promote resolution of disputes by negotiation directly between the parties involved, however, and thereby obviate resort even to arbitration, the parties should be required to pay into any such fund an arbitration fee on a sliding scale based on the amounts involved, in a manner similar to that at present employed by the American Arbitration Association. Irrespective of the manner in which such a fund were created, the cost would be far less than the current cost of litigation in courts or extended arbitration proceedings as now conducted.

Nonbinding arbitration, preferably conducted by specially qualified and long-term employed arbitrators as we have recommended but, in any event, provided for in the contract, is another method that should be given consideration. This procedure has been adopted in Europe with a provision that, although the determinations of such arbitrators are not binding, they are agreed to be admissible in any subsequent proceedings between the parties involved. The European experience is that both parties to such an arbitration put their best foot forward in presenting their cases, and although the findings and conclusions are not binding they are usually accepted because they are admissible in any future court proceedings. Further, and this is no small consideration to the European construction community, an owner who refuses to accept an arbitration determination acquires the reputation of being arbitrary and unreasonable, and a contractor who so refuses and takes the matter to a court becomes branded as a hardhead.

Notes

[1] This is a report of a study conducted by the Subcommittee on Contracting Practices of the U.S. National Committee on Tunneling Technology, Assembly of Engineering, National Research Council. The complete text is available from the National Technical Information Service, 5285 Port Royal Road, Springfield, Virginia 22161. Cite as report number NRC/AE/TT-77/1.

[2] The term "expert" is used throughout this report to refer to an impartial advisor, mediator, mediator-arbitrator, or arbitrator.

[3] Editor's Note: In October 1978, Robert Coulson, president of the American Arbitration Association, announced that a panel of approximately 75 arbitrators had been developed in accordance with the manner of implementation recommended here.

[4] Editor's Note: The Underground Construction Dispute Settlement Rules have not, to date, been published by the American Arbitration Association as a separate document. Parties may arrange to have their dispute administered in accordance with the procedures set forth in this report by filing a written agreement with the AAA citing the "Recommended Procedures for Settlement of Underground Construction Disputes" and specifying the settlement procedure that is being requested.

[5] One of the subcommittee members, a lawyer, recommended deleting the phrase "or relating to" from this clause, suggesting that with this phrase the clause permits an arbitrator to bind a party to matters concerning which he is *not bound* by any clause in the contract. The members of the task group noted that the clause, including the phrase "or relating to," had been used in the Construction Industry Arbitration Rules established by the American Arbitration Association and that experience in testing this clause over time had proved that it did not create problems in extending the arbitrators' jurisdiction. Therefore, the subcommittee consensus was to maintain the clause in the Recommended Procedures for Settlement of Underground Construction Disputes in the same form as has been used in the Construction Industry Arbitration Rules.

[6] *Ibid.*

[7] National Research Council, *Better Contracting for Underground Construction.* A report prepared by the Subcommittee on Contracting Practices of the U.S. National Committee on Tunneling Technology (Washington, D.C.: National Academy of Sciences, 1974). Excerpt from the section "Recommendations to Improve United States Contracting Practices," pp. 44–45.

Dispute?
Arbitrate, Don't Litigate

FRANK V. BONZAGNI

Because of the increased acceptance and popularity of arbitration (covered now under federal and 35 state statutes), the small contractor can expect to become involved in such proceedings with some frequency. He may find himself involuntarily summoned to arbitrate under a contract article or he may arbitrate on a voluntary basis through agreement between the parties where the original contract has no arbitration clause. In the latter case, he should weigh the advantages and disadvantages of arbitration versus a court proceeding. Here are some considerations.

Keeping Good Will

The contractor who has enjoyed good relations with an owner and architect may very well hesitate to jeopardize those relations with formal legal proceedings. He may feel that a meeting before an arbitrator in a hearing room, free from judicial trappings, will provide a more informal and more candid discussion of the problem. Under such circumstances, it might very well be possible to reach a settlement without and before a formal award by the arbitrator. In fact, appearance of the parties before an arbitrator may be, strange as it may seem, the first time all of the parties have met at the same time to seriously dispose of a claim. In this atmosphere, the contractor may well feel that a claim that may be weak under strict legal principles may have enough emotional or equitable appeal to produce practical justice. Some 40 percent of cases that reach arbitration are settled before hearing or award, which shows the value of getting the parties to meet and talk.

Selecting Arbitrators

Most successful business people would rather do business than argue and litigate. It is certainly better to proceed to a hearing when all the facts are

Reprinted with permission from *New England Construction.* © 1978.

fresh in the mind, witnesses are available, the decision must be made promptly, and payment can be expected reasonably quickly. Under existing American Arbitration Association rules, the Association, upon receipt of a demand for arbitration or submission agreement, will send to each party a list of qualified arbitrators from which each must, within seven days, indicate those satisfactory to him. If it is not possible for the parties to agree on arbitrators, then the Association will select an arbitrator, but not one whose name has previously been deleted from the list. Usually three arbitrators will be appointed (particularly in cases involving more than $50,000), but in its discretion or with consent of the parties the AAA may appoint a single arbitrator. The award customarily is to be made not later than 30 days after closing of the hearings or from the date of transmittal of the final statements and proofs to the arbitrator.

Lower Costs

In small cases, there seems to be no question that arbitration is considerably less expensive than a judicial proceeding. In simple cases that can be disposed of within two days, there will be administrative fees and expenses but no fee for the arbitrator unless the case is complex and demanding, in which situation the parties may agree to some compensation. After two days, the arbitrators will be compensated in any event. The contractor may or may not elect to have an attorney represent him, but these fees may not be as great as they might be for a prolonged trial. From the point of view of availability of witnesses, there may well be less effort required in marshaling the facts on a current problem than there would be in reviewing a situation that occurred some years ago. Costs for a hearing room and stenographers' services may be less. In very large cases where high stakes are involved, however, both parties may want to reserve their rights to pursue the case to the highest appellate court, regardless of administrative and legal fees.

Time Savings

Since arbitrators are prequalified on the basis of their previous experience in the construction business as contractors, architects, owners, or attorneys, it can be assumed that a case can be heard and disposed of more rapidly than before a judge and jury, who are not acquainted with the technical problems of design and construction. For this reason it is not necessary to repeat the same point again and again, nor to engage in tedious and unproductive cross-examination. Also, the arbitrator is not inclined to exclude evidence simply because it does not fit the usual legal requirements as to acceptability. On the other hand, a contractor would be unwise to assume that because of the arbitrator's experience it is not necessary to carefully prepare his case or that the arbitrator is an expert on any technical problem that will arise. The contractor must decide early in the proceedings whether his presentation is being understood and whether it is necessary to provide additional testimony or evidence.

Decisions Final

Awards that are made honestly and within the scope of the arbitrator's authority will be final and not subject to court review. Since the arbitrator is not required to write a decision supporting his award, the contractor may feel more comfortable with a court decision from which he can appeal.

After the decision to seek arbitration is made and the process of arbitrator selection has begun, the contractor must consider his approach to the hearing. The following points should be considered.

Documentation. Accumulate correspondence, pertinent documents, invoices, work records, exhibits, etc., and put them in a proper and logical order with an index of what they purport to say. You may wish to preface the documents with a statement of claim, which will objectively set forth the nature of the claim so that the arbitrator will have a clear idea of the problem. It must be remembered that until the hearing the arbitrator has only a minimum of information concerning the matter before him. The documents can be bound in a volume for the convenience of the arbitrator.

Chronology of Events. It is useful to set out in chronological order events which have transpired leading up to and concerning the claim. This is particularly important if the contract requires notice of claim or of differing site conditions, etc., since the respondent may well argue laches if there has been delay in seeking arbitration.

Witnesses. Interview witnesses and outline what their testimony will be. Consider who opposing witnesses will be and the nature of their testimony. Set up tentative answers or testimony to meet the thrust of anticipated opposing statements.

Site Visits. Arrange to visit the site before the hearing to ascertain the present condition of the building or work and consider requesting that the arbitrator visit the site together with the opposing party.

Transcript. A transcript is a necessity, except in very simple cases, since you will be called upon to furnish your summary of the case and your argument for relief.

The Hearing

At the hearing, after the witnesses are sworn, both the claimant and respondent are permitted to make opening statements. The purpose of an opening statement is to explain the nature of the case, what the claimant hopes to prove, and the relief he seeks. Usually the respondent reserves his statement until it is his turn to present the defense.

Both opening presentations are not only useful but also extremely important, since they set the direction, the scope, and the tone of the proceedings. Without being unduly long, the case should be stated simply and truthfully. You are not testifying as a witness at this point but are endeavoring to enlighten the arbitrator. You can state the facts you hope to prove and also illustrate your remarks by sketches, general site photographs, or models. These are known as "chalks" in legal proceedings and have the limited purpose of clarifying what the case is all about. If you use this occasion to attempt to testify and prove a case before calling your witnesses, you may rest assured the respondent will protest.

Presenting Witnesses

Presentation of witnesses should be in orderly fashion. You may wish to first present testimony to show how the contract came about and how the dispute arose; then present your superintendent, field engineer, or foreman to testify from field logs and from their own personal observation. These can be followed by expert witnesses. Experts, of course, after being qualified will usually respond to hypothetical questions and render their opinion as to what a particular set of facts means. For example, on a changed-condition claim they would testify from an examination of boring data, local topography, and the geological history of the area as to what a contractor, in their opinion, could reasonably expect to find.

Closing Statements

Finally, after presentation by both claimant and respondent, after witnesses have testified and been cross-examined, and after both sides have "rested," you will have an opportunity to make a closing statement summarizing your case in light of the testimony presented and to argue for a favorable award. If the proceeding has been lengthy and the transcript long, be sure to request sufficient time for reviewing all of the testimony. In your summary you should call attention to the testimony that has supported your position and show where the points made by the opposing party are not valid. In complex or extended cases, written summaries or briefs will probably be required. In such a situation, after reviewing the transcript you will need to write a brief somewhat along the following lines:

(1) List and summarize each claim separately.

(2) Each claim should contain:

(a) References to the transcript and exhibits which support your position; refute opposing party's statements in the transcript.

(b) Argument. Discuss the facts presented by both parties and reach a logical conclusion that the preponderance of evidence supports your position.

(c) References to supporting law or previous cases favorable to your case. If you do cite legislation or cases, be sure that the references are accurate and you have correctly stated their conclusions. Inappropriate or incorrect references could weaken your argument.

(d) Request for relief. In the light of the testimony and review of the documents, it is possible that the relief requested in your statement of claim should be changed by a revision of the figures, claim for interest, etc., so that a precise statement of what you claim is clear to the arbitrator.

Most participants in arbitration are generally satisfied with the outcome but may have some reservations as to whether the award is as large or small as they had hoped. At the very least, the process has been fast, the claim or defense has been understood by knowledgeable arbitrators, the parties have been able to speak without frustrating technical objections, and all can now concentrate on their business. The American Arbitration Association, which has grown with the increased demand for arbitration, continues to refine its procedures and has available for interested contractors extensive literature on the subject.

Arbitration—The Pros and Cons[1]

OVERTON A. CURRIE

Editor's Note: *In his address to the Conference on Construction Claims and Disputes (from which the following article is excerpted), Mr. Currie first examined the process of negotiation between the parties to a contract dispute. He pointed out that "even an unsuccessful conclusion to settlement negotiations leaves you with a great deal accomplished." Primarily, the parties will have gained a better understanding of the positions taken and have completed much of the preparation necessary for either litigation or arbitration. It is at this point, however, that a decision must be made about whether the claim is "worth [any] further expense and trouble . . .Looking at your claim as essentially an investment, you will have to decide whether to proceed with one of your last resorts: arbitration or litigation." The following is Mr. Currie's discussion of "Arbitration—The Pros and Cons," including preparation prior to the arbitration hearing and the presentation of the claim.*

• • •

If an acceptable negotiated settlement to a controversy is not possible, a decision must be made about where and by whom the dispute will be heard. If the contract contains a clause requiring the parties to submit their disputes to arbitration, this duty will be enforceable if:

(a) The contract involves interstate commerce and, therefore, the Federal Arbitration Act applies (9 U.S.C., §§1–14); or
(b) The dispute arises in a state whose law makes the duty to arbitrate enforceable; and
(c) The contractor is not guilty of waiving or being in default in asserting the right to arbitrate.

Reprinted with permission of Engineering News-Record and Conference & Exposition Management Co., Inc. from *Construction Claims & Disputes: How to Profitably Complete the Job.* © 1979.

If the contract does not provide for arbitration or if the parties choose not to exercise the right of arbitration, the attorney handling the claim will initiate an appropriate civil action in a court of competent jurisdiction. From the standpoint of strategy and convenience, it is generally to the contractor's advantage to be the plaintiff and have the option of selecting the forum. The selection most likely to favor the contractor's interests will, of course, depend on the circumstances of the case; but doubts as to whether to initiate the action should generally be resolved in favor of being the plaintiff.

Construction claims arising from large projects are frequently tried in federal court on a diversity basis because of the national scope of many contractor's businesses and the large sums involved. Federal court gives the parties the benefit of the federal rules, including the new rules of evidence. The shorter waiting periods in some state courts may be a factor to consider, however. In many cases it is preferable to try the case in the vicinity of the project because of easier access to evidence and witnesses.

In the case of a trial, a related initial decision concerns whether to submit the case to a jury, have it decided by a judge, or to seek or resist the appointment of a special master. A jury can be a valuable ally in cases where the contractor seeks to overcome a purely technical legal obstacle, such as failure to give written notice as required by the contract or unusual difficulty in establishing damages. Juries tend to take the equitable position that an honest worker should be paid for the work he has done or the injury he has suffered rather than insisting upon strict compliance with the contract or rules of quantum of proof. The result may well be different, however, if the claim is so technical and complex that the contractor has trouble proving liability in the first instance.

The type of project involved may also have a bearing on this decision. For instance, a local jury may prove disastrous if the case involves the construction of a public facility such as a school or hospital, particularly one funded by local property taxes or levies. A similar result would be likely to occur if the party being sued is a local business concern, for example, a subcontractor or supplier.

Other factors favor the choice of a bench trial. A judge sitting alone would be more likely to consider disputed evidence even though it might have been excluded from the jury's consideration. Many judges take the position that it is better to allow for doubtful evidence than to face an appeal. In such a case the judge relies on his own ability to give the evidence only the weight it deserves.

On the other hand, a judge is often more likely to follow the letter of the contract and the law and less likely to be swayed by sympathy or fairness considerations—two factors that often work to the benefit of a litigant who chooses to present his case to a jury. Of course a sympathetic ear is always a possibility where the litigant is a local citizen of good reputation.

The determining factor may ultimately be that many construction cases are simply too complex for the average jury, although some trial attorneys will argue that they are also too complicated for most judges, who are not familiar, through experience or background, with construction principles. In any event, the complexity of the matter and the relative advantage that may be gained by simplification or, on the other hand, by confusion, are factors to be weighed in deciding whether to proceed before a judge or a jury.

The Growth of Arbitration as an Alternative

Today contract clauses providing for arbitration of disputes are the rule rather than the exception in construction industry contracts. For example, the American Institute of Architects (AIA) standard form contract (AIA document A201, 1970), which is widely used, provides for arbitration in accordance with the Construction Industry Arbitration Rules of the American Arbitration Association (AAA). International construction contracts are frequently governed by arbitration rules promulgated by the International Chamber of Commerce.

This increase in the popularity and use of arbitration in the construction industry reflects a "veritable explosion" in the use of arbitration in all phases of legal practice.[2] Arbitration is not the panacea that one might imagine, as indicated by a closer examination of the relative merits of arbitration and litigation as means of dispute resolution.

Speed of Resolution

Proponents of arbitration are fond of pointing out that arbitration allows the participants to avoid congested court calendars and thus provides a quick means of resolving disputes. Indeed, judicial proceedings are frequently criticized for the inherent long delays. Arbitration can also prove to be a lengthy process, however, particularly if one party resists or "drags its feet." For example, the system of exchanging lists of arbitrators until both parties agree on a panel (a procedure utilized by AAA) can result in significant delays.

There is also the difficulty in continuously scheduling a series of sessions. Arbitration is characterized by long intervals between individual sessions.

In addition, the panel of arbitrators may grant adjournments or postpone-
ments on its own initiative or at the request of one or both of the parties.

The end result is that, while the informal nature of arbitration provides
a vehicle for the quick resolution of disputes, the actual time savings
depends upon the parties involved and the complexity of the issues.

Cost Savings

As is the case with comparative time savings, the cost of arbitration is
ultimately dependent on the parties and on the scope and complexity of
the issues. The cost of arbitration can be significantly less than the cost of
a court proceeding. In some simple cases, attorneys may not have to be
involved. In construction cases this would certainly appear to be the
exception rather than the rule, however, and in most cases the presence of
counsel is highly desirable.

Arbitration can also be expensive, since the prudent attorney will prepare
as carefully for one of these sessions as he would for trial. The use of
expert witnesses will increase the cost. In addition to attorneys' fees, the
parties pay arbitrators' fees, ranging from $200–300 per day, AAA fees,
and the cost of hearing rooms and of a transcript if one is desired by the
parties.

Technical Expertise of the Arbitrators

One of the points that makes arbitration such an appealing alternative
to litigation is the opportunity to have the dispute heard by a panel of
arbitrators with expertise in the field of construction, rather than by a judge
or jury with only a layman's knowledge of technical points. The ideal three-
person panel for most construction disputes probably includes a contractor,
an architect or engineer, and a lawyer well versed in construction law. In
such a case the persons making the final determination would be able to
draw on technical knowledge, experience, and a familiarity with industry
customs in making their decision. Such technical expertise is particularly
valuable when the situation requires interpretation of complicated engineering data and reports. In addition, jury members rarely have a chance
to question witnesses. Not only do arbitrators have this opportunity, but
their familiarity with the subject area puts them in a better position to ask
the right questions to clarify complex facts and arguments.

In short, able arbitrators are a necessity if the maximum benefit of
arbitration is to be realized. Competent arbitrators are generally available

if the parties can agree on the panel among themselves; however, if they cannot agree and where AAA rules are in effect, the AAA tribunal administrator will make this decision for them, and some of the possible benefits may well be lost in the process. Tribunal administrators frequently have only a limited knowledge of the construction field. As a result, a truly qualified panel may not be selected. For example, most lawyers have scarcely more familiarity with construction procedures and construction law principles than do laymen. As a result, contractors (both general and sub), architects, and engineers are a better choice for the panel.

Ideally, the party selecting arbitrators will look not only at the background of prospective panel members but also at the nature of the case in relation to that background; for example, a hospital construction case requires somewhat different experience from that needed to decide a road-building case. Where precautions are not taken to ensure suitable selections, the final panel may have no more expertise than would a judge or jury.

Privacy

Arbitration does have the advantage of privacy. This is important because few companies benefit from having their management procedures and financial condition become a matter of public record. This privacy factor also prevents the ultimate outcome of the proceedings from becoming a precedent for future disputes.

Avoidance of Legal Technicalities

In arbitration many of the technical rules that govern legal proceedings in the courts are avoided. Strict rules of evidence do not apply, and arbitrators are usually liberal in receiving evidence, particularly since the refusal to hear evidence, after proper objection, may constitute grounds for vacating the award. This makes possible easier and faster presentation of records, documents, pictures, opinions, and testimony of witnesses. The action of the arbitrators in receiving evidence is not, however, necessarily indicative of the weight or credit that they will give it in the disposition of the case. The arbitrators may ultimately choose to disregard an item of evidence even though it has been admitted for consideration.

Lack of Discovery

There is generally no discovery in connection with arbitration unless specifically authorized by statute, and most arbitration laws are silent on this point. The inability to compel discovery is generally cited as one of the biggest drawbacks of arbitration although, in particular cases, it might be viewed as an advantage. Note, however, that discovery may be allowed in some jurisdictions, even where no special need is shown, provided that it does not delay the proceedings. [See *Bigge Crane & Rigging* v. *Docutel Corp.*, 371 F. Supp. 240 (E.D.N.Y. 1973), applying the United States Arbitration Act.] This result is nonetheless unusual, and most courts still require a showing of necessity rather than convenience in those rare instances where discovery is allowed.

Subpoenas may be issued by the arbitrators and, depending upon the applicable law, by the attorneys of record in the arbitration proceedings. Under most state arbitration laws the arbitrator's subpoena power is coextensive with that of a judge in a civil lawsuit. The U.S. Arbitration Act contains a similar provision allowing arbitrators to issue subpoenas to compel the attendance of witnesses and the production of documents. [See 9 U.S.C. §7.] Subpoenas may be directed to strangers having information relevant to the proceedings as well as to parties, and in the event of a failure to respond to the subpoena the issuer may move an appropriate court to compel compliance.

Location of the Arbitration

Another of the factors frequently mentioned in favor of arbitration is the ability of the parties to select the location of the proceedings. In contrast, the location of court proceedings is determined by complicated and relatively inflexible rules of jurisdiction and venue. Agreement on this issue at the time of contracting can reduce inconvenience, delay, and costs, as well as afford a better opportunity for a complete presentation.

The AAA rules provide that the parties may mutually agree on the place where the arbitration proceedings are to be held. In the event that the parties are unable to agree, however, the AAA will make the final selection. The result in such a case may well be less convenient than the parties had anticipated. The criteria to which the AAA looks include: (1) location of parties, with preference to filing party; (2) location of witnesses and documents; (3) location of construction site and its relevance to the dispute; (4) relative cost to the parties; (5) place of performance of the contract; (6) laws applicable to the contract; (7) place of any previously commenced court action; and (8) location of most appropriate panel.

Even when the parties themselves set the place for arbitration, a location that seemed acceptable or even ideal when the contract was signed can later prove to be very inconvenient and costly. For instance, a Georgia subcontractor was held to be required to arbitrate in New York because the subcontract so provided, even though the construction site was in Georgia. The prime contractor, located in New York, had prepared the contract and initiated the arbitration proceeding [*U.S. f/u/o Mosely* v. *Electronic and Missile Facilities, Inc., et al.*, 306 F.2d 554 (5th Cir. 1962), 374 U.S. 167].

Waiver of Jury Rights

Although arbitration may be the best solution for a highly complex technical case, it also deprives a party of the right to explain his case to a jury of his peers. This effectively eliminates the availability of an emotional appeal in cases hinging on a legal technicality or where equitable considerations predominate.

Limited Scope of Judicial Review

Because the arbitrators function in a quasi-judicial role, their award will not generally be overturned by a court unless there is evidence of fraud, corruption, or gross negligence. This means that even an award based on errors of fact or law will usually be affirmed. In addition, since arbitrators do not have to set out the reasons for their decision, no findings of fact are available from which to predicate an appeal to a court on the merits of the dispute, even if such an appeal route were available. This is, of course, in contrast to the court system with its time-consuming and costly appellate system.

Enforcement of the Arbitration Clause

It should not be assumed that the presence of an arbitration clause in a contract guarantees freedom from litigation. Even where the contract specifically provides for arbitration of future disputes, the provision may be unenforceable under state law, although because most construction contracts involve interstate commerce, arbitration is enforceable under the Federal Arbitration Act. In addition, arbitration itself can spawn litigation, for example, where one party attacks the arbitrator's award or contends that the dispute is altogether outside the scope of the contract's arbitration clause.

Arbitration is a relatively modern development in dispute resolution. At common law, the courts were so jealous of their jurisdiction and so protective of a person's right of access to the courts that they would not enforce agreements to arbitrate disputes unless the arbitration process had already been completed and had resulted in an award; that is, either party could nullify the arbitration agreement by withdrawing its consent at any time before the arbitrator issued his award. [See, e.g., *Wm. C. Blanchard Co.* v. *Beach Concrete Co.*, 297 A.2d 587 (N.J. Sup. 1972).] Today, however, the overburdened court system has made alternative methods of dispute resolution a necessity, the result being that many jurisdictions now have statutory schemes making common-law arbitration agreements specifically enforceable. [See, e.g., *Park Construction Co.* v. *Independent School District No. 32*, 296 N.W. 475 (Minn. 1941).]

In addition to these developments in the common law of arbitration and award, many states have enacted statutes providing that arbitration agreements that comply with applicable statutory requirements and formalities will be enforceable. These statutes are generally held not to abrogate the common law of arbitration and award but to provide concurrent, if not parallel, remedies. [See, e.g., *Freeman* v. *Ajax Foundry Products, Inc.*, 159 A.2d 708 (Pa. 1960); *Robinson* v. *Navajo Freight Lines*, 372 P.2d 801 (N.M. 1962).] Thus, an arbitration agreement that does not comply with the applicable statutory provisions may nevertheless support an award that is enforceable under the common law [*French* v. *Petrinovic*, 54 N.Y.S.2d 179 (1945)].

Many states have enacted statutory schemes similar to the Federal Arbitration Act, 9 U.S.C. §1 *et seq.*, and others have patterned their statutes after the New York Arbitration Law or have adopted the Uniform Arbitration Act. Only two states, Oklahoma and Vermont, have no arbitration statutes, while fifteen states have semimodern laws that provide for specific performance of agreements to submit existing disputes to arbitration but not potential future controversies not existing at the time of signing the agreement.

Despite the drawbacks of many state laws, construction arbitration agreements are generally enforceable under the Federal Arbitration Act because of the involvement of interstate commerce. The federal act makes valid, irrevocable, and enforceable a written arbitration provision in a contract governing a transaction involving "commerce," except in certain situations.

In the context of construction disputes and the Federal Arbitration Act, there are many cases that deal with this "commerce" requirement. For example, in *Electronic & Missile Facilities, Inc.* v. *United States*, 306 F.2d 554 (5th Cir.1962), the Fifth Circuit Court of Appeals held that transactions such as are generally involved in a large project were within the scope of the Federal Arbitration Act. In that case the prime contractor had contracted with the United States Government to build certain missile facilities at two locations:

> It is clear, first of all, that since the construction of the missile facilities in Georgia required *substantial interstate movement of materials and personnel*, the contracts herein issued come within the purview of the Arbitration Act as contracts "evidencing a transaction involving commerce." Metro Industrial Painting Corp. *et al.* v. Terminal Construction Company, Inc., 2 Cir. 287 F.2d 382. (Emphasis added.)

As numerous cases indicate, there is a federal policy favoring arbitration and, therefore, the Federal Arbitration Act is to be liberally construed in favor of arbitration. The result is that when any possible interpretation of the contract will allow the dispute to be submitted to arbitration, the federal court will order arbitration rather than requiring action through the courts. [See, e.g., *Metro Industrial Corp.* v. *Terminal Construction Co.,* 287 F.2d 382 (2d Cir. 1961), *cert. denied*, 368 U.S. 817 (1962). See also *Prima Paint Corp.* v. *Flood & Conklin Mfg. Co.*, 388 U.S. 395 (1967), where the United States Supreme Court held that allegations of fraudulent inducement to contract were subject to arbitration under a contract provision that called for arbitration of "any controversy or claim arising out of or relating to this agreement or the breach thereof."]

While there are ways for a party to waive the right to arbitration, such a waiver will usually not be easily established. For example, in *Hilti, Inc.* v. *Oldach*, 392 F.2d 368 (1st Cir. 1968), the First Circuit Court of Appeals overruled the lower court judge and held that a party had not waived the right to arbitrate even though it had answered a complaint on the merits in a pending court action involving arbitration disputes and despite the fact that it had delayed nearly two years in demanding arbitration.

Court actions involving the attempt of one party to enforce an arbitration agreement against a resisting second party are of three basic types: (1) motions to compel arbitration; (2) motions to stay arbitration; and (3) motions to stay pending litigation brought in violation of the arbitration clause contained in the contract.

A successful motion to compel arbitration generally requires a showing of (1) an agreement to arbitrate, (2) allegations regarding the existence of a dispute, and (3) a statement that the opposing party has refused to honor the promise to arbitrate. In deciding on this motion, the judge will look to whether there is a valid arbitration agreement and whether there has been a refusal to arbitrate. He will not explore the merits of the dispute, which is the sole province of the arbitrator, and thus allegations that a claim lacks merit will be ineffective to prevent the judge from granting the motion.

Motions to stay arbitration will be granted, once the arbitration procedure has been initiated, where it appears to the court that the arbitration agreement is not valid, or that the matter in controversy is not capable of resolution by arbitration because of statutory preemption or public policy. A motion to stay litigation pending arbitration is granted when court action has been initiated in violation of the arbitration agreement.

Arbitration—Some Other Considerations

Contract Requirements

There are many different forms of arbitration agreements and provisions. Some merely provide that disputes "may" or "shall" be arbitrated. This is the language of minimum effectiveness, essentially requiring the parties to again agree at the time of the dispute that arbitration is an acceptable settlement method. This language, while legally sufficient to permit court enforcement of arbitration, does not necessarily encourage out-of-court settlements. It also leaves unanswered many of the questions that arise in connection with arbitration. A better contract provision is that set out in the AIA General Conditions (AIA document A201, 1970):

> 7.10.1 All claims, disputes and other matters in question arising out of, or relating to, this Contract or the breach thereof, except as set forth in Subparagraph 2.2.9 with respect to the Architect's decisions on matters relating to artistic effect, and except for claims which have been waived by the making or acceptance of final payment as provided by Subparagraphs 9.7.5 and 9.7.6, shall be decided by arbitration in accordance with the Construction Industry Arbitration Rules of the American Arbitration Association then obtaining unless the parties mutually agree otherwise. This agreement to arbitrate shall be specifically enforceable under the prevailing arbitration law. The award rendered by the arbitrators shall be final, and judgment may be entered upon it in accordance with applicable law in any court having jurisdiction thereof.

The AAA recommends a similar provision:

> Any controversy or claim arising out of or relating to this contract, or the breach thereof, shall be settled by arbitration in accordance with the Construction Industry Arbitration Rules of the American Arbitration Association, and judgment upon the award rendered by the Arbitrator[s] may be entered in any court having jurisdiction thereof.

The language of each of these provisions has several immediate advantages. First, it clearly delineates which disputes shall be arbitrable. Second, these provisions have received a substantial amount of judicial interpretation. Third, they incorporate rules that are uniform nationally and that answer many questions that arise in connection with less specific clauses.

For maximum effectiveness, in addition to the AIA or AAA provisions or similar language, the contract should also specify, where desired, the location of the proceedings, the names of particular arbitrators, or the preservation of particular legal remedies.

Multiparty Disputes

One of the most interesting questions in the arbitration area focuses on the feasibility of multiparty arbitration, for example, the consolidation of arbitration proceedings involving various parties when all disputes arise out of a common situation or fact pattern. Although multiparty arbitration would appear to provide the most expeditious of dispute resolution procedures in the construction area where disputes are complex and rarely involve only two parties, very few construction contracts presently provide for multiparty arbitration.

It has been previously noted that arbitration of construction disputes is frequently governed by the Construction Industry Arbitration Rules promulgated by the American Arbitration Association. Although these rules do not specifically provide for multiparty arbitration, it is clear that AAA has the authority to order a form of third-party arbitration under the general authority set out in section 3 of the rules:

> When parties agree to arbitrate under these Rules, or when they provide for arbitration by the American Arbitration Association, hereinafter called AAA, and an arbitration is initiated hereunder, they thereby constitute AAA the administrator of the arbitration.

Despite this broad general grant of authority, AAA has so far declined to join arbitration proceedings in what is essentially analogous to third-party practice in the judicial system, even where the contracts of all parties provide for arbitration. This stance is in accord with the traditional rule that without contractual consent to a multiparty arbitration, a court is without authority to order the consolidation of separate arbitrations, even though they concern the same issue of fact and contract interpretation and even though separate arbitrations could lead to inconsistent results. [See *The Stop & Shop Co.* v. *Gilbane Building Co.*, 304 N.E.2d 429 (Mass. 1973). But see also *Chariot Textiles Corp.* v. *Wannalancit Textile Co.*, 221 N.E.2d

913 (N.Y. 1966) and *Vigo Steamship Corp.* v. *Marship Corp. of Monrovia*,
257 N.E.2d 624 (N.Y. 1970), *cert. denied* 400 U.S. 819 (1970), which
indicate that, at least in New York, a court has the power to order
consolidation of two arbitrations where there are common issues of law
and fact.]

It is easy to imagine numerous situations where waste of effort and even
injustice can be avoided by joining all affected parties in a common
arbitration proceeding. For example, suppose a subcontractor claims
against the prime for extra work and recovers for certain items. Subsequently, in a separate proceeding and before a different arbitrator, the
prime loses its claim against the owner on the same issue. The inconsistent
awards result in injustice to the prime. Significantly, several federal courts
have recently realized the possibility of this type of situation and have
broadly construed the AIA standard form arbitration clause and subcontract "flow-down" clauses to authorize and compel multiparty arbitration,
even where the subcontracts contain separate arbitration clauses that are
materially different from the prime contract arbitration clause. [See *Gavlik
Construction Co.* v. *H.F. Campbell Co.*, 526 F.2d 787 (3d Cir. 1975);
Uniroyal, Inc. v. *A Epstein & Sons*, 428 F.2d 523 (7th Cir. 1970) and
Robinson v. *Warner*, 370 F. Supp. 828 (R.I. 1974).]

Although multiparty proceedings may lead to a more equitable result,
they do tend to decrease one of the primary advantages of arbitration,
namely its ability to provide for a more economical, efficient, and expeditious method of resolving disputes than is available in the courts. The
increase in the number of parties and counsel inevitably complicates the
entire process and leads to delays in the ultimate resolution of the dispute.

While arbitration is generally favored by prime contractors, it is considerably less popular with design professionals—the architect and engineer—
who object to being required to arbitrate with parties with whom they have
no contractual relationship. The design professional typically objects, for
example, that in an owner-contractor-architect proceeding the owner stands
in the position of a stakeholder, leaving the architect and contractor to
"fight it out," even though their duties and obligations under their
respective contracts are not necessarily reciprocal.

Applying the general rule that an architect does not warrant a successful
product and is not liable for faults in construction absent negligence, in a
leaky roof situation the fact that the contractor followed the plans and
specs does not necessarily mean that the architect was negligent. These
divergent paths of proof—for example, negligence and failure to comply
with plans and specifications—have little in common and are one major
basis for the design professional's objection to a joinder of this type of
procedure. A better case for multiparty arbitration, from the design

professional's point of view, would be one where the owner is claiming against the architect who, in turn, is claiming against the structural engineer for a design defect. This arrangement is preferable because the responsibilities of the design professionals are basically the same and negligence must be proved in both cases.[3]

Arbitrating with Government Entities

Although arbitration may be an available remedy in some government contracts, it has found considerably less acceptance in this area than in the private contract sector. Governmental reluctance to enter into binding agreements to arbitrate future disputes stems from the ancient concept of sovereign immunity and the underlying idea that the public welfare would be adversely affected if the state could be sued without its consent. Sovereign immunity has, however, to a large extent been waived by state and local governments as well as by the federal government, as in connection with the Federal Tort Claims Act. Accompanying this gradual erosion of sovereign immunity has been an increased recognition of the value of arbitration agreements in private commercial contracts and of the probable advantages to be obtained by their inclusion in government contracts.

The traditional rule in the United States has been that government bodies could not be bound by agreements to arbitrate. For example, the early case of *United States* v. *Ames*, 24 Fed. Cas. 785 (Cir. Ct. D. Mass. 1845) held that the federal government was not bound by the willingness of its own officials to submit to arbitration. This decision was based in part on the theory that the executive branch of the government could not agree to oust the jurisdiction of the courts any more than a private party could agree to such an ouster. Although the rules have changed dramatically where only private parties are involved, the stance of the federal government remains that unless Congress has specifically ordered arbitration or unless some technical loophole can be found, a governmental body cannot be bound by an agreement to arbitrate. This position is based on (1) public interest considerations, i.e., the fear that private tribunals will not always resolve disputes in a way protective of the public interest, and (2) fear of loss of the benefit of uniform law found in judicial precedents.[4]

Today the standard disputes procedure in federal contracts substitutes for any type of arbitration provision. The length of time necessary to appeal contracting officer decisions to the various boards of contract appeals and ultimately to the courts, however, has led some commentators to argue for the substitution of an arbitration proceeding after an initial agency decision.[5] Offered for additional support is the argument that there is a real question as to the impartiality and independence of the boards of contract appeals.

While the suggestion that arbitration be used in disputes involving federal government contracts would seem to have merit, it remains to be seen whether such an alternative will be made available. The prospects for future use of arbitration in state and local contracts is even less certain, given the hold of sovereign immunity in some states and its piecemeal waiver in others.

Arbitration of Prime-Sub Disputes

Arbitration provisions are as common in construction industry subcontracts as they are in contracts between the owner and the prime contractor. The subcontractor may specify a form of arbitration that differs from that in the prime contract. More commonly, the method of arbitration specified for disputes between the owner and the prime will "flow down" to the sub and be binding on him also. An example of this type of clause is the provision in the standard AIA subcontract form (AIA document A401, 1976), which reads as follows:

> 14.1 All claims, disputes and other matters in question arising out of, or relating to, this Subcontract, or the breach thereof, shall be decided by arbitration in the same manner and under the same procedure as provided in the Contract Documents with respect to disputes between the Owner and the Contractor except that a decision by the Architect shall not be a condition precedent to arbitration.

Preparation Prior to Formal Presentation of the Claim

If the claim is submitted to arbitration, it should be prepared along lines similar to those previously described for the preparation of a negotiated settlement. That is, all of the facts at hand should be marshalled and prepared for presentation in a favorable light; the damages should be determined and summarized, and the supporting documents made available; and, the applicable legal authorities assembled. In short, preparation for an arbitration hearing is very similar to that for a trial. There is one essential difference, however: in arbitration, provisions are not usually made for pretrial procedures such as discovery and pretrial conferences, whereas those procedures *are* available in formal litigation. Generally *both* parties to an arbitration must agree before such procedures are permitted.

Discovery

Once litigation has been instituted, the construction attorney will be heavily involved in the discovery process as a vehicle for eliciting facts, narrowing issues, and analyzing the contentions of the opposition. In most cases, neither skilled oratory nor extensive knowledge of the law can make up for the inadequate use of discovery.

Although the subject of discovery is one familiar to most attorneys handling construction litigation, a quick review of its objectives and techniques may be of value. Discovery pursuant to Federal Rules of Civil Procedure will be briefly discussed since they not only apply in the federal courts but have been adopted in large part by many states as their rules of civil procedure.

There are a number of available devices by which an attorney handling a complicated construction case can ascertain facts, narrow issues, eliminate contentions, and prepare for trial. First, there is the opportunity to take the deposition of persons whose knowledge and perspective are important to the case [Federal Rules of Civil Procedure §§30, 31, 32]. The deposition is perhaps the most effective way to compel a candid revelation of facts and opinions. These transcripts may then be used for certain specified purposes at trial, but more importantly as a means of uncovering and exploring all facets of the case.

Two other important methods of ascertaining the facts and narrowing the issues go hand in hand—namely Interrogatories and Requests for Production. These two discovery techniques are governed by rules 33 and 34 of the Federal Rules of Civil Procedure. While Interrogatories can be a valuable tool, it should be remembered that answers are prepared or reviewed by opposing counsel. This makes them less useful than depositions when candid responses are sought. The rule 34 method of obtaining the Production of Documents or Other Things is often utilized in conjunction with Interrogatories and with the taking of depositions as a method of obtaining access to files of information or key articles that will be involved in the trial. As a general rule, later discovery is more efficient and effective if examination of documents comes first in the discovery process. A Motion for Entry upon Land pursuant to rule 34 (a)(2) may also be useful in certain areas.

It is not unheard of for a contractor to build his case from his opponent's records. In fact, this may be the preferable method. The availability of the

Production of Documents device also means that a contractor need not abandon a claim just because crucial documentation has been lost or destroyed.

Finally, rule 36 of the Federal Rules provides for one party to make Requests for Admissions to the other party. This request can be used to compel the admission of facts as well as admissions regarding the authenticity of documents. Once again, however, the participation of counsel in answering Requests for Admissions frequently makes the device less valuable than envisioned by the drafters of the Federal Rules.

As a means of implementing the letter and the spirit of Federal Rules of Civil Procedure, the drafters provided for certain Sanctions in rule 37. Basically, these sanctions may be invoked when a party unjustifiably refuses to permit discovery or otherwise impedes the discovery process.

One final issue that should always be considered in connection with the topic of discovery is whether an attorney should undertake discovery so extensive in scope that it results in the education of the opposing side on all the points and details of the client's case. Attorneys are split on this issue, but it is one that warrants consideration.

As previously noted, the lack of discovery, except in unusual situations, is one of the primary drawbacks of arbitration. This forces the construction attorney to do an even closer analysis of his side of the case in order to recognize, find, and fit together any missing pieces.

Pretrial Conferences

The value of a pretrial meeting is that it gives the parties an opportunity to dispose of potential issues that can be resolved before trial. As a result courtroom time is saved and the attorney's burdens during trial are lessened. Issues that lend themselves to resolution at this stage in the proceedings frequently involve the statute of limitations (37 ALR 2d 1125), lack of written notice (66 ALR 649), and the applicability of "no damages for delay" clauses (10 ALR 2d 789). Normally a motion for summary judgment (with supporting affidavits and documentation) is appropriate to dispose of issues of this type.

A complicated construction case often involves rather novel legal issues and, to the largest extent possible, questions of this nature should be taken up with the court in advance of the trial. This helps to ensure that the contractor's planned method of presenting evidence does not become sidetracked. It also minimizes the need to do legal research during the trial when time can be better spent with witnesses and otherwise conducting the proceedings. It is especially important that a determination be made in advance that the planned method of proving damages is adequate. This is typically the most difficult aspect of a construction case, and a number of courts have imposed very stringent requirements as to the method and quantum of proof. Impact or disruption damages, for example, can be very difficult, if not impossible, to isolate and directly relate to a single delay.

In any case, to the extent practicable, counsel should obtain stipulations as to all matters on which he and opposing counsel can reach agreement. Stipulations are always appropriate regarding: (1) facts concerning which there is no dispute; and (2) document authenticity, thereby eliminating the time consuming necessity of establishing the authenticity of all documents introduced into evidence. It should be noted that a procedure similar to the pretrial meeting is available, though infrequently used, in connection with arbitration under AAA rules.

Presentation of the Claim

The final step in the claim process is, of course, presentation of evidence at trial or to the arbitration panel as a means of establishing the claimant's right to the relief requested. Obviously the tactics and strategies in either situation are a function of the choice of the individual attorney and of the relative strengths and weaknesses of his case. As previously stated, however, it is almost always best to simplify the complex, a task that is never more difficult than it frequently is in a complex construction case.

The presentation will involve, broadly speaking, two issues—liability and damages. It is frequently of substantial benefit to bifurcate these issues, with the presentation on liability first, and the damages presentation following the determination on liability. It may also be of great benefit to try these issues together, however, so that the quantum of damages suffered can influence the decision on liability.

Liability—How Do You Prove It?

To prove liability, counsel must first establish the parameters—the rights and duties—within which he will establish the alleged claim. As indicated below, in most instances this will entail a careful and detailed study of the contract, its provisions, and the factual circumstances constituting a breach of its obligations. In addition, it will be appropriate in many circumstances to make references to other standards and legal duties, such as the implied duty to cooperate and not interfere with the contractor's operation [see, e.g., *Peter Kiewit & Sons Co.* v. *U.S.,* 138 Ct.Cl. 668, 151 F. Supp. 726

(1957)]. Essentially, the road map to be followed is what the contract provides. It is the construction attorney's job to present factual evidence supporting the allegation that the requirements reasonably contemplated in the contract have been breached.

The Contract

The contract sets the boundaries: What does it say? What does it mean? Was it breached? It will be necessary to introduce the contract into evidence so that the obligations contained therein are part of the proof in the case. The attorney should then carefully analyze that document and outline each provision or condition, expressed or implied, that is alleged to have been breached. By proceeding in this fashion, he will have a ready-made checklist of categories on which proof must be presented to support the claim.

Witnesses

Live testimony is generally the most persuasive element of proof. For maximum effectiveness witnesses should be prepared well in advance of the trial, both to ensure that they are familiar with all facts about which they will testify and that they are, in fact, competent to establish the intended points. Adequate advance preparation also gives the witness an opportunity to feel familiar, confident, and comfortable with his role.

In selecting witnesses, it is necessary to determine who has first-hand knowledge of the facts. In this regard, often it is not the president who has the most thorough familiarity with the facts, but staff members, such as job superintendents, who are "in the trenches" on a daily basis, fighting the war that ultimately ends up in the courtroom or in arbitration. Another important point is that these individuals—who use the unique language of the construction industry in expressing themselves—frequently make excellent witnesses. They have the capacity to translate complicated construction problems into simple, everyday language that is quite frequently both colorful and persuasive.

The logical sequence of presentation of witnesses is, in most instances, chronological. First, call the individual who initially "sold" the job, made the estimate, and negotiated—or bid—and signed the contract. Follow this chronological sequence for the entire presentation.

Documentary Evidence

Documentary evidence plays an important role in most construction cases because of the necessity to make out a *prima facie* case. This is done by offering into evidence numerous writings (such as notice of claim, subsurface conditions, etc.) that are required by the contract in order to have a valid claim.

From the standpoint of convenience, a good practice is to obtain a stipulation of authenticity of documents, exchange exhibit lists, and make all potential exhibits available for inspection by the other side prior to trial or arbitration. This will enable the use of photostatic copies and will eliminate the cumbersome and time-consuming requirement of placing on the stand a witness to prove the authenticity of each document.

A word of caution regarding documentary evidence is necessary. It is sometimes difficult to resist the temptation to engage in a "paper war" in a lawsuit. This is counterproductive, since it is all too easy to become lost in paper with the net result being that none of the documents have any meaning for the trier of fact. For this reason great care should be exercised in determining what documentary evidence will be presented and the sequence in which it will be presented, so that only that documentary evidence essential to the case will be offered.

Summaries, Charts, Maps, and Other Demonstrative Evidence

Exhibits of this nature have the special advantage of presenting, in "picture" form, abstract, complicated, and extensive facts. Two examples will illustrate this point: First, assume that the contractor alleges that, through interferences by the other side, his labor forces have experienced a significant loss of productivity, with a resultant increase in labor costs and damages. It is appropriate in these circumstances to prepare a chart that depicts the curve of labor efficiency anticipated on the project and compares that curve with another curve depicting labor efficiency actually experienced. The data contained on the chart represents, of course, a compilation and summary of other evidence, either adduced with a witness or obtained from appropriate business records, such as payrolls, daily manpower reports, foreman's logs, or (if possible) the records maintained by the project architect or engineer. Displaying this information in an attractive visual form, in conjunction with live testimony, is doubly convincing.

Another example involves the use of a very simple set of drawings depicting the procedures and sequence for the construction of a building.

The first drawing would show the excavation for the foundation portion of the building, next the pouring of concrete, the erection of the walls, and so on. A clear understanding of how a contractor puts a building together can be of immeasurable value in establishing the economic consequences that result when that preplanned procedure and sequence cannot be followed because of some adverse act on the part of the owner or another party.

The usage and admission of such charts and exhibits is within the discretion of the trial court, and its action will not be reversed unless it commits an abuse of discretion in ruling upon questions of admissibility [*United States* v. *Brickey*, 426 F.2d 680 (8th Cir. 1970)].

Photographs

If the proper procedures for preserving the facts have been followed, photographs should be available for use in the presentation. These will enable the trier of fact to see the construction site and follow the progress of construction; this will, in turn, create interest and understanding where there would otherwise be only "talk" during the trial.

Expert Testimony

The use of expert witnesses has become commonplace in construction litigation, especially in the steadily growing number of complex "delay damages"-"interference"-"impact" construction cases. It is common practice in such cases for an expert to be utilized for the purpose of analyzing the validity of the schedule relied upon by the contractor in submitting his bid, as well as in the preparation of an actual schedule depicting where and how the job "went wrong." Testimony from such an expert is highly important in establishing both the impact of the breach of contract and the contractor's "correctness" in relying upon the original schedule.

There are two general prerequisites to the introduction of an expert's testimony. First, the subject testimony must involve questions beyond ordinary experience and knowledge. In the language of the Federal Rules of Evidence, expert opinion testimony will be allowed only if it "will assist the trier of fact to understand the evidence or to determine a fact in issue . . ." Second, the expert must be qualified "by knowledge, skill, experience, training or education. . ." [Federal Rules of Evidence, rule 702].

The qualifications of an expert must be presented to the court before he will be allowed to testify as such. An expert must similarly be qualified before an arbitration panel. There are no fixed rules regarding the prerequisites that must be met in order to qualify one to testify as an expert. Whether one has the requisite skill is in the discretion of the court or panel to determine, and that determination will not be disturbed absent an abuse of that discretion. [See *Grain Dealers Mutual Insurance Co.* v. *Farmers Union, et al.,* 377 F.2d 672 (8th Cir. 1967).]

The qualification of an expert simply involves an explanation of the unusual knowledge, skill, experience, training, or education that he purportedly brings to the matters being present. Generally the qualification will involve explaining to the court the facts that need to be proved and their relation to the qualifications of the witness, which give him the ability to assist in the understanding of those facts.

On many occasions, especially where the expert has outstanding credentials likely to impress the trier of fact, opposing counsel will attempt to stipulate to the qualifications of the expert in order to avoid a presentation of the credentials that will enhance his image. In situations where the contractor's expert has outstanding credentials, an offer to stipulate to this qualification should be rejected so that the court or panel can be exposed to his background, experience, and qualifications.

The opinion testimony of an expert may be based upon facts that are within his personal knowledge or upon hypothetical facts which he assumes to be true. It is preferable, however, for the expert to render his opinions based on facts which he has learned as a result of his involvement with the particular construction project. Frequently an expert's testimony will be rebutted by attacking the source material upon which his opinion is based, rather than his qualifications or his opinion itself. See, for example, *Chaney & James Construction Co.,* 421 F.2d 728 (Ct.Cl. 1970), where expert testimony and CPM diagrams were rejected by the court because the expert had failed to review the data upon which the diagrams were based. Without any independent knowledge of the facts, he could say only that the diagrams appeared to be logical and valid. Thus, where the expert does not have personal knowledge of the underlying facts, extreme care should be exercised to ensure that his opinions are based upon reliable data and that he has reviewed available factual information before testifying.

In terms of costs, it may be more expensive to economize on expert fees by involving the expert at a late stage in the proceedings rather than to have retained his services as soon as the possibility of a claim was recognized. With regard to fee arrangements, the contractor should be careful to avoid a contingency fee arrangement, which could impair or destroy the credibility and objectivity of the expert. As a general guideline, experts' fees vary from $20 to $60 an hour plus expenses. Such money is well spent if the expert can simplify the complex and be persuasive as to those facts on which recovery depends.

Computers and the Claims Presentation

Some contractors and their consultants, expert witnesses, and attorneys recommend the use of computers in the preparation and presentation of a claim. Depending on the type and sophistication of the computer, it can collect and hold a great deal of information, quickly and accurately sort or index it into many groups and subjects, and make computations in a fast and efficient manner. It can be used for CPM printouts and schedule comparisons and for all kinds of calculations of quantities, costs, time, and damages. The computer printout, however, is no better than the facts or data fed into it and the program or logic used to collect or compute the data.

Some experts, attorneys, and businesses are using computers in litigation, especially where there are many documents, witnesses, or complicated combinations of variables that relate to the disputed issues. Complex antitrust litigation and equal employment opportunity litigation with many statistics are areas in which the computer is useful.

In complicated litigation, such as a multimillion dollar construction case involving many disputes and hundreds of documents and details, there is a need to keep and control all related information and to index and cross-index the subjects, witnesses, and documents. To enable the attorney handling the case to retrieve every letter and every memorandum on any subject, use of the computer may be practical and warranted.

Damages—How Do You Prove Them?

At the outset, it must be stated that the problems inherent in proving damages can be substantially reduced, and perhaps eliminated, by initiation of proper job cost accounting at the time the breach of contract is first discovered. It is frequently possible to establish accounting measures whereby breach-generated costs can be segregated and separately maintained. If such a procedure is followed, subsequent proof of damages entails little more than presentation of evidence of these separate accounts.

It is recognized, however, that this "ideal" situation seldom exists. Either the problem is not recognized in time to set up separate accounting procedures, the maintenance of separate accounts is simply not possible because of an inability to isolate costs, or no attempt is made to establish the requisite procedures. In these circumstances it becomes necessary to develop some formula that is sufficiently reliable to permit the court or arbitration panel to allow its use as proof of damage. The development of such a formula is especially difficult in "interference-impact" cases because of the frequent inability to isolate additional costs generated by the breach of contract. The problem is not unlike separating the yolk from the white of the scrambled egg.

Delay Damages

At the present time, in the normal delay case the lawyer's principal task is to establish and isolate the period of delay attributable to the adverse party. Once that is done, proof of damages involves the itemizing of those fixed (ongoing) costs that were incurred during that period of delay. If the period of delay itself is not isolated in this manner, however, the ensuing problems can become quite difficult. For example, it is generally held that the courts will not make any effort to apportion damages in a situation where both parties are found to have contributed to the delays in completion of the contract, so that the causes for delay are concurrent. [See *U.S.* v. *United Engineering Contracting Co.*, 234 U.S. 236 (1914).] The question, thus, is essentially one of liability—necessitating the establishment of the key fact that the other side is solely responsible for the particular period of delay involved. Once this is done it is then incumbent to demonstrate the amount of damages incurred for fixed cost items, such as:

(a) Job and general home office overhead (as extended by the delay).
(b) Items of equipment allocated to the project (the cost of which is directly proportionate to the time spent on the job).
(c) Salaries of supervisory personnel (whose presence was required on the project for the extended period of time).
(d) In addition, if it can be established that as a direct result of the extended performance period, cost increases were experienced in material purchased for the job or by way of increased wage rates, then those items of damage would also be recoverable.

Impact-Disruption Damage

The impact-disruption case presents a different problem. In these situations it is virtually impossible to segregate the additional costs incurred as a result of the delay. Therefore, various approaches have been utilized, sometimes in conjunction. One of these is the so-called "total cost" approach, whereby all additional costs generated on the job over and above the original estimate are treated as being attributable to the breach of contract. The "total cost" theory may be accepted by a court where (1) it can be adequately demonstrated that there are virtually no other causes except the delay that could have created the additional costs incurred by the contractor, (2) the costs appear reasonable, (3) the issue of liability is clear, and (4) the failure to permit the use of such an approach would deny recovery [*J.D. Hedin Construction Co., Inc.* v. *U.S.*, 171 Ct.Cl. 70 (1965)].

It is possible to prepare demonstrative evidence (based upon the actual records maintained during the course of the job) depicting this type of information and, thus, offering a comparison with optimum expectable performance. Once this is done, a recommended procedure then entails:

- Production of fact testimony from witnesses establishing that a particular impact or disruption produced a specified result (such as, for example, a necessity for acceleration of the schedule) and thereby caused overtime work, addition of personnel, and incurrence of increased costs per unit of work.
- The next witness should then establish that there was a time period during the job wherein no acceleration occurred and that, during that time period, labor costs for similar work units were significantly lower than those occurring during the acceleration period.
- Then, expert *opinion* testimony is adduced to show that, in the professional opinion of the witness and based upon his experience, the additional costs occurring during the period of acceleration were, in fact, attributable solely to the acceleration.
- Last, having established the factual reasons for the acceleration (breach of contract by the other side), a simple comparison is then made as to your client's costs during the nonacceleration period. The measure of recovery is the difference.

The acceptability of this type of approach is widely recognized. [See *Frank Sullivan Company* v. *Midwest Sheet Metal Works*, 335 F.2d 33 (8th Cir. 1964).]

Keep in mind that once liability is established, the fact that damages cannot be proved with mathematical certainty does not necessarily defeat the right to recover [*Rusciano Construction Corp.* v. *State*, 37 A.D.2d 745 (N.Y. 1971) N.Y.S.2d 21 (1971)]. Thus, if the fact of damage is shown with reasonable certainty, then the extent of damage may be left to the drawing of reasonable inferences by the jury or finder of fact.

Additional sources from which damages may be ascertained include the estimates or bids of other contractors, the owner's estimate (if any), the estimate of actual costs of the contractor, charts of planned and actual job methods, man loading tables, payment records, progress and completion schedules, and similar records. All may be used to show the reasonableness of the contractor's expectations concerning unexpected problems, economic results, losses, and damages.

When analyzing potential remedies and damages proof problems, consideration must be given, as one alternative, to the articulation of a claim in quasi contract. Thus, if there has been a material breach, the election of the contractor to rescind and seek recovery in *quantum meruit,* or the reasonable value of the benefits furnished, may be advantageous. The articulation of a claim under such a theory may sometimes render proof of damages easier, avoid the problems inherent in seeking a "total cost" recovery on a pure contract breach theory, and bring about a recovery in excess of actual contract prices. [See *Susi Contracting Co.* v. *Zara Contracting Co.,* 146 F.2d 606 (2d Cir. 1944).]

Conclusion

In summary, it is essential for the contractor and his counsel to understand, in detail, the facts of the case. This need is constant, regardless of whether the presentation is made to a judge, jury, or panel of arbitrators. The contractor and its personnel must know and understand what was reasonably expectable by and of them under the contract, so that a determination as to the existence of a breach of those expectations may be made in their favor.

Documentation, through the adducing of job diaries, photographs, expert reports, correspondence, progress charts, payment records, and other writings is essential. Proof of the existence of a breach by resort to this documentation, along with expert testimony and the use of demonstrative evidence, will be necessary. Damages, though not necessarily subject to calculation with specificity, must be rational, reasonable, documented, and capable of articulation through an understandable formula and by a means establishing a connection to each breach.

Notes

[1] This is excerpted from an article entitled "Presenting and Defending Claims in Arbitration and Litigation."

[2] Gerald Aksen, "What You Need to Know about Arbitration Law—A 'Triality of Research,' " *Forum,* vol. X (Winter 1975).

[3] For a comprehensive discussion of multiparty arbitration from the perspective of the design professional see Jerome Reiss and Carl M. Sapers, "Multi-party Construction Claims," *Constructor* (August 1974).

[4] See John P. Cogan, Jr., "Are Government Bodies Bound by Arbitration Agreements," *The Arbitration Journal,* vol. 22 (1967): 151–160.

[5] See Samuel Katzman, "Arbitration in Government Contracts: *The Ghost at the Banquet,*" *The Arbitration Journal,* vol. 24 (1969): 133–142.

The Often Overlooked Use of Discovery in Aid of Arbitration and the Spread of the New York Rule to Federal Common Law

LOUIS H. WILLENKEN

Counsel involved in drafting arbitration agreements, administering contracts that provide for arbitration, and presenting cases in arbitration fail to take advantage of many of the procedures that can be used to obtain discovery in aid of arbitration. Traditionally such discovery was only available upon a showing of extraordinary circumstances. In recent years, however, courts have been more inclined to grant prearbitration discovery. Despite this increased availability, the possibility of obtaining such discovery is often overlooked. Frequently, by the time prearbitration discovery is sought, the party seeking it has little time to study the options and has already made decisions that affect his ability to obtain discovery. Failing to take advantage of available discovery procedures, although an economically sound decision in certain cases, can other times severely prejudice a party's position. Thus, from the time of drafting the contract through the presentation of any evidence, counsel should be cognizant of the status of the law regarding discovery in aid of arbitration.

In an effort to apprise counsel of the legal status and the practical aspects of prearbitration discovery, this article includes the following topics:

1. State Laws
2. Federal Courts
3. Analysis of Categories of Rules
4. Factual Considerations
5. Discovery by Subpoena
6. Letters Rogatory
7. Collateral Discovery
8. Providing for Discovery in the Arbitration Agreement

State Laws

Generally a court may order discovery in connection with a proceeding before it, for example, as in a motion to compel arbitration.[1] By statute, courts in some states may also hear an application for prearbitration discovery in a proceeding instituted solely for that purpose.[2] The existence of procedures that permit discovery in aid of arbitration does not mean that the courts are bound to grant applications for such relief. In New York, courts have traditionally refused to grant discovery in aid of arbitration absent a showing of extraordinary circumstances.

The general rule set forth in *Application of Katz (Burkin)*[3] is as follows:

> We are of the view that examinations before trial under court aegis should not be granted in such [arbitration] proceedings except under extraordinary circumstances such as the demonstrated need of reaching a witness or evidence which is unavailable without a court order. Necessity rather than convenience should be the test.[4]

The theory supporting the denial of disclosure in arbitration proceedings is that the parties, in opting to arbitrate, have sought to avoid the increased cost, time, and complexity that accompany court actions and statutory discovery procedures.[5]

There were some early exceptions in New York to the stringent *Katz* rule. For example, in *Interocean Mercantile Corporation* v. *Buell,*[6] the court stated as follows:

> [T]he moving papers show that the appellants have been unable to obtain the evidence they seek, even in affidavit form, because the witnesses are hostile. The appellants should have the opportunity to endeavor to obtain this evidence, as in their view of the case such evidence is most material. It follows that the motion should have been granted.
>
> The appellants furthermore urge that, because of the hostility of the witnesses, the commission should issue to take testimony upon oral questions, rather than upon written interrogatories. In this regard, also, the facts presented are sufficient. The appellants, however, should pay the expenses and the reasonable counsel fees of the respondents in the taking of said commission upon oral questions.[7]

More recently, unreported decisions have indicated a greater willingness on the part of the courts to order discovery in aid of arbitration. In so doing, the lower courts in New York appear to be reacting to the New York Court of Appeals holding that arbitrators do not have the power to order prehearing disclosure. Citing *De Sapio* v. *Kohlmeyer,*[8] a New York Supreme Court justice granted an application for depositions and document discovery in *Matter of Leo Nash Steel Corporation,*[9] and stated:

> Under the circumstances presented, namely, the sizable sums involved, the complexity of the claims made by the parties, the documentary proof to be adduced, the court is of the opinion that the relief sought is warranted.[10]

It thus appears that in New York the extraordinary circumstances rule allows the court latitude to permit discovery in aid of arbitration where warranted by the facts of the case.

The courts in a number of other jurisdictions have taken a position less sympathetic than that of the New York courts to the claim of extraordinary circumstances. In *McRae* v. *Superior Ct.*,[11] arbitration of a dispute over profits in the dissolution of a partnership had already been ordered when petitioner sought, and was granted, an order prohibiting the taking of his deposition for discovery purposes. The California court wrote:

> [I]t would be wholly incompatible with established policies of the law to permit the court ... to intervene in, and necessarily interfere with, the arbitration [by ordering the taking of a deposition].[12]

In *Lutz Eng. Co., Inc.* v. *Sterling Eng. & Const. Co., Inc.*,[13] the Rhode Island court declared simply that discovery would not be allowed in aid of an arbitration by a subcontractor against a general contractor for unpaid balance on construction work.

In New York, as well as in other jurisdictions, courts have shown some deference to decisions of arbitrators concerning discovery and have been willing to grant discovery where the arbitrators have determined it to be appropriate.[14] None of this authority seems to require that the arbitrators themselves have any statutory power to grant discovery.

In *Cavanaugh* v. *McDonnell & Co.*,[15] plaintiff, a securities salesman, sought discovery of defendant employer's records prior to arbitration, alleging that the latter had falsely represented the character of plaintiff's employment. The Massachusetts court indicated that it was for the arbitrators to decide the need for defendant's records and declared that "arbitration, once undertaken, should continue freely without being subjected to a judicial restraint which would tend to render the proceedings neither one thing nor the other, but transform them into a hybrid, part judicial and part arbitrational."[16] Similarly, a Florida court upheld an arbitrator's order requiring a deposition in *Frieder* v. *Lee Myles Associates Corp.*[17]

Section 2711.07 of the Ohio Arbitration Act[18] and section 16 of the Pennsylvania Arbitration Act[19] have codified a requirement that the courts may grant discovery only upon the request of an arbitrator to a court having jurisdiction. The foregoing statutes do not address the questions of whether an arbitrator's request is conclusive or what test a court is to apply in overriding the arbitrator's request.

Thus, in *Harleysville Mutual Casualty Co.* v. *Adair*,[20] the Supreme Court of Pennsylvania refused to allow discovery absent the request of the arbitrators, pursuant to state statute, stating: "When appellant [insurer], by its own contract, agreed to abide by the rules of the American Arbitration Association, it voluntarily surrendered the right to invoke any of the procedural devices which would be available in an action at law."[21] The court unfortunately did not set forth any test for granting or denying discovery when requested by the arbitrator.

At least one bar association has recommended that New York adopt a procedure somewhat similar to that of Ohio and Pennsylvania. Under the recommended procedure, arbitrators would be given discretionary power to require document discovery in advance of hearings; any application for broader discovery would be made initially to the arbitrators for an advisory opinion, after which the application for broader discovery would be decided in the courts.[22]

It appears that the implementation of the bar association's proposals would simplify document disclosure but make additional discovery procedures even more difficult. As a result, a claimant who has a legitimate need for discovery would have to overcome two hurdles—a procedure insuring delay where discovery is appropriate.

Federal Courts

Citing the doctrine of *Erie R. Co.* v. *Tompkins*,[23] the Supreme Court required that a federal court whose jurisdiction was based upon diversity apply state substantive law in a case involving arbitration [*Bernhardt* v. *Polygraphic Co.*[24]]. Accordingly, in answering the question of whether to allow discovery in aid of arbitration, a federal court in a diversity case is required to look to state law.

The United States Arbitration Act,[25] however, applies by its provisions to arbitration-related actions involving "commerce." The definition of "commerce" includes transactions "among the several States or with foreign nations . . . or between . . . any State or foreign nation. . . ."[26]

The question of prearbitration discovery in a "commerce case" appeared to be decided when a district court in New York denied as unwarranted a request for prearbitration deposition. In *Commercial Solvents Corporation* v. *Louisiana Liquid F. Co.*,[27] the court held that reliance upon state court cases was misplaced and that "pre-trial discovery clearly involves a matter of procedure which is within the power of the federal courts or Congress to prescribe."[28] The court then cited *Bernhardt*.[29] Thus, the court decided against prehearing discovery in arbitration, decided that state law was not applicable to the question, and decided that the issue was one of procedural law preempted by the United States Arbitration Act.

Since the United States Arbitration Act did not regulate all issues regarding arbitration, however, the choice of law question for unregulated issues was not answered by *Commercial Solvents*. The coverage of federal substantive arbitration law in cases involving "commerce" was incomplete because "what the Congress intended was merely to overrule by legislation long standing judicial precedent, which declared agreements to submit judicable controversies to arbitration contrary to public policy," according to the court in *American Airlines, Inc.* v. *Louisville & Jefferson C.A.B.*[30] The issue in *American Airlines* was whether a state agency could delegate decision-making authority to arbitrators. The court held that the issue should be decided under state law. Based upon the *American Airlines* reasoning, commentators argued that state law should govern the question of discovery in aid of arbitration in federal courts, even in cases involving "commerce," contrary to the holding in *Commercial Solvents*.[31]

The principle of state law governing discovery questions was followed in *Penn Tanker Co. of Delaware* v. *C.H.Z. Rolimpex, Warszawa*.[32] The court held that discovery on the merits of a controversy that will be referred to arbitration is generally not appropriate "except, perhaps, upon a showing of true necessity because of an exceptional situation."[33] The court relied upon a state court decision which allowed discovery in exceptional circumstances. It is interesting to note that the court cited with approval *Commercial Solvents*, which had held that the question of prearbitration discovery was not to be decided by state law.

This necessity or exceptional circumstances test was followed in *Ferro Union Corp.* v. *S.S. Ionic Coast*.[34] The court allowed discovery for use in an arbitration of sailors about to depart. The necessity test was again followed in *International Assn. of H.&F.I.&A.W., L. 66* v. *Leona Lee Corp.*,[35] in which the court allowed limited discovery on matters to be submitted to arbitration, finding that such discovery "effectuates the policy favoring arbitration."[36] It appears that federal courts have thus adopted the rule of necessity developed in New York State courts as a principle consistent with the United States Arbitration Act.

In *Bigge Crane and Rigging Co.* v. *Docutel Corp.*,[37] the court applied both state and federal law and permitted discovery in aid of arbitration in extraordinary circumstances. The plaintiff had brought the action in federal court to recover on a contract, seeking discovery *inter alia*. The defendant responded with a motion to stay the court action and to compel arbitration under the United States Arbitration Act.[38] The question presented was whether the stay of the trial in the federal court action under section three of the act also stayed discovery rights pursuant to the Federal Rules of Civil Procedure. The court, while interpreting section three to allow discovery at the court's discretion, did not limit its power to grant discovery in aid of arbitration to cases arising out of the stay of court proceedings. In interpreting the United States Arbitration Act to allow discovery, the court stated:

> The court recognizes the federal policy to interpret the United States Arbitration Act "so as to further rather than impede, arbitration. . . ." *Signal-Stat Corp.* v. *Local 475*, 235 F.2d 298, 303 (2d Cir. 1956). It must also be recognized, however, that the present federal rules governing pretrial discovery were initiated, after the original Arbitration Act, as an aid in reaching the truth and as a means of reducing both the length of trials and the element of surprise. These goals may be of equal help in arbitration, as well as court trials.[39]

The court viewed the absence of discovery as "a throwback to the outmoded 'sporting theory of justice.' "[40]
The court also cited state law, however, and clearly relied on it as part of the basis for its decision, as follows:

> The New York Rule, at least in the First Department, seems to be that the court has power to permit examinations before trial in arbitration proceedings, but that there must be a showing of necessity rather than of mere convenience.
>
> *   *   *
>
> Under the principles outlined above, the court believes that it should exercise discretion to permit discovery in this case because (1) discovery is particularly necessary in a case where the claim is for payment for work done and virtually completed, and the nature of any defense is unknown; (2) the amounts involved are so substantial that any expense in taking depositions is relatively small; (3) the action has proceeded to such a point that the taking of depositions can probably be accomplished without delaying the arbitration; and (4) only one of the five defendants has joined in the motion to stay the trial.[41]

Based upon the language of *Bigge Crane,* it was correctly predicted that discovery would be permitted in more federal cases by courts focusing on whether discovery would delay arbitration, rather than upon whether discovery was necessary.[42]

In *Bergen Shipping Co., Ltd.* v. *Japan Marine Serv., Ltd.,*[43] the court viewed an application for discovery as coming within the requisite extraordinary circumstances test in an arbitration by a shipowner against a service contractor for failure to provide a crew, on the grounds that:

> This was clearly a case of extraordinary circumstances. The allegations to the effect that the crew was about to leave the United States and be reassigned to vessels in international commerce were sufficient to meet the test of necessity.[44]

In *Vespe Contracting Co.* v. *Anvan Corp.*,[45] the status of remaining work and necessary repairs were in question in an arbitration between a subcontractor and the prime contractor. The court permitted discovery because:

> As progress continues at the construction site, evidence of Vespe's performance of the concrete work is "disappearing" behind the hotel's interior and exterior wall coverings. For all practical purposes, Vespe's work product will be inaccessible for future inspections. In light of the peculiar circumstances here, we think it proper to allow discovery to proceed at this time. The results of this discovery should be of great assistance during the arbitration proceeding.[46]

It should again be noted that Pennsylvania law requires the arbitrator to approve any request for discovery in aid of arbitration before the court will grant it. There is no mention of that procedure being followed or required by the federal court in Pennsylvania in *Vespe Contracting Co.*

The discovery question was again confused in a "commerce" case under the United States Arbitration Act in *Mississippi Power Company* v. *Peabody Coal Company*.[47] Plaintiff power company sought and received the right to prearbitration discovery and such discovery proceeded. Defendant coal company eventually objected to certain discovery requests, however, and plaintiff filed a motion to compel such discovery. The motion was heard by a succeeding judge. That judge, noting that some district courts have allowed prehearing discovery in exceptional circumstances and finding that the vast majority of the courts have concluded that prehearing discovery on the merits is inconsistent with the aims of arbitration, held that under the circumstances of that particular case prehearing discovery should not go any further.[48]

Analysis of Categories of Rules

The various statutory and court-made rules governing discovery in aid of arbitration can be classified as follows: disallowance of discovery; discovery based upon recommendations of the arbitrators; discovery based upon a showing of necessity or extraordinary circumstances; discovery based upon a showing of no delay; or discovery as a matter of right (a rule not adopted in its entirety in any known jurisdiction).

Whether the court purports to apply state or federal, statutory or case law, it will carefully review the facts before it to determine whether justice can be done in the absence of discovery and whether discovery in the particular case will further or hinder the purposes of arbitration. If the facts do not support a clear answer to the discovery question, then the outcome depends upon the court's interpretation of the purpose of arbitration and whether discovery serves that purpose.

That discovery has certain benefits is generally accepted. Discovery is used to disclose the real points of dispute between the parties and affords an adequate factual basis in preparation for trial[49]; discovery makes the trial "less a game of blindman's buff and more a fair contest[50]; discovery is of great assistance in ascertaining the truth[51]; and discovery makes evidence available at trial which might not otherwise be available or affordable.[52] At the same time, it is clear that discovery is frequently abused and may cause expensive and protracted litigation.[53] Indeed, there are proposals to place restrictions on the broad discovery which has been allowed in court proceedings in recent years.[54]

Since the bar appears convinced, after many years of experience regarding the question, that a certain amount of discovery serves the ends of justice, it is difficult to understand how allowing discovery in aid of arbitration can be inconsistent with the purposes of arbitration, as long as (1) the hearings are not delayed; (2) the party seeking the discovery bears *all* of the expenses involved, including the other party's clerical and even attorney's costs for such discovery; and (3) the discovery sought is consistent with the magnitude, complexity, and scope of the dispute.

Factual Considerations

Since the facts have influenced courts in many instances to allow prearbitration discovery, a summary of some of the particular facts relied upon by courts may be helpful in assessing the possibility of success in attempting discovery in any given case. The following have been cited by courts as a basis for allowing such discovery:

   a. Information exclusively within the possession of hostile witnesses.[55]
   b. Size of the claim.[56]
   c. Complexity of the claim.[57]
   d. Need for documentary proof.[58]
   e. Unknown defense.[59]
   f. Cost of discovery compared to magnitude of claim.[60]
   g. Potential to accomplish discovery without delaying arbitration.[61]
   h. Unknown identity of persons potentially liable.[62]

Before attempting to marshal those facts that might convince a court to allow prearbitration discovery, however, it may be prudent to consider whether other methods of obtaining disclosure will be more useful or appropriate.

Discovery by Subpoena

Under common law, arbitrators lacked the power to subpoena documents or witnesses to the hearings.[63] Presently, however, at least 26 states have enacted statutes that give the arbitrator the power to issue subpoenas.[64] In addition, the United States Arbitration Act vests an arbitrator with authority to subpoena material evidence.[65] Various rules of the American Arbitration Association also allow an arbitrator to issue subpoenas where authorized by law.[66]

Absent an agreement to the contrary, the subpoenaed witness must be questioned during the arbitration hearing.[67] This limitation in the subpoena process severely undercuts the use of a subpoena as a prehearing disclosure device. The arbitrators are free to recommend, however, that the parties agree to have witnesses questioned and documents produced in advance of the hearings and are also free to draw adverse conclusions from a refusal.[68]

The California arbitration statute,[69] an exception to the general rule, vests arbitrators with power not only to issue subpoenas but also to order depositions to be used as evidence—but not as a discovery device.[70] Once such a deposition is ordered, the parties would not be free to withhold and present such portions as they see fit and presumably the witness would not appear at the hearings.

The decision of an arbitrator as to whether or not to issue a requested subpoena is generally within his discretion.[71] The courts have stated, however, that arbitrators should call for the production of important documents in the hands of a party.[72] Failing to insure that the information in the hands of one party is fully and timely made available to the other may constitute a breach of duty by the arbitrators, where prejudicial.[73] Similarly, the quashing of a subpoena by an arbitrator can be an abuse of discretion.[74]

Arbitrators have the power to determine facts which go to the scope of their subpoena power. In *Great Scott Supermarkets, Inc.* v. *Local U. No. 337, Teamsters,*[75] after the arbitrator found that a party's attorney had not been acting in his capacity as attorney when he prepared certain documents, the court refused to overturn the subpoena of those documents. In a proper case, however, courts will substitute their judgment for that of the arbitrators with respect to the materiality of information sought.[76]

Other courts have devised special procedures to regulate the subpoena power of arbitrators. In *Minerals & Chem. Philipp Corp.* v. *Pan American Com.,*[77] the court ordered a court referee to supervise the inspection of documents described in the subpoena to ensure that confidential data not be unnecessarily disclosed.

The subpoena has territorial restrictions. The state in which the arbitration hearings are being held defines the limits of its court subpoena, while in federal court the district in or 100 miles from the place of the hearings is the applicable limitation.[78]

Letters Rogatory

Where arbitrators subpoena a witness not within the territorial United States or a court determines that the deposition of a witness not within the United States is proper in aid of an arbitration, it may be possible to obtain letters rogatory. United States district courts have inherent power to issue letters rogatory in litigation.[79] State courts generally have the same powers.[80] To date, there is no reported case which decides the question of whether letters rogatory may be issued in aid of arbitration.[81]

Collateral Discovery

In certain situations, it is possible to conduct discovery in a lawsuit that is related to the subject matter of an arbitration and use the fruits of that discovery in the arbitration.[82] Of course, it is best if the opponent in the arbitration is also a party in the lawsuit. Having had his chance at cross-examination during the lawsuit, the party will be unable to complain of unfair treatment if the arbitrators accept depositions. Even if the opponent had no chance of cross-examination, however, the statements under oath in the lawsuit may have sufficient weight to serve the purposes for which they are offered in the arbitration.

A dispute between the parties about the preliminary issue of whether there is an agreement to arbitrate offers yet another collateral manner in which discovery may be attained. It is not uncommon for a court to allow discovery regarding this preliminary issue.[83]

Finally, in applying for a provisional remedy, a party may be able to obtain some discovery in aid of arbitration. In connection with arbitration proceedings, courts have granted a variety of provisional remedies such as attachment,[84] mechanic's lien,[85] and preliminary injunction.[86]

Since courts have been receptive to discovery regarding the threshold question of whether there is an agreement to arbitrate, they may also be persuaded to allow discovery on such collateral issues as whether a provisional remedy is appropriate.[87]

Providing for Discovery in the Arbitration Agreement

For many years, lawyers were apprehensive with respect to the use of discovery in aid of arbitration. The basis of that apprehension is aptly summarized as follows:

> [Disclosure in advance of arbitration] could establish one party in a position to harass his opponent, indulge in a fishing expedition, obtain confidential information contained in his opponent's books (in no way germane to the issues) and, in general, engage in long, drawn-out pretrial examinations.[88]

Recently, however, there has been greater recognition of the need for discovery in large or complicated arbitrations. As one report concluded:

> The present limitations on discovery in arbitration proceedings result in substantial waste of time. Because of the lack of prearbitration discovery, the simplest of arbitrations requires more than one hearing. At the first hearing the claiming party will put in his evidence, which frequently will include documents seen for the first time by the other side and perhaps contentions made for the first time. The defending party then requires time to obtain evidence to meet the claimant's allegations. In a complicated case the development of this case in this fashion may well result in numerous hearings spread over a period of years. This is wasteful of the time of both the arbitrators and counsel, lengthens the arbitration, and, because arbitrators frequently base their fees on the number of hearings held, increases the cost of arbitration.
>
> The present situation also makes an arbitration a very risky business as frequently there is inadequate development of fact.[89]

The report recommended that discovery include prehearing depositions, interrogatories, and production of documents.[90]

The potential size and complexity of a dispute should be recognizable from the contract. According to one New York decision, *Local 99, ILGWU v. Clarise Sportswear Co.*,[91] the contract itself is therefore an appropriate and proper place to provide for discovery in advance of arbitration. By providing for discovery in the contract, parties may agree on the parameters in the hope of avoiding resort to the courts when a dispute arises. According to one lower New York court, the parties are free to make the discovery a right or to place restrictions thereon which "may not be ignored."[92] Beyond the holding of the lower New York court, there is no case law regarding the enforceability of a discovery clause in the arbitration agreement.

There is, however, no reason why an arbitration clause may not provide for discovery in matters in excess of a certain claim, or for more extended discovery if the amount in dispute exceeds a certain sum. As a safeguard against the inflation of claims to the threshold sums, the agreement can further provide for an award to include attorneys' fees and other costs where it is determined by the arbitrators that the size of a party's claim is inflated merely to obtain discovery. In the alternative, if the agreement provides that attorneys' fees as well as all costs of discovery must be paid by the requesting party in all instances, the cost will discourage discovery in respect of small claims.

The discovery provisions in an arbitration clause may be as varied as the particular contract warrants and the parties can agree upon. The following is a list of examples of discovery limits that can be provided by contract:

a. Discovery pursuant to the Federal Rules of Civil Procedure.
b. Discovery pursuant to the Federal Rules of Civil Procedure, except no depositions of independent witnesses.
c. Depositions of the two most knowledgeable persons who are officers, agents of employees of each party.
d. Disclosure of all related documentation.
e. Interrogatories to each party.
f. Affidavits from each witness and a copy of each document that is expected to be used at the hearing.
g. Disclosure pursuant to a selected body of rules. For example, article 11 (eleven) of the Rules for the ICC Court of Arbitration empowers the arbitrator, where such rules are silent and the parties have not agreed to an applicable procedure, to promulgate procedural rules governing the proceedings. Pursuant to article 11, arbitrators have ordered discovery.[93]

The contract should provide that any such discovery agreement is enforceable in court. It may also be prudent to require any discovery request to be served within a specified time after the demand for arbitration and that the process for selecting the arbitrators and even the hearings, where possible, will proceed simultaneously with discovery. Naturally, in providing for the laws of any state and the rules of any arbitration association to apply, consideration should be given to the discovery rights under that state's laws and that association's rules. It would be helpful if all arbitration associations provided optional rules for discovery that could be included in the contract. Such rules could provide one or more size limitations on a claim before discovery is allowed and could further provide timing of discovery that would not delay hearings.[94]

Where a right to discovery is provided either by contract or by association rule, the applicable provision should include a statement as to whether discovery questions are within the jurisdiction of the court or the arbitrator. The appropriate forum for discovery disputes depends, to some extent, upon the scope of the discovery right, as only the court has the power to compel third-party discovery or to effectuate depositions in other jurisdictions. If it is not specified who determines discovery disputes, the party seeking relief presumably has a choice of forum, unless the dispute both lacks diversity and is arbitrated in a state that requires that such matters first be determined by the arbitrator. There is, however, no law on the question of choice of forum where discovery is sought by contract right or association rule.

Another question that is unclear is whether an arbitrator who has made a decision regarding a discovery issue, submitted pursuant to association rule or contract provision, has the final say or whether his decision can be modified or reversed by the court and, if so, on what basis. In *Mobil Oil* v. *Asamera Oil*,[95] the New York Court of Appeals held, regarding an arbitrator's decision on a discovery request pursuant to association rule, that "for the court to entertain review of intermediary arbitration decisions involving procedure or any other interlocutory matter, would disjoint and unduly delay the proceedings."[96] Of course, the considerations may have been different had one party approached the court to enforce an arbitrator's discovery decision vis-à-vis a third party. It is difficult to perceive a reason, unless specified by rule or contract, for allowing the arbitrator the final say on the merits but not on discovery questions.

Whether a party seeks discovery pursuant to contract, association rule, statute, or court discretion, it should be made clear at the outset that discovery is being sought only as an aid to arbitration, to avoid claims of a waiver of the right to arbitrate.[97] Another advantage of having a discovery provision in the arbitration clause is that such a provision reduces the likelihood of a finding of waiver when seeking or participating in discovery.

The size and complexity of potential disputes, the likelihood that parties will arbitrate in good faith, and the nature and degree of material information likely to be in the hands of one party should be considered in drafting the arbitration clause. Unlike litigation, the discovery rights in arbitration can be tailored to the requirements of the most likely disputes.

Notes

[1] RLC Elec. Inc. v. American Elec. Laboratories, Inc., 39 App. Div. 757; 332 N.Y.S.2d 119 (1972).

[2] N.Y. Civ. Prac. §3102(c); see also §52–412 of the Connecticut Arbitration Act (Conn. Gen. Stat. Ann. §52–408, *et seq.* (West)). Where a state law allows an application for prearbitration discovery absent any other pending request for court relief, a federal court sitting in that state appears to also have jurisdiction over such an application, at least where there is diversity or federal question jurisdiction. Johnson v. England, 356 F.2d 44, *cert. denied* 384 U.S. 961 (9th Cir. 1966); Wright, Miller and Cooper, Federal Practice and Procedure §3721, 524–25 (ed. 1976).

[3] 3 App. Div. 2d 238, 160 N.Y.S.2d 159 (1st Dept. 1957). See also Gelbrish v. Castelluci, 46 App. Div. 2d 863, 361 N.Y.S.2d 672 (1st Dept. 1974).

[4] *Supra* n. 3, 160 N.Y.S.2d at 160–61. See also Katz v. State Dept. of Correctional Services, 407 N.Y.S.2d 967 (2d Dept. 1978); Int'l Components Corp. v. Klaiber, 54 App. Div. 550, 387 N.Y.S.2d 253 (1st Dept. 1976); MVAIC v. McCabe, 19 App. Div. 2d 349, 243 N.Y.S.2d 495 (1st Dept. 1963); 8 Weinstein-Korn-Miller, N.Y. Civ. Prac. ¶7505.06, 75–129 (ed. 1978); 31 *Lawyers' Arbitration Letter* 24, Aug. 15, 1967; "Developments in the Law—Discovery," 74 *Harvard Law Review* 940, 943 n. 7 (1961); 98 A.L.R.2d 1247 (1964).

[5] Wolff, "Disclosure Proceedings Opposed," *Bar Bulletin* 111–14, Nov.–Dec. 1960; "Arbitration and Award—Court May Permit Discovery on the Merits When It Will Not Delay Arbitration," 44 *Cincinnati Law Review* 151, 151–52 (1975).

[6] 207 App. Div. 164, 201 N.Y.S. 753 (1st Dept. 1923). See also Avon Converting Co. v. Home Ins. Co. of New York, 93 N.Y.S.2d 90 (Sup. Ct. 1949); Ehrlich v. Drake Constr. Corp., 92 N.Y.S.2d 711 (Sup. Ct. 1949); *In re* Universal Film Exchanges, Inc., 160 Misc. 416, 290 N.Y.S. 5 (Sup. Ct. 1936).

[7] *Supra* n. 6, 201 N.Y.S. at 755.

[8] 35 N.Y.2d 402, 362 N.Y.S.2d 843 (1974).

[9] N.Y.L.J., Aug. 1, 1977, at 11 (Sup. Ct. Kings Co.).

[10] *Id.*

[11] 221 Cal. App.2d 166, 34 Cal. Rptr. 346 (Ct. App. 2d Dist. Div. 2 1963).

[12] *Id.* at 171.

[13] 314 A.2d 8 (R.I. 1974).

[14] See, e.g., Allweiss v. Katz, 48 App. Div. 2d 872 (2d Dept. 1975).

[15] 357 Mass. 452, 258 N.E.2d 561 (1970).

[16] *Id.* at 564.

[17] Case No. 75–4417 (Cir. Ct. 11th Jud. Cir. Dade County, Fla. 1975).

[18] Ohio Rev. Code Ann. §2711.01, *et seq.* (Page).

[19] 5 Pa. Cons. Stat. Ann. §1, *et seq.* (Purdon).

[20] 421 Pa. 141, 218 A.2d 791 (1966).

[21] *Id.* at 794.

[22] 33 *The Record* 231, Assn. of the Bar of the City of New York (April 1978).

[23] 304 U.S. 64 (1938).

[24] 350 U.S. 198 (1956).

[25] 9 U.S.C. §1, *et seq.*

[26] *Id.*, §1.

[27] 20 F.R.D. 359 (S.D.N.Y. 1957).

[28] *Id.* at 363.

[29] *Supra* n. 24.

[30] 269 F.2d 811, 816 (6th Cir. 1959).

[31] See Erie, "Bernhardt and Section 2 of the United States Arbitration Act: A Farrago of Rights, Remedies and a Right to a Remedy," 69 *Yale Law Journal* 847, 860 (1960).

[32] 199 F. Supp. 716 (S.D.N.Y. 1961).

[33] *Id.* at 718.

[34] 43 F.R.D. 11 (S.D. Tex. 1967).

[35] 434 F.2d 192 (5th Cir. 1970).

[36] *Id.* at 194.

[37] 371 F. Supp. 240 (E.D.N.Y. 1973).

[38] 9 U.S.C. §§3–4.

[39] *Supra* n. 37 at 246.

[40] *Id.* at 245.

[41] *Id.* at 246.

[42] See n. 5, *supra.*

[43] 386 F. Supp. 430 (S.D.N.Y. 1974).

[44] *Id.* at 435 n. 8.

[45] 399 F. Supp. 516 (E.D. Pa. 1975).

[46] *Id.* at 522.

[47] 69 F.R.D. 558 (S.D. Miss. 1976).

[48] *Id.* at 566–68.

[49] Radio Corp. of America v. Solat, 31 F. Supp. 516 (S.D.N.Y. 1940); Hickman v. Taylor, 329 U.S. 495 (1947).

[50] United States v. Procter & Gamble Co., 356 U.S. 677, 682 (1958).

[51] 4 Moore's Federal Practice ¶26.02[2]; Ragland, Discovery Before Trial (1932).

[52] Moore's *supra* n. 51: "Report to the Advisory Committee on Rules of Civil Procedure," Field Survey on Federal Pretrial Discovery, Columbia University Project for Effective Practice (1965).

[53] "Tactical Use and Abuse of Depositions under the Federal Rules," 59 *Yale Law Journal* 117 (1949).

[54] See "Report of the Special Committee for the Study of Discovery Abuse." Section of Litigation. American Bar Association (rev. Dec. 1977).

[55] Interocean Mercantile Corp., *supra* n. 6.

[56] Leo Nash Steel Corp., *supra* n. 9; Bigge Crane & Rigging Co., *supra* n. 37.

[57] Leo Nash Steel Corp., *supra* n. 9.

[58] *Id.*

[59] Bigge Crane & Rigging Co., *supra* n. 37.

[60] *Id.*

[61] *Id.*

[62] *In re* Universal Film Exchanges, Inc., *supra* n. 6.

[63] Tobey v. Bristol County, 3 Story 800 (No. 14–065) (C.C. Mass. 1845).

[64] 16 *Lawyers' Arbitration Letter* 1, Nov. 15, 1963.

[65] 9 U.S.C. § 7.

[66] See §31, Commercial Arbitration Rules; and §24, Accident Claims Rules.

[67] North American Foreign Trading Corp. v. Rosen, 58 App. Div. 2d 527 (1st Dept. 1977); Di Maina v. New York State Dept. of Mental Hygiene, 87 Misc.2d 736, 386 N.Y.S.2d 590 (Albany Co. 1976); 8 Weinstein-Korn-Miller, *supra* n. 4 at ¶7505.09, 75–132; see also 9 U.S.C. §7.

[68] A Manual for Commercial Arbitrators, 11–12, Am. Arb. Assn. (Feb. 1977).

[69] Cal. Code Civ. Proc. §§1282, 1283.

[70] See Jones, "Problems of Proof in Arbitrations," *Proceedings of the Nineteenth Annual Meeting*, Nat'l Acad. of Arbitrators (1966).

[71] Atlas Floor Covering v. Crescent House & Garden Inc., 333 P.2d 194 (Cal. Dist. Ct. of App. 1958).

[72] Hyman v. Pottberg's Ex'rs, 101 F.2d 262 (2d Cir. 1939); Laurance, "The Common Sense of Arbitrations," 2 *Arbitration Journal* 113, 117 (1938).

[73] Chevron Trans. Corp. v. Astro Vencedor Compania Naviera, 300 F. Supp. 179 (S.D.N.Y. 1969).

[74] New England Petroleum Corp. v. Asiatic Petroleum Corp., N.Y.L.J. Nov. 15, 1977 at 12 (Sup. Ct. N.Y. Co.).

[75] 363 F. Supp. 1351, 1353 (E.D. Mich. 1973).

[76] Oceanic Transport Corp. v. Alcoa Steamship Co., 129 F. Supp. 160 (S.D.N.Y. 1954); Di Maina, *supra* n. 67.

[77] 15 App. Div. 2d 432, 224 N.Y.S.2d 763 (1st Dept. 1962).

[78] Commercial Solvents, *supra* n. 27.

[79] United States v. Staples, 256 F.2d 290 (9th Cir. 1958).

[80] See, e.g., N.Y. Civ. Prac. §3108.

[81] See Kuffler, "New York Charter Arbitration and Pre-Hearing Discovery: A Concept Whose Time Has Come," *Lloyd's Mar. and Com. Q.*, 557–59 (Nov. 1978).

[82] See United States Steel Corp. v. Seafarers Int'l Union, 237 F. Supp. 529 (E.D. Pa. 1965); but see Drivers, Chauffeurs, Etc. v. Akers Motor Lines, 582 F.2d 1336, 1341–42 (4th Cir. 1978).

[83] See *In re* Candee Cottons, Inc., N.Y.L.J. Jan. 18, 1960 at 13.

[84] Carolina Power & Light Co. v. URANEX, 451 F. Supp. 1044 (N.D. Cal. 1977); American Reserve Ins. Co. v. China Ins. Co., 297 N.Y. 322 (1948).

[85] Modular Technics Corp. v. Graverne Contr. Corp., 32 N.Y.2d 673 (1973); A. Sangivanni & Sons v. F.M. Floryan & Co., 262 A.2d 159 (Conn. 1969); Frederick Contractors, Inc. v. Bel Pre Medical Center, Inc., 334 A.2d 526 (Md. 1975).

[86] American Eutectic Welding Alloys Sales Co. v. Flynn, 161 A.2d 364 (Pa. 1960); but see *In re* New England Petroleum Corp. (Asiatic Petroleum Corp.), N.Y.L.J. Feb. 27, 1975 at 2 (Sup. Ct. N.Y. Co.).

[87] See Carolina Power & Light Co., a case in which resolution of a factual controversy was basic to the right of attachment, *supra* n. 84.

[88] Wolff, *supra* n. 5 at 111.

[89] *Interim Report* at 10. The Maritime Law Association's Standing Committee on Arbitration (Nov. 1975).

[90] See also Kuffler, *supra* n. 81; *The Record, supra* n. 22; 44 *Cincinnati Law Review, supra* n. 5.

[91] 44 Misc.2d 913, 255 N.Y.S.2d 282 (Sup. Ct. N.Y. Co. 1964).

[92] *Id.*, 255 N.Y.S.2d at 284.

[93] See Mobil Oil Indonesia v. Asamera Oil (Indonesia), 43 N.Y.2d 276 (1977).

[94] At present, neither the American Arbitration Association, the ICC Court of Arbitration, the New York Stock Exchange, nor the National Association of Securities Dealers has any rule nor any published position regarding discovery (other than the subpoena rules and the ICC Court of Arbitration Rules) allowing the parties or the arbitrator the power to fashion procedural rules.

[95] *Id.*

[96] *Id.* at 282.

[97] Unicon Management Corp. v. Pavcrete Constr. Corp., 259 N.Y.S.2d 598 (1st Dept. 1965); compare E.C. Ernst, Inc. v. Potlatch Corp., 462 F. Supp. 694, 695 n. 1 (S.D.N.Y. 1978).

Designing an Arbitration System for a Mass Transportation Construction Project

ROBERT T. GOLEMBIEWSKI, JEFFREY B. TRATTNER,
AND GERALD J. MILLER

Three major constraints faced the Metropolitan Atlanta Rapid Transit Authority (MARTA) in Atlanta, Georgia, in 1974 when staff members readied construction contract documents for bidding. First, plans called for an ambitious and optimistic schedule, with a no-frills budget. Second, the Urban Mass Transportation Administration (UMTA), the major federal source of funds, would approve contract awards and audit payments to contractors. This allowed UMTA to look over MARTA's shoulder, if not to second-guess, at leisure, decisions made in a fast-paced program. Third, the authority was an unknown contract manager in construction and equipment markets, with no track record in managing any construction projects, no less a $billion plus program.

Anticipating the Worst in Contract Disputes

Consequently, there was widespread uncertainty at this stage of the program. MARTA staff members were unsure about the degree of control UMTA would exert, as well as about the problems they would encounter in maintaining a strict budget and working with schedule constraints. Authority executives were concerned that the contractors might exact excessive profits and have an undue impact on the schedule. In addition, UMTA and contractors had their own misgivings. UMTA administrators assumed a major risk in granting the largest amount of federal transit dollars ever allocated to a local construction program. MARTA's tight schedule and budget counseled caution for contractors, especially in considering whether and how much to bid on MARTA work.

Experience in public works projects made it clear to the parties— MARTA, UMTA, and the contractors—that trouble would come, if anywhere, from contract disputes, with a possible loss in both time and

Reprinted with permission of the American Arbitration Association from *The Arbitration Journal.* © 1979.

money. To UMTA, disputes meant that generous awards might have to be made to contractors to avoid protracted delays. On the other hand, contractors could envision paltry profits and considerable agitation in getting the railroad built. A way of steering clear of such problems had to be found by the project managers. If they hoped to maintain the schedule and budget, avoid adverse second-guessing by UMTA, and obtain the confidence of contractors, they had to develop an equitable, inexpensive, and expeditious means of resolving contract disputes.

How Disputes Occur

MARTA's concern about a vehicle for resolving contractual disputes was well-founded. At worst the contract or the design may fail to show contractors clearly what work to do and how it should be done. At best construction plans often require additional engineering or design changes that force change orders. Change orders vary in their impact on the contract. The client will tend to seek updates of plans and designs, to benefit from hindsight, new experience, or more mature reflection. And contractors especially fear that change orders will result in added work without additional or adequate compensation. Disputes occur when a contractor disagrees with the engineer's interpretation of the work required in a construction contract and the additional payment due above what was agreed to in the original contract. MARTA indicated that it would revise contracts for five general types of changes.

Value Engineering

The potential for conflict is limited when the contractor suggests a change in specifications based on value engineering. By allowing the contractor to initiate changes, MARTA encouraged the contractor to think of better ways to accomplish the work. If contractors could alternatively meet or improve on specifications and also can prove that there is no sacrifice in quality, they could share in the savings.

Unexpected Field Conditions

A second change results from field conditions that differ from initial expectations or assumptions, a common situation that provides ample potential for honest differences, not to mention sharp dealing. For example, plans may require a contractor to compact ground to a certain density. The ground might cover a long-forgotten garbage site, however, limiting the degree of compaction possible. The standard density set in the contract would be impossible to achieve, and the contract must be changed.

Engineering Errors in Original Plans

A third change occurs when a contractor finds that engineering plans contain mistakes. The sources can be legion. The language in the specifications may be incorrect, field conditions may differ, or there may be an error in the drawings.

Changes of Mind or Will

MARTA could also decide to change plans of engineering concepts for approaching a project. These changes were likely to arise from the demands of outside interests—especially railroads, telephone, electric, gas, and other utilities, as well as the city, county, and state governments with which MARTA worked. For example, railroads are sensitive to a potential impact on their tracks. If MARTA needed to impose on their rights-of-way, railroads might force MARTA to work with their specifications. Also, the Georgia State Department of Transportation controls interstate highways and must approve plans that call for altering routes or controlling traffic. Similarly, the cities control changes affecting sewer and water lines. Many lines were built around the time of the Civil War and would disintegrate if in the path of construction. MARTA agreed to replace them, meeting present standards.

The cities or counties might also ask for other changes after city planners had approved the original design plans. One MARTA staff member stated that "We're in a hurry with the building program, and no one else is. They were here before MARTA construction and will be here afterwards." Many local agencies are chronically understaffed and cannot deal in timely ways with the volume of plans that MARTA produced. Most government agencies sign off when the drawings are made and then later require changes, as field conditions become clearer or after they have been able to really review the plans.

New Ways Bring Changes

The final type of change order occurs when, after contracts have been let, MARTA engineers find a better way of doing things. In other words, as technology advances, MARTA takes advantage and changes contracts accordingly.

Reducing the Chance of Disputes

The inevitability of change requires special attention in contract documents. The MARTA contract has two parts. The first part—the general contract—specifies general conditions under which work is to be done. The second is a special-conditions section tailored to the particular construction project. A change can occur in either. Although the special-conditions section seeks to anticipate problems, some always resist prediction.

Stresses on the Contracting Process

In such projects, there is not much leisure to solve problems. Construction is dynamic, and changes must be made quickly to keep the project going. To exacerbate the problem, MARTA's construction schedule was tight. A MARTA observer concluded that the schedule may have been "overly optimistic. It did not leave enough room for mistakes or contingencies for bad weather, labor problems, natural disasters, and so forth, which, in fact, did occur in many contracts."

In addition, a large number of MARTA contracts were bid in depressed economic circumstances. The recession of the mid-1970s initially favored MARTA and resulted in lower bids, assuming that contractors made bids on contracts only high enough to keep their firms going. Thus, MARTA's initial advantage might fade as the Atlanta economy improved, and the inevitable change orders would give contractors opportunities and motivation to reopen the bargaining on contracts.

MARTA executives wanted desperately to maintain schedule, while also realizing that this left them more vulnerable in negotiating the costs of changes. Keen competition in a tight economy often had kept bids unexpectedly low, but there would be no competition to control pricing among contractors when changes occurred at a later date. Well-placed observers feared that contractors might bludgeon MARTA at the negotiating table. Also, the changed bargaining relationship forced MARTA engineers to evaluate critically the need for every change. The ever-present question in the minds of construction project managers was, Do we want the change very badly?

The impact of contract documents on the change process also was affected by the funding formula. The contract with MARTA included a face amount and a contingency fund. The contingency was generally 10 percent, and provided an obvious target for increasing the amount a contractor could get paid as a result of contract changes. For a time, street talk also proposed that MARTA would retain a substantial "surplus" because of its favorable bidding experience, and MARTA executives were concerned that this erroneous, but oft-repeated, rumor might encourage contractors to seek aggressively hefty settlements for change orders.

Lack of Knowledge among Contractors

Another problem was a lack of information crucial to bidding among contractors. Contractors analyze past agency contract management in bidding on a new project. They look at the track record of the buyer and determine how conflicts were resolved in the past. If its record reflects arbitrariness or delay the agency may receive bids with a great deal of slack, as contractors increase their bids to compensate for anticipated problems involving agency interpretations of the contract. Given the fact that MARTA was new, all contractors suffered in their ability to estimate with sophistication. This lack of knowledge acted as a counterweight to economic conditions and strong competition, authority executives realized, and increased the possibility of problems arising in negotiations over change orders.

Strategies Sought to Reduce Disputes

Although inevitable, MARTA executives believed that contract disputes could be prevented in some instances, and that they could be restricted to reasonable boundaries in almost all cases. It initially sought ways to eliminate some of the more obvious causes of contractual disputes.

First, MARTA chose to assume the liability for contractor accidents, both those involving construction workers and those between contractors and third parties not connected with the work. For example, MARTA would pay claims for workers' compensation and also claims resulting from accidents between an Atlanta resident who happened to be in the area and a contractor's vehicle while the driver was at work.

Second, MARTA decided to use federal contract language, a decision influenced by two factors. In the development of the contract documents for the MARTA construction program, authority executives gave greatest consideration to UMTA's reserved right to approve various contract actions, either prospectively or through the audit process, based on federal regulations. With this fact firmly planted, the need for as much certainty as possible in contract documents was manifest. A common source of legal knowledge and experience would lessen the likelihood of divergent opinions regarding the propriety of various actions MARTA might take in administering contracts.

MARTA executives also attached considerable importance to the size, scope, and experience of would-be contractors. Consequently, most construction and equipment companies bidding on MARTA projects would be national firms rather than local ones. Contractors might not be familiar with Georgia law or Georgia contracting practices, but they would more than likely be familiar with practices used by federal agencies. Many contractors would be afforded a certain degree of comfort if MARTA contract language and practices were rooted in federal rather than state law.

These two factors convinced MARTA staff members to model MARTA's contract documents—especially as to general conditions—after federal contract documents, as far as practicable. This key decision sought to maximize stability. In addition, federal contracting processes and regulations were the most sophisticated and extensive available.

MARTA executives also relied on a third method to avoid construction delays. Once a change was decided on, MARTA wanted it implemented whether the contractor agreed or disagreed. MARTA executives thus inserted clauses in contracts requiring work to proceed while the contract dispute worked its way to resolution. Therefore, with or without agreements over changes, contract disputes would not have an impact on the schedule. The contractor had the option of filing a claim for payment, of course. No change could stop work, however, and no claims would result from schedule stoppages occurring over disputed changes.

MARTA Evaluates Strategies to Resolve Contract Disputes

While some disputes could be avoided at the outset, others, involving a great deal of money, could not. MARTA executives searched for a method to handle those disputes that would be inexpensive, expeditious, and fair.

Several important legal considerations influenced this decision. Although state law normally governed contract administration, the heavy infusion of federal dollars and the presence of UMTA review warned MARTA executives that federal law and regulations would govern the project as much as state law, if not more so. In handling disputes, one eye had to focus on Washington. In addition, there was no settled body of state law governing sophisticated construction contract disputes. An existing, but relatively undeveloped, body of Georgia law would not suffice. Finally, most parties sought to keep disputes away from relatively unsophisticated judges and juries whose inexperience might jeopardize a prompt and fair disposition of the case and be costly to MARTA and the contractors.

Thus, MARTA executives evaluated informal methods of dispute handling, reevaluated judicial methods, and finally concluded that an independent panel could best settle disputes through arbitration.

In-house, Informal Approaches

The legal problems in dispute handling initially led MARTA executives to consider nonlegal or informal methods, specifically handling the disputes in-house. MARTA's general engineering consultant—Parsons-Brincker-hoff, Tudor, and Bechtel (PBTB)—had supervised disputes during the San Francisco Bay Area Rapid Transit (BART) construction. MARTA executives investigated the utility of a similar arrangement in Atlanta.

The BART/PBTB model had definite advantages. This approach kept the disputes out of the courts and sidestepped the federal-local law problem. Moreover, the general engineering consultant not only had experience in handling contract disputes but also was familiar with MARTA contracts and contractors. In addition, PBTB had sufficient staff to deal with contract disputes, while MARTA would have to hire additional staff if it took on the job. Adopting the BART/PBTB model could save valuable time and capitalize on existing experience.

This approach, however, also had severe disadvantages that could threaten the budget and the quality of contractor work. First, the approach lacked built-in safeguards to cut costs. To avoid litigation, PBTB might be encouraged to settle disputes through bargaining with contractors who wanted to increase their pay-out. PBTB had little bargaining power and might be exposed to allegations that it had to buy its way out of disputes. Second, PBTB's contract with MARTA was a cost-plus-percentage arrangement based on the overall cost of the project, which also might encourage allegations of convenient settlements. Third, PBTB's additional design role—the design of stations and rail lines for MARTA—might conflict with its dispute settlement role. Having no incentive to decrease the number of changes, PBTB engineers and architects might be accused of concealing design flaws and mistakes in changes.

Jeffrey Trattner, MARTA staff counsel, concluded that the disadvantages of the BART/PBTB model outweighed the advantages. Dispute settlement, he believed, had to be handled outside MARTA to avoid conflicts and additional costs. Furthermore, to control change orders he suggested and got approval for locating authorization of change orders within MARTA rather than PBTB.

Reevaluating the Courts

MARTA executives next reevaluated the courts for handling contract disputes. Here the constraints proved overwhelming. State courts would prove unworkable due to the complexity of contract cases and the possible bias of those who would hear the case. Basically, complicated contract documents could overwhelm the already-burdened courts, with consequent time lags. In addition to the detailed and specialized language of the contract, complex drawings and charts could swamp the courts with information. A jury must be educated to the basic elements of contracts, as well as to their application in the particular case. This takes a great deal of money and time. In contrast, with an educated audience, or one having a degree of familiarity with construction, parties can rely on a certain level of assumed knowledge. Both parties can conduct more meaningful discussions. A resolution of the dispute is more likely to result from an informed discussion of the merits of the case. In addition, a jury's decisions can be made as a result of ephemeral considerations. Overloaded with information, it may decide on factors other than the merits of the case. Persuasive arguments aside, for example, the lawyer's personality might become a large issue in itself. According to Trattner, "No one in Atlanta is neutral on the subject of MARTA." The climate of opinion could work for or against MARTA; but the contractor would be cautious because "most are outsiders, not Atlanta natives, who might be viewed as carpetbaggers by a jury." Finally, local courts might invite UMTA suspicion. Since granting more than $800 million to MARTA encouraged close oversight, the inexperienced local courts could reinforce UMTA's motivation to exert tight control.

So the MARTA decision was not difficult. Local courts lacked the necessary training and experience. Reliance on local courts also might encourage more detailed pre- and postdecision review by UMTA. Consequently, MARTA executives doubted the wisdom of using state courts as dispute handlers.

The WMATA Model

MARTA staff members next looked to the Washington Metropolitan Area Transit Authority (WMATA). WMATA used the U.S. Army Corps of Engineers Board of Contract Appeals (EBCA) on an ad hoc basis, contracting with the army board to hear contract disputes when necessary.

Trattner found that this arrangement had drawbacks for MARTA. First, EBCA had less experience than other government boards of contract appeals with many of the types of contract disputes that MARTA would encounter. Second, MARTA executives disliked the tentativeness of EBCA's decisions. Under the contract clause that gave jurisdiction to EBCA, its decisions were *not* final and binding on the WMATA Board of Directors, who could reject the decisions of the army panel. In practice this has never occurred but, according to a WMATA observer, the threat remains and could work to undermine confidence in the process. This problem could be eliminated by vesting finality in the engineering board by contract. Third, WMATA bore the entire cost of using the engineer board to hear its disputes. The EBCA performs the service on a cost-reimbursable basis, at an estimated rate of approximately $50,000 a year. Fourth, the EBCA decisions could be appealed to the U.S. District Court but that court has little expertise in disputes arising under federal contracts, which are usually within the jurisdiction of the U.S. Court of Claims. MARTA's problem with state courts might reappear in federal guise if it were to follow the WMATA model.

Board of Contract Appeals at DOT

MARTA executives also investigated other federal agency methods and looked in detail at the Board of Contract Appeals in the U.S. Department of Transportation. Several advantages of that approach seemed obvious. Basically, since MARTA would be dealing with UMTA in the administration of the capital grant, some authority staff members thought that the Department of Transportation Board of Contract Appeals (DOTCAB) might prevent some UMTA second-guessing. DOTCAB would fit MARTA well for two other reasons. Many federal procurement specialists rated the DOT board as excellent in overall ability and professionalism. The board thus had a reputation for competence. Moreover, the board had wide-ranging expertise. Due to the many different transportation specialties among DOT agencies using DOTCAB, the board had achieved sophistication in dealing with construction contract claims.

As a result of procurement specialists' ratings and his own analysis of the cases facing the DOT board, Trattner moved ahead to solicit DOT interest. The move met with both agreement and opposition. Some DOT staff members regarded the use of DOTCAB as innovative and managerially advantageous. DOTCAB participation in MARTA contract claims settlement would encourage uniformity and reduce duplication in UMTA audits/ reviews. Simplification of audits and oversight also might decrease the need for interference or over-control by UMTA in local decision making. Other DOT administrators, however, opposed DOTCAB participation for two reasons. First, they believed that DOTCAB had no legislative authority to review MARTA contract disputes. A DOT order, in fact, stated that specific legal authority would be necessary to enter into an agreement with a local government. Second, DOT officials expressed concern that DOTCAB would have to apply Georgia law to many of the contract disputes, a condition DOT officials felt that DOTCAB was not competent to satisfy.

MARTA's staff counsel argued that specific DOT orders and regulations did allow DOTCAB participation. Trattner's assistant, Bruce Bromberg, stated that these rules even encouraged DOTCAB intergovernmental agreements. Moreover, Trattner explained that federal contract language would remedy the state law problem. Contractors and MARTA, as a result of federal contract language, would agree to use federal procurement law to govern the handling of disputes. Although he offered rebuttals to UMTA officials' argument, Trattner failed to convert the DOT opposition, who prevailed over the DOT pro-innovation group.

The attempt to involve DOT—although superficially simple—actually covered six months, from May to October 1975. During this time MARTA awarded two contracts without any clause specifying ways of settling disputes over claims. Other contracts would be awarded shortly, also with no such clause. Without a method to which both the contractor and MARTA were bound by contract, both parties might have to deal with the issue of *how* to settle a contract dispute, as well as with settling the dispute itself.

Arbitration

After receiving DOT's final decision, Trattner began looking at other alternatives. "Fortuitously," he recalled, "someone suggested (or I had it in the back of my mind) the possibility of using arbitration. I had received some literature on the American Arbitration Association (AAA) that described what it called its construction industry panels—for arbitration." Trattner found that AAA had set up specialized panels to deal with construction disputes. The panel concept, AAA style, already had gained wide support from major associations in the construction industry, such as the American Institute of Architects and the Construction Specifications Institute.

Wide endorsement stoked Trattner's interest. He and Bromberg met for initial discussions with AAA's then general counsel, Gerald Aksen, to explore the possibility of using AAA for dispute settlement. In the first meeting, Trattner examined the AAA processes and experiences with construction contract litigation. To learn more about AAA arbitrators' expertise in construction, Trattner searched the files of available AAA arbitrators at random to ascertain their qualifications and background. He found that AAA had numerous qualified people available to hear disputes, and that their track record was good.

Trattner also expressed concern about state legal barriers to arbitration. Could state law hinder reliance on the process? Trattner reviewed his research on state arbitration law and found that some states had enacted arbitration legislation, while others had not. Georgia was in between, in a gray area in which there appeared to be a conflict as to whether courts could compel arbitration without a state statute. That is, where two parties agree initially to arbitrate a dispute but one of the parties refuses later, could the other party go to court to order arbitration? Trattner found one case that seemed to say that the courts could not compel arbitration, while another opinion stated the opposite.

Acknowledging the conflict, AAA's Aksen suggested another approach. He observed that federal arbitration law applied when the parties engaged in interstate commerce. The interstate commerce provision could be relevant in MARTA's case because most authority contractors are out-of-state contractors and because 80 percent of its money came from federal funding. Trattner subsequently confirmed that out-of-state contractors and federal grant funds constituted enough of an interstate connection to apply federal, rather than state, law.

Trattner's conversations with Aksen and especially Trattner's own research on both legal and financial implications of arbitration for MARTA convinced him that the now crucial problem with contract disputes might get solved. Other obstacles remained, however. Particularly, how would the MARTA top management and its board react?

Gaining the Approval for Arbitration at MARTA

Trattner had to get approval for this approach from both MARTA General Manager Alan Kiepper and the MARTA Board of Directors. Trattner developed his strategy around two major points—the probable lower cost of arbitration as opposed to other methods, and the favorable opinion of MARTA construction staff about arbitration.

The most compelling argument in favor of arbitration, Trattner believed, would be the money saved. "In the long run, arbitration might turn out to be the least costly alternative. For example, using EBCA, we would have to enter into a contract to bear the expenses of all parties." With AAA arbitration, in contrast, a minimal registration fee would be paid. In addition, who pays additional costs would be decided by arbitrators assigned to a specific case, based on a fee schedule.

No less important an argument, MARTA staff members—especially Assistant General Manager for Transit System Development (AGM/TSD) William Alexander—favored arbitration. Past experience with arbitrating disputes convinced construction managers that it could work at MARTA. Staff members' reactions reflected general favor in the construction industry, as Trattner found. Almost unanimously, moreover, construction staff wanted to avoid the courts.

Following the talks with Aksen at AAA, Trattner met with General Manager Kiepper. Trattner explained the arbitration process, reported the reasons why he thought it would work, and also recommended that MARTA use the AAA. Kiepper approved Trattner's request to propose arbitration to the Development Committee of the Board of Directors.

Trattner did some prepresentation visiting and talked with three board members to explain the situation. His first stop was with Lyndon Wade, chairman of the Development Committee. Wade reacted positively and encouraged Trattner. The chief staff counsel then talked with Harold Sheats, a new board member and also development committeeman. Sheats had been a lawyer and Fulton County attorney for 25 years, in and around public construction for much of that period. He expressed no feeling about AAA arbitration either way. Sheats, however, was concerned about another related issue, the size of legal services fees and billings from law firms outside MARTA. Arbitration would use an in-house staff—Trattner's Office of Staff Counsel—to handle all arbitration. The reduced costs promised by Trattner attracted Sheats, who became an advocate for AAA arbitration.

Trattner's visits to board members were not all positive, but all proved informative. The third Development Committee member Trattner talked to was Fred P. Meyer, also an attorney. Meyer opposed arbitration because he supported reliance on outside counsel for MARTA.

Meyer's opposition seemed indicative of the position of many other attorneys in two respects. First, opposition to the process of arbitration develops from a practitioner-lawyer because, according to Trattner:

> As a general rule, the practitioner-lawyer would rather handle the case in court than arbitrate. Arbitration, generally speaking, among practitioners does not have a particularly good name, due to misinformation and a lack

of recent information about the process and how it developed over the years. In Georgia, particularly, arbitration has gotten some bad press because of the conflicting court decisions and the uncertainty that unsettled law produces. Also, practitioners point out that arbitration is always final and conclusive with no right to appeal except in very rare instances. Most attorneys by nature don't ever like anything that has no right of appeal. They don't particularly care to put all their eggs in one basket.

Trattner also found that some attorneys oppose arbitration for three additional reasons: the lack of valuable court rules, such as discovery; use of affidavits rather than actual testimony; and its common inapplicability to subcontractors, as well as to prime contractors. Practitioner-lawyers favor counsel's right to look at the opponent's case before the hearing to avoid surprises. Under arbitration, discovery does not usually apply, while courts make it available and apply it quite liberally. Attorneys proceed blindly under arbitration, only guessing the strategy and evidence that will be used by the other side. Moreover, arbitration usually allows ex parte affidavits rather than the presence and live testimony of witnesses. Affidavits might limit cross-examination and consequently the full development of the issues in dispute. Finally, attorneys object to the limited applicability of arbitration, that is, to prime contractors only. Since prime contractors typically subcontract to many other firms, the limited use of arbitration reduces its potential for problem resolution, perhaps severely. In fact, many disputes occur between the buyer (such as MARTA) and a subcontractor, leaving the buyer to deal with the subcontractor through court proceedings and the prime contractor through arbitration. The complexity of the process increases costs and neutralizes the prime contractor's ability to deal with change.[1]

Trattner made mental notes to tailor MARTA's use of arbitration to respond to most of the practitioner-lawyers' concerns, but counsel was not persuaded about Meyer's advocacy of outside lawyers for two basic reasons. First, in-house counsel has more familiarity with the problem to be arbitrated. Second, Trattner argued that the Office of Staff Counsel was organized to handle contracts. Given this background, according to Trattner, "It would have been extremely costly to turn a partially developed arbitration package over to an outside attorney who was not working in construction at all. Even with our background, we still spend many, many hours preparing when we go to arbitration."

Trattner's next stop was the full Development Committee. Because initial reaction among construction staff members had been good, Trattner asked Transit System Development (TSD) head Alexander to accompany him before the committee, so that Alexander could help answer questions. On December 3, 1975, Trattner, Alexander, and other TSD staff members met with the Development Committee. Trattner explained the pros and cons of arbitration; Meyer raised questions about in-house or outside counsel responsibility for arbitration (but the issue failed to excite other members); and Alexander expressed satisfaction with the proposal. After discussion, the committee voted to approve the use of arbitration.

The Development Committee reported the proposal favorably to the full Board of Directors on December 8. The board routinely passed a resolution unanimously approving arbitration.

Implementing Arbitration at MARTA

Having secured board approval, Trattner and Bromberg began implementing arbitration by drafting a contract clause that met the complaints raised by the practitioner-lawyers. In addition, Trattner sought to solve three other key problems by guaranteeing a legal presence in arbitration cases, resolving the conflict between federal and state law, and avoiding premature resort to arbitration. (For details of MARTA contract features related to arbitration, see Appendix 1.)

Trattner dealt with the first practitioner-lawyer objection by preparing a basic arbitration clause that allowed the use of federal rules of discovery. Opposing sides in a contract dispute were granted the right to examine the other's evidence before the arbitration hearing. Second, the clause prohibited ex parte affidavits. Third, the arbitration clause became mandatory in all subcontracts.

In addition to meeting the practitioner-lawyers' objections, Trattner acted on three other potential problems. The new contract clause provided that at least one member of the arbitration panel must be an attorney, in part to ensure that the panel enforced rules of discovery. Trattner felt that only an attorney could adequately deal with each side's desire for fairness in applying federal rules for reciprocity in revealing evidence. To further ensure the presence of an attorney, the clause required a one-person panel—a lawyer—for disputes under $25,000. Disputes involving more than $25,000 would be heard by a three-person panel, one of whose members would be a lawyer.

To prevent the uncertainty resulting from unsettled state law, a second potential problem, the arbitration clause provided that all questions arising under contracts must be governed by and decided according to the law applicable to U.S. government procurement contracts. This linked MARTA disputes with 30 years of federal precedent. In addition, the link allowed for introduction of evidence, representation by counsel, and other normal federal requirements of due process.

Trattner also set up a triggering procedure for arbitration that prevented a third problem, the premature resort to the process. Under this procedure, contractors cannot resort to arbitration until they receive a final decision from MARTA denying a contract claim. In effect, MARTA executives must state that their decision is final, except insofar as the contractor has a right to demand arbitration.

MARTA's Arbitration Model in Action

The Change Process: The Setting for Disputes

As previously noted, the process of changing the work outlined in engineering designs and undertaken by a contractor who wins an award begins when one of five conditions obtains. (1) The contractor may find a better way of doing work. (2) Field conditions may differ from those assumed in engineers' plans. (3) Alternately, the contractor may find mistakes in original designs or plans. (4) MARTA engineers also may decide to change plans as a result of a request or demand from some other agency, such as a railroad, or the state, counties, or cities. (5) Finally, MARTA engineers may change plans to take advantage of new technology.

The Initiating Change Notice

A change notice based on one of the five conditions initiates the process of changing work. A change notice essentially outlines the change needed and provides for review by MARTA staff members and negotiation with the contractor.

From Change Notice to Change Order

A typical facilities contract change notice—based on a request originating either with the contractor, MARTA, or the authority's general engineering consultants (now Parsons, Brinckerhoff and Tudor, or PBT)—starts with the resident engineer (RE), who prepares the notice with a justification and preliminary cost estimate. The notice goes up MARTA's TSD chain of command for approval.

Three factors guide TSD officials' review of a change notice. First, these officials want to create and maintain a reputation for fairness and flexibility in dealing with contractors. According to TSD's Alexander, MARTA reviewers have the power to break contractors through inflexibility in administering changes. The injudicious use of such power backfires, however, and results in higher bids as word gets around in the contracting community. Second, TSD officials want to motivate contractors to finish work quickly. Inflexible change-notice reviews could provoke contractors to resist time-saving measures for which they might otherwise go unrewarded. Third, smooth day-to-day operating relations between MARTA construction managers and contractors are a premium not to be recklessly threatened. Inflexibility and unfairness in handling changes would create adversaries out of parties who could cooperate. Thus, the TSD approach to change-notice review is based on the goals of expediting work and maintaining cooperation with contractors.

The change notice also goes to the Office of Staff Counsel for review as it goes up the TSD hierarchy. Two basic reasons explain the involvement of the staff counsel. First, UMTA reserves the right in all prime and subcontracts to audit under certain conditions for a period up to three years following payment. The potential costs to MARTA are great. As Trattner explained, "If we process a change order, and we take a position, settle it, and pay a claim resulting from the change order, the federal government can come back a year later, review the paperwork and say that we have not justified this change order. They will, therefore, declare this change order ineligible for federal participation or for 80 percent payment. You can't stand too many of those."

Second, the Office of Staff Counsel provides an independent review by an in-house staff member with no direct involvement in construction and, thus, who is beyond subtle conflicts of interest. MARTA negotiators should ask themselves: "Are we enforcing our contract rights; are we paying for things that we otherwise should not be paying for?" The Office of Staff Counsel acts as objective reviewer, analyzing contract documents for both legal and engineering implications. To handle both substantive and legal aspects, the Office of Staff Counsel has a civil engineer/lawyer. This ambidexterity "makes us both useful and potentially troublesome," Trattner believes. "From the engineering standpoint, there is not much we can't understand. No matter how complex the change order, we can usually decipher what they are talking about. We can read the drawings and the technical specifications and decide whether or not they make sense."

Both UMTA second-guessing and the necessity of an overall view explain the pivotal role the staff counsel's office assumes in contract matters. According to Trattner:

> The staff counsel is the one point within the authority where all the pieces come together, short of the general manager. We are independent of everybody else. We are the only office that has an overview of the whole program.

Most important, if there is a problem with UMTA auditors, we wind up defending the matter. If something goes to arbitration, we wind up handling the arbitration. It is only right that we should know what is happening in advance and concur in it.

The staff counsel reviews the change notice initially to determine whether contractors are entitled to extra payment or whether they are already obligated under the terms of the contract to perform the change. In addition, the counsel analyzes the notice for form and substance. This involves answering such questions as is the language clear, are the references accurate, and are we citing the right authority for proceeding with the change? The initial review by staff counsel also points out other implications of the change, such as the effect on any contracts. Finally, counsel determines whether authority and funds exist to issue the change notice as such.

After staff counsel review, the notice goes to the contractor. The contractor replies with a proposal, which is returned to the staff counsel for review. Counsel then provides engineers with an opinion on whether the cost is allowed, including the question of any additions as well as whether proper credit is received when deleting items.

The engineers then negotiate with the contractor. If the two parties agree, a change order is drafted. At this point, the staff counsel again reviews to assure that the negotiated position is consistent with prior reviews. After this review, the order goes to the AGM/TSD for final approval.

Handling Disputes

The change process may, of course, provoke disputes between contractors and MARTA engineers that are not amenable to negotiations. For instance, based on a legal position taken by the staff counsel, the MARTA negotiator may not accept the contractor's cost estimate for a contract change and the contractor may refuse to sign the change order without the price concession. MARTA engineers then issue a unilateral change order that directs the contractors to perform, giving them 30 days to protest the order by submitting a claim. In another instance, MARTA engineers may issue a letter change order, directing the contractors to perform the change. If contractors think they are entitled to additional funds for their work, they may then submit a proposal for negotiation. If, after negotiation, contractors disagree with MARTA's position, they are directed to perform the change and file a claim.

The process for attempting to resolve any disputes involves a number of steps, of which arbitration is the last and final one. (For details about the procedures through which contractors can make a claim against MARTA, see Appendix 2.)

As a first step toward that final resolution, resident engineers examine the contractor's claim. The REs, the TSD representatives at the work site, provide a factual analysis of the contractor's claim. They present the circumstances objectively in a report to their superior—in this instance, the project engineer. After developing the facts, the resident engineers may deny the claim. Otherwise, they remain silent. The contractor, in either case, then submits the claim through the resident engineer to TSD's Division of Construction. The division evaluates the claim, along with TSD's Division of Engineering and the staff counsel. If all three groups recommend the contractor's position, the assistant general manager of TSD signs approval. If one recommends denial, the claim goes back down the chain of command to the RE who informs the contractor that the claim is denied, and that the contractor has a right to request a final decision.

The final decision constitutes the unsatisfied contractor's last step before arbitration. This triggers a process set up as MARTA's fail-safe mechanism, one in which more MARTA staff members get involved in the decision-making process. When the contractor requests a final decision, the RE again reviews the claim and adds any additional information found since the original analysis. From the RE, the request goes to the project engineer, and then to the staff counsel. The attorney in the Office of Staff Counsel who originally reviewed and denied the claim prepares another analysis and reviews his or her work. If the same conclusion is reached, the staff counsel requests the AGM/TSD to convene MARTA's "Gray-Haired Council." Final decisions are to be rendered within two weeks after the contractor's request.

The Gray-Haired Council consists of a group of senior MARTA employees who act as advisors to AGM/TSD Alexander in making the final decision on the contractor's request. The name was inspired by Alexander, who observed that in such cases MARTA "needed some gray hair involved in settling disputes, some wisdom of the ages." The council's formal membership included MARTA's director of construction and director of engineering, the PBT project director, the PBT director of construction, and Trattner as staff counsel. Other PBT engineering staff members may take part, depending on the subject matter. In addition to the usual members, the Gray Hairs convene with the attorney who did the research, the TSD project engineer, and the resident engineer. The council examines the drawings and the contract documents; the attorney presents the case and his or her recommendation; and then the floor opens for discussion. According to one member:

> It is a pretty free-wheeling discussion. It tries to introduce practical considerations. For example, while we may think we may have a good legal position, we start to get into the practicalities of who is going to be the expert witness. What kind of witness would the resident engineer make? What kind of documentation do we have to support our position? From the standpoint of the arbitration panel, how reasonable a case does the contractor have? Is there more than one reasonable interpretation? What's the industry practice? Are we stipulating something that is out of the ordinary?
>
> We throw all of these things out for discussion. We call for more information, such as whether we have interpreted this particular clause differently on other contracts. The discussion ranges from ten minutes to two hours. At the end of it, I think we hash out almost everything. Then we say, "Let's go around the table and see where we stand."

The council's final decisions to date have been unanimous, but variable in direction—sometimes in favor of the original staff counsel decision, other times agreeing with the contractor's request, or even some middle position for negotiating a settlement.

The council serves three major purposes in maintaining the integrity and momentum of the MARTA rail construction program. First, the council brings more than 100 years of construction-contract expertise to bear on a particular problem. Second, it brings together people who had nothing directly to do with the original decision, and who can provide a fresh approach to the problem. Third, it provides flexibility at a high level in dealing with contractors. The group may meet some of a contractor's objections, while dismissing others.

Going to Arbitration

A few disputes reach the final stage of resolution—arbitration. Both MARTA and the contractor agree in signing the original contract that the decision of the arbitration panel will be final.

The arbitration process gets triggered after an adverse final decision from Alexander, when the contractor may choose to initiate the arbitration process by filing a notice with both MARTA and the American Arbitration Association. The notice spells out the specific issue over which the contractor and MARTA are in conflict.

AAA then handles the administration of the case. The Association provides MARTA and the contractor with a list of arbitrators—including in the list background information and areas of expertise—from which the parties choose a panel. Identical lists are furnished to all parties. The parties review the lists, strike those who are objectionable to them, and rank all of those acceptable in order of preference.

The process of striking arbitrators may involve gamesmanship, a thrust-and-parry to bargain over who will hear the dispute. The information provided by AAA about the proposed arbitrators' backgrounds is limited and encourages guessing about their probable inclination. Depending upon the nature of the claim, there are at least five different areas of expertise represented on the AAA list. AAA may propose attorneys who have only general legal experience and some or no construction background, as well as attorneys with a construction background—such as a patent attorney who is also a mechanical engineer. Some proposed arbitrators may come from the contractor community, including owners of construction companies, for instance. AAA also may propose academicians, such as a professor of civil or mechanical engineering. Architect-engineers are often included, particularly those who work as consulting engineers for design, with no involvement in construction. Finally, there are government employees who would be counsel-equivalents at state, local, or federal levels. Depending on the subject matter of the claim involved, the parties must decide which mix of arbitrators is most acceptable. Trattner observed that

> It's akin to selecting a jury. In one sense, you've got much less information because you can't question these people as you can potential jurymen. In other senses, you have much more information about panel members. You've got a little biographical blurb, and advice solicited from people in MARTA and PBT who have backgrounds in construction and engineering. Those people know something about what backgrounds predict what decisions; and they may even know people on the list. It comes out to an educated guess.

Limits do get placed on AAA in proposing panel members to encourage objectivity—a problem usually caused by a conflict of interest. "We have insisted from the beginning," noted Trattner, "that we did not want anybody on the list from the Atlanta area, because the odds are that we would have a conflict sooner rather than later. It's inevitable; the project is so large." Trattner related one example. "The certainty of a conflict was proven very dramatically when we recently received a list that included the name of a local attorney. On that same day, he filed a lawsuit against us."

The striking of names may continue, according to MARTA's arbitration procedure, through two lists of ten names each. If AAA finds agreement impossible, it imposes a panel. As yet, AAA has not imposed a panel.

At the same time the parties select panel members, they begin the discovery process. The parties interrogate one another in writing to ascertain anything relevant to the claim. If either party fails to provide information the other party or parties find necessary, the matter gets referred to the attorney member of the panel whose decision is final.

All preliminaries concluded, the parties schedule an arbitration date with AAA and file pretrial memoranda with the panel members, if necessary.

The panel meets with the parties, who can call witnesses and examine and cross-examine them. All witnesses must appear before the panel, as a rule. If attendance is impossible, a witness may be examined at another time and a deposition taken, providing that the party examining the witness gives reasonable notice to the other party of the place and time this will occur.

After hearing the evidence, the panel allows further memoranda from the parties. Finally, the arbitration panel decides the issue and assesses cost.

Having instituted arbitration as the ultimate method of settling contract disputes, MARTA managers also have continually assessed the process. The short experience with arbitration so far suggests that both managers and contractors perceive that the entire process has resulted in fair settlements and that the process has helped expedite construction and reduce delays. But more important, the arbitration process has helped overcome the wicked triple bind—constricting budgets and schedules, potential federal agency intrusion, and watchful, even skeptical, contractors—that faced MARTA managers at the start of construction.

Appendix 1

MARTA CONTRACT CLAUSES RELATING TO ARBITRATION

1. Any dispute concerning or arising out of or in connection with any decision, determination, or other action by the Authority or its duly authorized representatives, or arising out of or in connection with the warranty of the Work, shall be decided by arbitration in accordance with the Construction Industry Arbitration Rules of the American Arbitration Association then in effect. For this purpose, arbitrators shall be appointed by the American Arbitration Association in accordance with Section 13 of the said Rules. If the amount in dispute is less than $25,000, one arbitrator, who shall be an attorney, shall be appointed; if the amount in dispute is $25,000 or more, three arbitrators, at least one of whom shall be an attorney, shall be appointed, and all decisions and awards shall be made by a majority of them, as provided in Section 28 of the said Rules. The arbitration proceedings shall be governed by and conducted in accordance with this Article, the said Rules, and Title 9 of the United States Code. The parties stipulate and agree that this Contract evidences a transaction

involving commerce within the meaning of Section 2 of the said Title 9 of the United States Code.

2. The Authority will finance the Work in part by means of a grant under the Urban Mass Transportation Act of 1964, as amended, administered by the U.S. Department of Transportation under a capital grant contract between the Authority and the United States. In order to ensure that the Contract is performed in all respects in conformity with the said capital grant contract and with the laws and regulations governing the same, all disputes subject to this Article, and all questions arising in connection therewith, shall be governed by and decided according to the law applicable to U.S. Government contracts.

3. Arbitration in good faith of all disputes subject to this Article shall be a condition precedent to the commencement by either party of any action at law, suit in equity, or other proceeding involving any such dispute, and this Article shall be specifically enforceable under the applicable arbitration law. The arbitrators' award, and their decisions of all questions of law and of fact in connection therewith, shall be final and conclusive, and their awards shall be enforceable as provided in Title 9 of the United States Code.

4. Notice of the demand for arbitration shall be filed in writing with the other party to the Contract and with the American Arbitration Association. In the case of a dispute arising out of or in connection with any decision, determination, or other action by the Authority or its representatives, no demand for arbitration shall be made until the Contractor has received written notice explicitly stating that the decision, determination, or action involved is final subject only to arbitration in accordance with this Article. In all such cases the Contractor shall file his notice of demand for arbitration within thirty days next after he has received such notice, unless, in the case of the particular decision, determination, or action this Contract prescribes a different time, in which case such different time shall control. In the case of a dispute arising out of or in connection with the warranty of the Work, the notice of demand for arbitration shall be filed within a reasonable time, not in excess of one year, after the dispute has arisen. In the case of all other disputes subject to arbitration under this Article the demand for arbitration shall be filed within a reasonable time after the dispute has arisen, but in no event more than six months after the Authority has formally accepted the Work as provided [elsewhere]. Failure to file a timely notice of demand for arbitration of any dispute subject to arbitration hereunder shall constitute a waiver of all claims and rights in connection with such dispute.

5. The parties mutually promise and agree that after either has filed a notice of demand for arbitration of any dispute subject to arbitration under this Article, they shall, before the hearing thereof, make discovery and disclosure of all matters relevant to the subject matter of such dispute, to

the extent and in the manner provided by the Federal Rules of Civil Procedure. All questions that may arise with respect to the fulfillment of or the failure to fulfill this obligation shall be referred to an arbitrator who is an attorney for his determination, which shall be final and conclusive. This obligation shall be specifically enforceable.

6. Arbitration under this Article and all hearings in connection therewith shall be held in Atlanta, Georgia. All witnesses who testify at such hearings shall be sworn and subject to cross-examination by the adverse party; depositions may be used if, in the discretion of the arbitrator or arbitrators, the deponent is not reasonably available to testify thereat, and provided that the deposition offered in lieu of his testimony was taken under oath and after reasonable notice to the adverse party of the time and place thereof; notwithstanding sections 31 and 32 of the aforesaid Rules, an *ex parte* affidavit shall in no event be considered over the objection of the party against whom it is offered.

7. The Contractor promises and agrees that the provisions of this clause shall be included in all subcontracts into which he may enter for labor to be performed on, or materials or supplies to be delivered to, used in, or incorporated into the Work, and that if any dispute subject to arbitration under this Article involves labor, materials, or supplies furnished under any such subcontract, the rights and liabilities of the Authority, the Contractor, and all subcontractors who are or may be involved shall be determined in a single arbitration proceeding.

8. The Contractor shall carry on the work and maintain the progress schedule during any arbitration proceedings.

Appendix 2

MARTA PROCEDURES FOR CONTRACTOR CLAIMS

1. *Contractor Claim*
   1. Immediately after receipt from the Contractor, [Resident Engineer] prepares a factual analysis, without recommendations, and submits to Construction Division. Negotiations will not be conducted with Contractor, although additional information may be requested.
   2. Staff Counsel and Engineering Division advice sought and decision reached. Communicate to Resident Engineer.
   3. Proceed as directed by the Authority to:
      a. Initiate change notice, or
      b. Communicate denial to the Contractor indicating right to appeal to the Authority submitting any additional documentation in support of his claim. Resident Engineer's letter to Contractor will *not* indicate that the decision or determination is "final, subject to arbitration" or words to that effect.

2. *Contractor's Request for Final Decisions*
   1. Submit to MARTA Construction Division.
   2. Directors of Construction and Engineering, MARTA and [PBT], Project Director, Engineer and Chief Staff Counsel will evaluate basis of dispute and will meet with Assistant General Manager for Transit System Development to provide him with recommendations.
   3. If so decided by the Assistant General Manager for Transit System Development, Construction Division in coordination with Staff Counsel shall prepare a Final Decision for the signature of the Assistant General Manager for Transit System Development.
   4. Delivers Final Decision to Contractor and records date, time and name of Contractor's representative receiving Final Decision.
   5. Foregoing will be accomplished within 2 weeks (where possible) from Construction Division's receipt of Contractor's request for a Final Decision.
3. *Contractor's Request for Arbitration*
   1. Forward all related documents to MARTA Construction Division. Assist in evaluation and preparation of arbitration package.
   2. Coordinate preparation of arbitration package, and provide necessary support of Staff Counsel.

Notes

[1] Editor's Note: In practice, many of these objections to commercial arbitration have been overcome. First, while no prehearing discovery is called for, most arbitrators will adjourn after the first hearing to allow the parties time to exchange important documents. Since this exchange takes place after arbitration is initiated, controls can be maintained on the time allotted to this function. Second, while commercial rules indicate that arbitrators may accept affidavits, they may also reject their submission and insist on direct testimony when necessary. Third, many prime contractors today have included arbitration clauses in their contracts with subcontractors to avoid the necessity of taking their disputes into court.

A Contractor Looks at the Causes of Construction Contract Disputes

MAX FELDMAN

To understand the causes of construction contract disputes, it is necessary to understand the roles of the various parties involved and how those roles contribute to the creation of controversy. Similarly it is necessary to analyze the realities, timeliness, and reasonableness of the various instruments used to bind the parties together, which in all probability, if more prudently prepared, exercised, and interpreted, would lead to significantly less controversy and far more productive, cooperative effort.

Far too often today the initial and usually prevailing attitude on both private and public works is the "antagonist" approach rather than the productive "teamwork" attitude that should prevail. Too often the architect or resident engineer presents a lofty or completely diametric and sometimes even hostile attitude toward the contractor from the very onset of the project. The cause of friction is thus instantaneously sparked and remains throughout the project. Without involving oneself too deeply in the psychiatrics that may exist, it is time that the architect-engineer team and the contractor recognize that they are equals and not adversaries, that the contractor is not a devious, unscrupulous, unprofessional roughneck any more than the architect-engineer is a moral, scrupulous, all-knowing ego above question, criticism, or reproach.

It is also necessary for the industry to recognize that times have changed. The traditional institutions and approaches require drastic reformation to withstand the onslaught of increasing controversy stemming not only from the old problems but from the new challenges that are emerging from today's socioeconomic changes, ecological demands, population explosion, dilution of human and natural resources, the introduction of new materials and concepts that are in total conflict with heretofore traditional construction, the impact of union restrictive practices, and the introduction of more and more government intervention and control. The architect-engineer and the contractor must set aside past differences and approach the new problems as partners in a common search for more workable methods.

In this context it is possible to set forth the genesis of the major problems of controversy in the construction industry, which basically stem from

Reprinted with permission of the American Arbitration Association from *The Arbitration Journal.* © 1972.

three generalized areas: the design, the contract documents, and the construction.

Design

Role of Architect-Engineer

He or she is the *designer* of the plans and specifications, who may or may not provide field supervision of the contract work. While his role may not have significantly changed in relationship to the owner or client, the extent of his work in the design and detail of the plans and specifications has become exceedingly more complex and involved. He has become the "middleman" between the owner and contractor in obtaining the end results and, therefore, more often than not becomes in fact the agent of the owner, even if he lacks the legal right to this role. He rarely performs as the *designer only* of the plans and specifications. Because he is a businessman seeking new work, or volunteering to protect his client, or as a strong ego refusing to admit to errors or omissions in his own plans and specifications, his findings understandably are not always unbiased, detached, or impartial, and the ensuing findings or opinions oftentimes represent his vested interests.

Architect-Engineer Fees

It is time, therefore, to recognize that many of the problems that lead to disputes arise out of lack of appropriate staff or consultants, and that this arises out of inadequate architectural fees. It may seem strange for a contractor to become the advocate for increased fees for professional services, but then who is most affected by the results of inadequate staff and knowledge due to low fees; who is most affected by incomplete, unconformed plans and specifications; and who has more day-to-day intimate knowledge of causes of controversy and the usual impractical, arbitrary, or unknowledgeable means employed to resolve them or ignore them, which lead to greater delay, confusion, indecision, and greater losses or damages to one or all of the parties involved?

The professional's performance is a direct function of the adequacy of his fee. Too often the best talent in the architect's-engineer's office is directed to design with the least attention to detail and specifications. The fee structure is outdated and inadequate, and by sheer economic necessity the architect is compelled to minimize his services and use a "cookie cutter" approach to plans, taking details from prior projects and pasting them onto the new project without appropriate modification, or failing to provide sufficient detail drawings for construction, or failing to coordinate and conform the architectural, structural, and mechanical plans, and the specifications of the project.

Use of Paraprofessionals or Sales Representatives

Too often major details of the drawings and portions of the specifications are provided by "considerate" sales representatives of special products, equipment, building material, and the like. Many such "special interest" specifications are written more by sales representatives than by independent qualified architects or engineers, which often leads to exclusivity for the product, preempting competitive bidding. In many instances such procedures lead to specifying inappropriately tried and tested materials or products. Too often the specification stipulates a specific product and stimulates use in accordance with manufacturer's specifications or requirements whereby the architect abdicates his responsibility of design and attempts to transfer it to others not involved in or responsible for design.

When an architect-engineer decides to use a new product, the responsibility for its use must remain with the architect. The responsibility of amply researching the product must be that of the professional; if he cannot suitably assure himself of its performance, then adequate guarantees not only of the performance of the product but also its effects on other portions of the work or its use in occupancy should be carefully and stringently spelled out so that the manufacturer assumes the appropriate responsibility. The mere replacement of the material, product, or equipment probably is an insufficient remedy. Since the use of the material or product is exclusively decided by the architect-engineer under his design prerogative, the responsibility of its performance, except for its installation in accordance with the manufacturer's or architect's requirements, cannot and should not be imparted to the contractor but must lie with the manufacturer and the architect.

The Specification Writer

Too little attention is directed to this vital arm of the architectural team. The very nature of the work requires unusual expertise not only in the technology involved but also in legal knowledge, union practices, and proficiency in technical writing. In most architectural offices, however, the least attention and salary expenditure is directed to the specification writer. Apparently the very nature of the work attracts the least imaginative, experienced, and knowledgeable of the architectural or engineering technocrats.

While this phase of work is as important as any other in the total concept, and certainly more demanding and rigorous than any of its counterparts, it suffers most from inattention and inexperience. It suffers from insufficient dialogue with the designers and engineers, and often is assembled without regard for the specific needs of the project. To what extent are most specification writers reduced to "scissors specialists" attempting to tailor specifications from other jobs and other sources to the specific job on hand, without correcting preexisting errors and without recognizing that the specifications or portions thereof are being used out of context? This common practice, together with the often low caliber of experience and knowledge, almost always leads to errors or omissions, or ambiguities between the plans and specifications, and to the nonconformed set of specifications.

The Contract Documents

The private sector provides the greatest flexibility in selecting the type of contract best suited to its needs and consequently is much less vulnerable to dispute. The built-in flexibility usually controls the selection of the architect and contractor and provides the necessary fees to permit the professionals and contractors to furnish full and complete services. It also lends itself to the teamwork concept of owner-architect-contractor, which tends to resolve problems at the outset and minimize their impact on costs and controversy.

It is axiomatic that public bidding suffers the most from controversy and is the most exposed to arbitrary and even capricious rulings. Correspondingly the public agency, because of the structure of the system and the salaries involved, is usually least serviced by either competent staff or staff with sufficient authority at all levels for the immediate, decisive action that could mitigate damages and delays. Public bidding is further aggravated by the introduction of its own General Conditions, Supplementary General Conditions, Typical Details, Standard Details, Standard Specifications, and the like, which add to the similar and other voluminous documents prepared by the architect-engineer for the specific job. Obviously this creates duplication, confusion, ambiguity, and a series of catch-alls deliberately intended to protect the public by confusing everyone and covering everything. Needless to say this practice does not save the taxpayer's money since the initial bids are higher than should be. This practice also does not avoid controversy, and it is probably true that more contractors are bankrupted on public works projects than in any other sector of the economy. Obviously higher bids do not protect against many "catch-alls" or "grandfather" clauses as are used in public bid documents.

If the mere contract documents in public bidding were not preemptive enough, the effects are compounded by the awarding of multiple or of separate prime contracts for the major items of work such as plumbing, heating-ventilating-air conditioning, electrical, structural steel, elevators, and general construction. Separately awarded contracts, according to the agency involved, may be administered by the architect, a resident engineer, a construction manager, or the general contractor. No matter who supervises the prime contractors, invariably conflicts arise over the ambiguities in the plans and specifications, delays and disruptions to the work of others by one or more of the contracting parties, or by changes in the scope of work that may have effects and costs far surpassing the cost of the physical change itself. The decision of the supervising agent, whether by caprice, arbitrariness, indecision, inexpertise, or other reason, may be catastrophic to the economics and timing of the project and may lead to controversy, increased costs, disharmony, and even to bankruptcy of the contracting firms. Litigation is a court of last resort, and often innocent firms cannot last while awaiting the outcome of litigation.

It must be recognized that if the supervising agent on such prime contract awards is the architect or general contractor, he does not have the authority to compel compliance by any defaulting prime contractor because of the lack of privity of contract and, therefore, lacks the financial threat to hold over the head of the defaulting party. When the supervising agent is a resident engineer or construction manager for the owner, as agent for the owner he is empowered to take the necessary steps to control and direct the prime contractors and costs. If his efforts tend to be either dictatorial or indecisive, however, he can effectively disrupt the job progress.

The Contractor

The contractor is the force that translates the thought and word into physical reality, converting the plan and specification into "bricks and mortar." He is not the designer, nor does he interpret the plan and specification. He constructs what is shown and contracted for—nothing more and nothing less. That he may be an engineer or architect himself or employ such professionals in no way changes his responsibility or obligation.

The contractor today is more and more a conglomerate of subcontractors, material suppliers, union affiliations, accountants, engineers, and technicians, and less and less the image of 30 to 50 years ago. The contractor no longer is the Lord of the Fief, performing virtually all the work with his own labor force which he totally controlled and exploited. The contractor of the 1970s and 1980s is a far cry from his predecessor, and it is time that this different image was recognized. It is time that contract documents between the owner and contractor are appropriately reformed to reflect the realities of today's society. The contractor cannot control forces over which he has no authority; he cannot assume responsibility over work forces, laws, events, and designs over which he has no control and which operate in total independence of the contractor, and which often are even counterproductive to his own efforts. This lack of awareness by the owner-architect of the limitations imposed on the contractor is one of the primary root causes of disputes arising out of the contract documents.

The basic effectiveness of a general contractor lies in establishing sequence of work, selection of subcontractors, coordination of the work of subcontractors and his own work forces, and providing, where the contract permits, a centralized authority and quality control on the site. But his authority stops here!

In most larger centers of population, one subcontractor has become the main contracting force because of his ability to specialize and keep his work force and equipment constantly employed. His work load, attitude, and competence may well be the controlling criteria on the job.

But in actuality, both the contractor and the subcontractor are subservient to the role of labor. The worker comes from a union hiring hall. This union has usurped the role of the contractor who historically was the entrepreneur and employer. The union now generally decides how many men are required, what caliber of men will be provided, what productivity will develop, how much nonproductive, standby labor force will be imposed, and what the wages will be. There is no such thing as realistic collective bargaining any longer between contractor and union. The union has and controls the manpower resource and therefore contains the power and decision making. It effectively dictates to the contractor the terms under which he will work, and these terms can significantly change as union contracts are renegotiated while the project is under way. By this control it not only determines the economics and scheduling of the job, but it also establishes the quality of workmanship.

Erosion of the original anticipated conditions constantly takes place. New products, equipment, or methods that could lead to reduced costs are often restricted or prohibited by the union. Materials and methods of construction may be specified in the plans and specifications and the job accordingly bid, yet the union may well be the final determining factor as to how the job will be done and what materials will be used. Obviously the contractor can thereby be placed in serious financial jeopardy.

Other major and new factors have also entered today's picture, such as Equal Employment Opportunity, where neighborhood minority action groups in concert with governmental agencies have propounded new requirements on the hiring practices and work forces to be used on the project, in conflict with prevailing union practices. Again the contractor exerts less and less control over production or quality control and even the economics of the job.

Adding to these problems, governmental directives from federal, state, and local agencies spew forth with ever increasing, rigorous requirements, and insert and demand new, sometimes drastic, uneconomic and unobtainable concessions from general contractors. The devices used to impose miscellaneous requirements are the usual, vague catch-all contractual clauses. Instead of relying on legislative practice to obtain social reform and confront those who make and can change the operating rules, namely government and labor, it is found more expeditious and less controversial to impose these demands and requirements on the most unlikely and least influencing party, the general contractor, to accomplish the desired ends. But the wrong conduit is being used as the means; the use of "privity" to withhold payments merely penalizes the general contractor, who cannot accomplish the social changes mandated, and improperly adds another onerous provision to the contract documents that does not belong. This does not mean to imply that the contractor should not contribute to the commitment of nondiscrimination and Equal Employment Opportunity, but it cannot be made the scapegoat of the failure of the body politic to implement effective plans of affirmative action. Politicians issuing executive orders to governmental agencies, who promulgate these into contractual scripture, only lead the contracting parties into further controversy, impotence, and polarization, and divert attention from the proper focal points.

The Catch-All or Grandfather Clauses

The number and type of "catch-all" clauses used in the General Conditions, Supplementary General Conditions, or Supplemental Conditions are legion. Among the most common and troublesome are those that attempt to provide for a complete job regardless of errors and omissions that may exist in the contract documents. Typical of these problem-creating clauses are:

> Para. 1.2.3. of the AIA General Conditions. "Execution Correlation, Intent and Interpretations" which states ". . . It is not intended that work covered under any heading, section, branch, class, or trade of the Specifications shall be supplied unless it is required elsewhere in the contract documents or *is reasonably inferable therefrom as being necessary to produce the intended results."*

Other such typical devices commonly used are:

> The contract documents, as listed in the Form of the Agreement are complementary, and *it is the intention of those documents to include all work necessary for the proper completion of the project.*
>
> *The Contractor will be furnished additional instructions and detail drawings as necessary to carry out the work included in the contract.* The additional drawings and instructions thus supplied to the Contractor *will coordinate with the Contract Documents and will be so prepared that they can be reasonably interpreted as part thereof.*

Such provisions invariably lead to dispute. Design is the inherent responsibility of the architect and his consultants. The contractor's obligation is to build what is in the plans and specifications, not to interpret them. The contractor's bid is predicated on what is shown on the plans and specifications, not on what his interpretations of those plans and specifications might be. It must be recognized that the architect and his professional consultants have spent months designing and drafting the plans and specifications—their knowledge of the project is unique and intimate and complete, and the contractor in the few weeks of preparing a bid can never be as knowledgeable of these factors and concepts and, therefore, in no way can assume any responsibility for the errors or omissions or the lack of conformance of these documents. It is also reasonable to conclude that if the information had been appropriately shown at the time of the bid, all bids would have accordingly reflected the costs and the owner would have knowingly paid for it. What justification can therefore be offered for such attempts by the contract documents, and the architect in his findings, to obtain unjust enrichment to the owner at the expense of the contractor?

A typical illustration of such failure of the architect-engineer to fulfill his obligation lies in the design and development of sprinkler systems for buildings. In many projects no design or details for the sprinkler systems are provided; instead an outline or performance specification is written wherein the contractor is required to design the system in accordance with the various authorities or agencies having jurisdiction. Often this requires an award to a subcontractor based on a series of assumptions that can prove erroneous and costly. The design and construction must meet with the approval of numerous agencies, including the mechanical engineer, the local building department, the local fire department, the Fire Insurance Rating Bureau, the owner's fire insurance company, which may involve Factory Mutual, F.I.A., or other Fire Rating Bureaus. Tests must be run on the water pressure in the city mains to determine whether or not pumps are required. Study must usually be made of all other related mechanical and electrical work to avoid interference and provide headroom requirements. All of this requires intensive design and meetings with engineers of the various regulating agencies to obtain approvals leading to the final development of drawings. Not only is this time consuming, but it is rightly a function and responsibility of the architect-engineer.

Obviously all the above conditions are costly and may lead to substantial claims for extras. The lack of pressure in city street mains on one job led to additional costs of $100,000, while the determination of the owner's insurance company preempted the decision of the Fire Rating Bureau on another job changing the sprinkler head locations from 130 feet on centers to 100 feet on centers, adding $32,000 to the job costs. Both of these developments resulted in claims for extras and unnecessary litigation, which would have been avoided if the mechanical engineers had provided a complete design with the contract documents.

Ambiguities or Conflicting Conditions

Again, the instrument utilized in the Contract Documents is the "catch-all" clause to overcome the conflicting conditions and ambiguities that often exist as shown in extracts from typical General Conditions for projects:

> Title to divisions and paragraphs in the specifications are introduced merely for convenience and are not to be taken as a correct or complete segregation of the several units of materials and labor. No responsibility, either direct or implied, is assumed by the architect for omissions or duplications by the Contractor or his Subcontractors, due to real or alleged error in arrangement of matter in these specifications.

> Any provision in any of the Contract Documents which may be in conflict or inconsistent with any of the paragraphs in these General Conditions shall be void to the extent of such conflict or inconsistency.

Other more controversial and all-inclusive forms of interpretations to overcome ambiguities or errors and omissions are seen in some typical extracts from General Conditions public bid work, such as:

Drawings and Specifications are intended to agree and be mutually explanatory and shall be accepted and used as a whole and not separately. *Should any item be omitted from the drawings and be herein specified, or vice versa, it shall be executed the same as if shown and contained in both at no extra cost to the Board. Should anything be omitted from the drawings and specifications necessary for the proper construction of the work herein specified, or should any error or disagreement between the specifications and drawings exist or appear to exist, the Contractor shall not avail himself of such manifestly unintentional error or omission, but must have same explained or adjusted by the Architect before proceeding with the work in question. The Architect reserves the right to change the design of any architectural details shown on the contract documents without additional cost, provided that there is no increase in the amount of materials or workmanship,* or cost to the Contractor.

Other such examples are:

During the course of the work, *should any errors, omissions, ambiguities or discrepancies be found on the drawings or in the specifications, or should there be found any discrepancies between the drawings and specifications to which the Contractor has failed to call attention before submitting his bid, then the Architect will interpret the intent of the drawings and specifications* and the Contractor hereby agrees to abide by the Architect's interpretation and agrees to carry out the work in accordance with the decision of the Architect. *The Contractor will be held to have included in his proposal the most expensive material or method of construction wherever the intent of the Drawings or Specifications is not indicated clearly.*

The architect-owner is quite willing to recognize that he can make mistakes in the preparation of the plans and specifications but is unwilling to recognize the same human frailty in the contractor, even though the contractor lacks the intimate knowledge of the contract documents that only its designer and creator could know. Thus, the architect and owner attempt to shift fault by catch-all clauses in the specifications. There is, however, no substitute for the responsibility of the architect and his consultants. There are no two bites of the apple for the architect-owner any more than there are for the contractor. The responsibility for complete and proper design cannot be delegated to the contractor by the architect, nor can the contractor be expected to pay for the ambiguities or errors or omissions in the design. The contractor in presenting his bid warrants he will faithfully construct what is shown in the plan and specification—he has no right to deviate from the contract documents, no matter how much more he may think he knows than the architect, and apart from bringing out structural or architectural deficiency or incongruity when and if he has discovered same, his obligation is to follow precisely the plans and specifications. The Board of Education of the City of N.Y. unfairly ignores these concepts when it states:

It is the intention that these specifications and the drawings accompanying same, shall provide for the erection of a building complete in all its parts. Any work shown on the drawings and not particularly described in the specifications, or vice versa, or any work which may be deemed necessary to complete the contract shall be furnished by the Contractor as a part of his contract.

During the course of the work should any ambiguities or discrepancies be found on the drawings or in the specifications, or should there be found any discrepancies between the drawings and the specifications, to which the contractor has failed to call attention before submitting his bid, then the Superintendent will interpret the intent of the drawings and specifications, and the Contractor hereby agrees to abide by the Superintendent's interpretation and agrees to carry out the work in accordance with the decision of the Superintendent. It is expressly stipulated that neither the drawings nor the specifications shall take precedence, one over the other, and it is further stipulated that the Superintendent may interpret or construe the drawings and specifications so as to secure in all cases the most substantial and complete performance of the work as is most consistent with the needs and requirements of the work, and of that question the Superintendent shall be the sole judge.

Without question, one-sided, arbitrary determinations of this kind cannot find justification in equity nor can they avoid controversy. The erection of such protective screens is immoral, if not illegal, and converts legitimate bidding on public works to a veritable game of Russian roulette.

"Or Equal" Clauses or Substitutions

To avoid restraint of trade and permit true competitive bidding, honest and fair evaluations of alternative products or materials is mandated of the architect where substitutes have been offered by the contractor for specified products or materials. The "special interest" specification, written by a sales representative or particular manufacturer in "assistance" of the architect, works in reverse and often precludes substitutions even though bids may be based on use of substitutions or equals. Injudicious review or protective reaction by the architect can lead to major controversy on a project.

The evaluation of equivalence must be judiciously done to insure the appropriate performance and compliance to the plans and specifications. Too rigid an interpretation, however, can lead to exclusivity in lieu of competitive bidding. A recent public bid project contained a performance specification for a particular curtain wall, although the bidding documents permitted alternatives or equals. Because of the inability of any other manufacturer, regardless of his quality, reputation, and performance, to comply with the special restrictive clauses, the bids for the curtain wall were more than one million dollars higher than other competent and equivalent manufacturers would have bid. Obviously the public interest was not served by this restrictive practice.

Other typical devices written into the General Conditions or the Specifications are:

> *Substitution Proposals*: It is the intent of these specifications to establish an appropriate level of desired quality and style and design conformity for materials and equipment installed, under the base bid. *It is also the desire of both the Owner and the Architect to encourage price, management, and technological competition*: therefore, if the Contractor desires, he may submit a request to use any materials or products other than those specified. No extra costs resulting from a substitution proposed by the Contractor shall devolve upon the Owner, the Architects, or another Contractor.

The technique resulting from this type of restrictive paragraph is to make the contractor responsible for design; substituting a material or product from that specified will be at the full expense of the contractor not only to investigate its suitability and equivalence but to exempt the architect from all responsibility if the product or material fails in its use. Again, it must be recognized that design is the responsibility of the Architect and that substitutions or equals, when used in accordance with the contract documents and approved by the architect, must remain the responsibility of the architect as if he originally specified it.

Shop Drawings

A typical specification relating to the architect's responsibility regarding Shop Drawings is:

> The Architect's approval of such drawings or schedules shall not relieve the Contractor from responsibility for deviations from drawings or specifications, unless he has in writing called the Architect's attention to such deviations at the time of submission, nor shall it relieve him from responsibility for errors of any sort in shop drawings or schedules. Checking of shop drawings is to be regarded as gratuitously assisting the Contractors and the Architect does not thereby assume responsibility for errors or omissions or for dimensions or the fit of completed work in place. Where errors or omissions are found later, they must accordingly be made good by the Contractor, irrespective of any approval by the Architect.

The controversy that usually develops between contractor and architect is the denial of the architect to assume any responsibility for the review and approval of the shop drawings. The architect's service almost invariably includes checking of shop drawings as part of his design responsibility. Certainly one of the principal functions of the architect is to insure compliance with his plans and specifications, yet by such escape clauses he attempts to divorce himself from his own directives to the contractor to prepare and submit for approval all necessary shop detail drawings to adequately demonstrate the work to be performed. Interestingly enough, one of the greater benefits accruing from shop drawings is the coordination of major elements of the work with all the subcontractors or prime contractors involved. Disparities in clearances and interferences in the works of mechanical and architectural trades are often disclosed, requiring architectural decision and determination and often leading to claims for extras. Curiously, an attempt is made to pass on to the contractor alone this vital area of work, which involves the heart of design consideration. Actually it should be a joint responsibility of architect and contractor.

Mutual Responsibility of Contractors

Herein lies an attempt by the architect-owner to ordain the rights of the contractor with second- and third-party disputants, whether or not privity of contract exists between the various parties. The typical language of this clause reads as follows:

> If, through acts of neglect on the part of the Contractor, any other Contractor or any Sub-Contractor shall suffer loss or damage on the work, the Contractor agrees to settle with such other Contractor or Sub-Contractor by agreement or arbitration, if such other Contractor or Sub-Contractor will so settle. If such other Contractor or Sub-Contractor shall assert any claim against the Board on account of any damage alleged to have been so sustained, the Board shall notify the Contractor, who shall defend at his own expense any suit based upon such claim and, if any judgment of claims against the Board shall be allowed, the Contractor shall pay to satisfy such *judgment* of claim and pay all costs and expenses in connection therewith.

In general, this clause is aimed at separate prime contracts on public bid works to attempt to force the prime contractors to resolve the differences themselves. What is overlooked in this case, however, is the privity of contract and, further, that the claim often is made by the contractor against the owner for failure to enforce compliance of contract provisions and responsibilities. In such instances only the owner can allocate responsibilities to other prime contractors if they are involved, and certainly only the owner wields the financial capability and contractual weapons to deal decisively with the defaulting prime contractors; hence, the very concept of trying to compel the prime contractors to mutually resolve the problems and exclude and exonerate the owner becomes unlikely, improbable, and sometimes impossible. The device, however, is frequently used by the architect and owner to withhold payments and coerce the contractors and tends to further exacerbate the controversy.

The Changed Condition or Changes to the Contract Work

Perhaps the most common, most abused, most confusing, and least understood by both the architect-owner and the contractor is the changed condition to the contract documents. The same statement to varying degrees might also apply to members of the legal profession, depending on their exposure to construction law.

There is no question that every contract anticipates disputes and in one fashion or another attempts to provide mechanisms for resolving them. There is no question that every contract anticipates changes, whether as a result of modification to the contract documents during the construction period or as a result of errors and omissions, ambiguities, or conflicts in the plans and specifications. In recognition of the necessity to provide for changes, the usual contracts include clauses regarding changes in the work, such as:

> No extra work or changes shall be made unless in pursuance of a written order from the Board to the Architect, and a written order from the Architect stating that the Board has authorized the extra work or change, and no claim for an addition to the contract sum shall be valid unless so ordered.

The problems regarding changed conditions do not emanate from the provisions of the contract documents but rather from their interpretation and means or lack of application. To most, changed conditions relate to physical departures or modifications to the plans and specifications, promulgated by the architect-owner, leading to the issuance of a change order for an add or deduct to the contract amount. In this context, there is no argument except to insure prompt, authentic decision and authorization. In such works projects as shown in the above quoted paragraph, written authorization from the owner must precede the performance of the change even when agreed to by the architect. When hundreds of men are standing by and the disruption of work affects progress, efficiency, and costs, delay in obtaining written authorization from the owner may have drastic, costly, and far-reaching effects, often far in excess of the value of the change. Needless to say, a major cause of controversy is in the making.

Changed conditions appear in the work as well as in the contract documents under other guises as well, such as those clauses entitled "Boring

Data," "Existing Site Conditions," "Acceptance of Site and Previous Work," and "Subsurface Conditions Found Different." Typical illustrations of these provisions commonly found in contract documents are:

> The designs for this project are based on information from test borings made at the site. The boring logs are shown on the drawings. Bidders are warned that reliance upon these borings is at the Bidder's own risk and that the Owner assumes no responsibility for their accuracy, nor shall any claim be made if actual conditions differ from those indicated by these borings, or existing grades or conditions.

> The Drawings showing the logs of soil borings made on the site are available for examination by the Bidders, but are not to be made a part of the Contract. Bidders must interpret for themselves the soil conditions underlying the surface of the ground.

> The Contractor shall accept the site and previous work "as is" at the time of the signing of the Contract, and starting of work will be interpreted as a waiver of any claim to the contrary.

> The Contractor shall completely familiarize himself with existing site conditions, sub-surface soil conditions as shown on borings, and most feasible, expeditious and economical method of coping with same. The Architect makes no guarantee and accepts no responsibility for sub-soil conditions shown on borings.

> All proposals are received and the contract for this work will be made with the understanding that the Contractor has carefully examined the plans, specifications and borings and has visited and thoroughly inspected the premises and is familiar with all existing conditions and accept the site "as is." It is understood that neither the Owner, Architect, nor any City, State or Federal Agency has made any representation as to any conditions existing upon or underneath the surface of the plot or in connection with adjoining property.

By these catch-all devices putting the onus of responsibility solely on the shoulders of the contractor, a major source of controversy develops. During the many months involved in the design of the project the architect has surrounded himself with a series of engineering consultants and specialists, has retained soil consultants, obtained borings and other subsurface data, and has developed a design based on this information and expertise. This obviously is the intent and obligation of design. Yet in the contract documents, every effort is then made by the architect-owner to detach himself from his own design decisions and make the contractor, who not only cannot design, by law or by the contract documents, responsible for whatever changes may take place in the subsurface conditions as they are exposed. As stated earlier, the contractor's only obligation is to construct what is on the plans and specifications, not to interpret them, not to depart from them. Certainly it must be agreed that the contractor does not have more expertise than the designer. It must also be admitted that the engineer has availed himself of all the preponderance of available information and analyzed this mass of information in order to design the structure, while the contractor spends but a few weeks taking off the quantities of the job and pricing them. How can these knowledges be compared? How can the responsibilities be shifted? Certainly at best the contractor would not have any further knowledge or ability to forecast the subsurface conditions of the site than the licensed, professional engineer-of-record who prepared the design. In this context, any and all unanticipated subsurface changes should be admissible changed conditions leading to appropriately adjusted contract costs, thereby eliminating one of the major causes of construction controversy. Boring data must be considered as much a part of the contract documents and owner's responsibility as any other feature of the design of the project, and if the answer to better boring information lies in better techniques of taking borings under the supervision of licensed, professional engineers, then the design criteria should be appropriately tightened up in the planning of the project by the designers.

The concept of changed conditions is taken by many to relate solely to "bricks and mortar" type changes. In other words these are construed as constructive changes, since physical work is involved and the change involves an addition or deletion to the work emanating from a design change or a design defect. Most architects and owners can immediately relate to this condition and sometimes take necessary action to remedy the situations. These are, however, a series of changed conditions that are far more subtle in their nature and consequence and are as much the reason for modification of the contract costs as the obvious constructive change. In this connection, the architect-owner must recognize the effects of disruption and delay in the contractor's work and performance which require change orders as much as the "bricks and mortar" type of changes. In fact, these changed conditions are usually far more expensive in their impact on the project by means of extended field and home office overhead, lost efficiency, exposure to escalation, and lost profits.

Consider the effects of delays in processing shop drawings in reasonable time in today's highly escalated labor market. Consider the ramifications of improper untimely performance and progress by a prime contractor on public bid jobs as it affects the work of all other prime contractors.

A private housing development project was scheduled, financed, and committed to start in July 1969. In actuality, because the architect was unable to complete the plans and specifications within the scheduled time and obtain the necessary agency approvals, the construction start was pushed forward six months in time. The project therefore moved into a wage escalation that amounted to $1.2 million in unanticipated added costs.

Community action in a project being constructed in the New England area caused local authorities to revoke the building permit, even though substantial work had been completed in excavation, driving of piles, and placement of foundations. The structural steel was completely fabricated awaiting shipment to the job site when the stop-work order was issued. After fourteen months of delay, during which time the structural steel was sold at auction for salvage value, new plans were prepared with community participation, the project building permit was reissued, and work on the job was restarted. Needless to say, the costs of damages involved to the owner, contractor, and subcontractors were enormous. For each of the participants in this experience, the end result was a series of changed conditions which, of necessity and right, had to include escalation, disruption, lost efficiency, change in labor conditions, interest charges on financing, and extended field and home office overhead, in addition to the physical changes to the plans and specifications.

The intent herein is to demonstrate that changed conditions are not necessarily a physical departure from the contract documents, whether it be subsurface conditions found different than anticipated or shown, pile obstructions, design defects, plan changes, or similar situations, but also that these include the more major causes of dispute in the more abstract type of items such as delay, disruption, escalation, change in government regulations, involvement of community action groups, and the like.

The Construction

The Testing Laboratory

Major restructuring of the methods of testing and qualification of testing personnel is long overdue. Serious efforts have been made in recent years to improve techniques; the responsibility of testing and inspection for quality control has shifted from the contractor to the owner; but the results remain essentially the same. The testing laboratories still use inexperienced, unqualified personnel in the field and plant due to insufficient fees. Many methods of testing leave much to be desired so that reasonable doubt exists as to the veracity of the test. In fact some renowned testing laboratory owners openly state that 20–40 percent of concrete cylinders can be expected to show below-strength concrete even though the concrete is probably sound, because of poor handling, curing, and testing of cylinders by their own personnel. Plant and field control is less than rigorously applied, mixing water temperatures in the truck tanks are rarely checked, aggregates are rarely washed and cooled before compliance, cylinders are usually taken from the truck rather than from in-place concrete on the deck, and many of the other specified checks of dry and wet weight and mix temperatures are questionably performed. Cube tests of masonry mortar are notoriously misleading and, like the concrete cylinders, show inaccurate results because of the sampling and handling techniques. In winter work by the time the cylinders or cubes reach the laboratory, they have been overexposed to freezing weather, and in hot weather work are exposed to rapid drying without proper curing.

The design mix for concrete is prepared by the testing laboratory by licensed professional engineers. The ingredients to be used are specified by the engineer-of-record. These parties, as well as the inspectors, are in the employ of the owner and under the direction of the architect-engineer. Yet how many concrete specifications attempt to shift the responsibility of design to the contractor by use of such clauses as:

> Preliminary designs and tests for the purpose of determining concrete mixes for concrete, in accordance with Section C26-1478.0 of the New York City Building Code, and tests of cement, sand and other concrete materials will be made by a laboratory selected by the owner. It shall be the responsibility of the contractor to satisfy himself that concrete mixes, based on the results of the preliminary tests, will produce concrete strengths as required by the contract and he shall so state in writing to the architect before pouring concrete.

No one questions the contractor's responsibility when bad concrete develops as a result of obvious improper use of ingredients or as a result of poor field handling. The problem under discussion, however, occurs when poor concrete develops even though no departure from the plans and specifications has been evidenced. Several years ago, six or more jobs in the city of New York were seriously affected almost simultaneously by below-strength concrete, with essentially the same design mixes and ingredients having been used, and yet the same mixes had previously been successfully used on numerous jobs. Rightly the architect-owner replied that the mix had been successfully used and proven on many other jobs. Just as rightly the contractor replied that "I used the specified materials in the specified fashion under the inspection of the owner's independent testing laboratory in the plant and field, and under the close examination of the owner's supervising professional engineer in the field; therefore the problem and remedy are not mine."

The answer to avoiding this serious controversy is to have more qualified personnel and to require licensing of all inspectors. In addition, higher fee structures would permit employment of more qualified personnel and equipment, and development of better testing techniques.

The Inspector and Clerk of the Works

The role of this representative of the owner is vital to the smooth functioning of the project. While many inspectors are extremely knowledgeable and cooperative, just as many are unknowledgeable and unscrupulous and become a major source of friction on the job. When an inspector acts the "frustrated contractor" and starts to run the job and interpret the plans and specifications, a major cause of controversy develops. Too often the inspector, particularly on public works jobs, interferes with the administration and coordination of the job by issuing orders directly to the subcontractors and workmen instead of working through the construction superintendent of the contractor. Equally disturbing is the inspector who passively watches work being improperly done, but much later "discovers" it and causes the problem to be corrected at great expense. While it is true that the deficiency warrants correction, cooperative efforts would minimize errors and corrective work and keep the job running smoothly.

There is no substitute for a knowledgeable, conscientious inspector whose scrutiny and efforts can be enormously beneficial to the owner, architect, and contractor. In the private sector, inspectors or clerks of the works are screened by the architects, usually are higher paid, and are equipped with sound construction knowledge; but on public works, the tendency to find similar competence and cooperative attitude is less likely and, more often than not, the inspector tends to be bureaucratic, dogmatic, and even punitive. Many is the time the contractor wishes to protest the abusive practices of these capricious inspectors but rarely does so, knowing that the agency will counter to protect its own image or stand behind the inspector to instill a loyalty complex within the structure. In the long run this attitude is self-defeating, but the contractor lives with the day-to-day operations, and the capricious attitudes and acts of the inspectors can prove costly and seriously delay occupancy, acceptance, and final payments. Much remains to be done in the field of inspection to avoid controversy, delay, and unwarranted costs.

The Punch List

One of the most abused or misused construction activities is the punch list. At the outset let it be clear to all that the owner is entitled to obtain good workmanship and quality, and that the contractor is responsible to properly construct the work and fulfill the standards required. Any contractor or subcontractor would be foolish to deliberately encourage or incorporate substandard or sloppy workmanship, since he knows full well he will be required to correct it. At today's wages for labor with its corresponding lower productivity, the punch list is assuming greater financial hardship than ever before and becomes a source of greater irritation between owner-architect and contractor.

Because of vandalism, malicious mischief, personal antagonism or sabotage by workmen on the job, carelessness, lack of pride, and a variety of similar reasons, punch lists grow longer each year and, correspondingly, the costs of correction rise. A better understanding of the problem would occur if the owner, architect, or tenant would look into his own house, and his own performance, and compare the workmanship of his own staff—the housemaid performs less and less work than before, secretaries produce less and are susceptible to more errors and carelessness, manufactured products (automobiles, appliances, and the like) have more built-in defects and improperly assembled parts than ever before. The problem of the punch list is universal to all parties and industries and, while no one would make a brief in defense of poor workmanship, a greater understanding of the problem must develop on all sides. More patience must be exhibited in the correction of the work and, it is hoped, a greater awareness and sense of responsibility in the trades would emerge to parallel the sense of pride and accomplishment that used to exist 30 or 40 years ago.

While all the above is admission of a great problem facing the industry, the problem is often manifestly compounded by the inspector, particularly on public works, and to a lesser degree by the architect on private works. The inspector is more concerned with protecting himself against the possible criticism of his superior and becomes over-exacting, "fly-specking," and sometimes vindictive or punitive in his actions. He now becomes the sole determiner of the standards of performance. And when this attitude is carried to the ultimate by the inspector or architect, numerous punch lists are presented instead of a one-time, all-inclusive punch list. By numerous punch lists, the expense of corrective work is greatly magnified and frictions increase.

It is time that inspectors on public works and their superiors, as well as architects, recognize that there are different standards of construction. Low-cost public housing certainly does not warrant the same degree of perfection or quality control as a high-cost institutional facility. The degree of quality control is built in by the tone and content of the specifications, and the cost of the job accordingly recognizes the difference in quality performance. If punch lists are distorted by the failure to recognize these vital differences, then controversies develop, the public or owner will not be served in their best interests, and certainly the contractor and subcontractors are being unduly penalized.

Payments and Acceptance

By and large, in the private sector, little problem develops regarding monthly payments and only occasionally is the final payment unduly withheld. In the public sector, however, some agencies are notorious for their slow, untimely payments, aided and abetted by a never-ending supply of bureaucratic inefficiencies and demands. Other public agencies, of course, are as prompt and efficient in the monthly payments as the private sector and deserve the highest acclaim for their understanding of the urgent necessity that the contractors be promptly paid.

It is to the detriment of public works projects, or any project, that payments be unduly withheld. In these cases the contractor and subcontractors are compelled to borrow large amounts of money, often in excess of their usual credit lines. Pressures then begin to mount, since the high rates of interest, tight money markets, and lack of payments to material suppliers, subcontractors, internal revenue service, and insurance companies start to come into play and choke off the credit lines. Financially solvent contractors, as well as the smaller and weaker contractors, are thus put into serious jeopardy and sometimes into bankruptcy.

Although few factors are as onerous to the construction industry as the improper payment problem, acceptance of the construction and the final payment are equally troublesome. It is rare that a written final acceptance is issued on projects even though numerous punch lists have been completed and guarantee periods have expired. The most usual approach is to let the project "fade away," which avoids possible criticism from the owner at a later date had a written acceptance been issued. What this overlooks is that the contractor by contract and in writing has guaranteed his work for the stipulated period as set forth in the contract documents. It also overlooks the fact that in most jobs, 100 percent payment and performance bonds have been posted by the contractor, which is additional insurance that defects will be remedied.

Because of the lack of acceptance, and the continuing nitpicking on punch lists, excuse is often found by the owner or agencies to avoid timely final payment on the project. Final payment on some public jobs has been delayed for as much as six to seven years without adequate cause. Indecisive public officials, living in constant fear of criticism, or the arbitrary public official who interprets contract documents to suit his whims, convenience, or caprice, or the owner who is undercapitalized, are the usual causes for withheld final payments. Other reasons may be stated publicly and even distorted, but the facts usually demonstrate arbitrary or calloused bureaucratic inefficiency and a never-ending series of diversions and dilatory practices.

The retained moneys on final payment usually vary with the value of the project. On multimillion dollar projects, it is obvious that the withheld final payment can be in the hundreds of thousands and even millions of dollars. Usually this money, if the job has been successful, represents the contractor's and subcontractor's profits and their operating capital. If these funds are tied up for long periods of time on a number of the contractor's projects, it is equally obvious that substantial sums become involved affecting the operating capital, borrowings, credit line, growth potential, bondability, and financial statements. The harm thereby generated can be devastating. The public interest can never be served by unjustly withholding payments, especially when protected by surety bonds or insurance, when in the final instance it is the public that becomes affected, either by getting higher bids than warranted on its work or by creating hardship in bankruptcies that erode the tax base and create unemployment and decreased capital improvements.

Conclusion

There can be no doubt that the construction industry is unique in every aspect; that it draws upon virtually every segment of our society; that it brings together more diverse groups than any other industry; that its problems are many; that its contributions are great. But like every other industry or sector of our economy, reform is required. Because so many different vested interests are involved, the urgency of reform is even greater and yet more difficult to obtain.

Certainly no one can say that contractors are all good and architects or owners are all bad, or vice versa. Each side has its problems and points of view. But it must be agreed that one thing can be done at once—that a teamwork approach can be used on every project, where all interests meet on an equal footing and work together for the common good. Each party has the responsibility to mitigate damages. To prevent work stoppages, faster means to resolve disputes must be developed, by impartial bodies such as the American Arbitration Association, while the work is going on. Contract documents must be reformed to delete or correct all objectionable problems such as those referred to above. The contractor's problems and points of view regarding the plans and specifications must be listened to more responsively. The plans and specifications must be better prepared. The inspectors must be better trained, oriented, and restricted only to inspecting. Payments must be properly made. From these, the construction industry could move forward with far less controversy and with far more productive effort.

... ...

Subcontractors and Arbitration

ROSEMARY S. PAGE

Various factors make arbitration agreements by and with subcontractors unique. The subcontractor is, by definition, one who contracts to do a part of a whole. The subcontract document, if any, therefore, is one of a series of other documents. By definition, the subcontractor's agreement is auxiliary to the main contract documents. These factors and others, which will be discussed later, have resulted in case law which specifically addresses the issue of arbitration as it relates to the subcontractor under construction documents.

A number of court decisions analyze the impact of the interrelationship of construction contract documents to the subcontractor's entitlement to arbitrate or to be bound by the agreement to arbitrate. The doctrine of incorporation by reference is sometimes a factor in this context. Other decisions deal with the impact on arbitration of governmental concern in protecting the economic interests of subcontractors, laborers, and materialmen. Still other court opinions interpret the effect on arbitral rights of attempts by the contracting parties—usually the general contractor and the subcontractor—to modify, either by design or by happenstance, the language in an otherwise broad arbitration clause.[1] An examination of a sampling of these court decisions may offer some guidance in drafting arbitration clauses relating to subcontractors.

Courts have held that the intention to arbitrate and the words which express it must be clear and direct and may not be found by construction or implication.[2] Questions have been raised in some of the cases discussed herein whether those principles also apply to arbitration clauses relating to subcontractors. For example, is it possible by implication to find an agreement to join parties in the consolidation of arbitrations? May the right to arbitrate be based upon the incorporation by reference of the dispute resolution clause located in another contract and, if so, what language is required? What effect, if any, do federal or state statutes have upon the doctrine of incorporation by reference or election of remedies? May a nonsignatory—that is, a person who has not entered into a provision agreeing to arbitrate—compel arbitration? May a contingency proviso in an otherwise broad arbitration clause be activated so as to defeat a subcontractor's right to arbitrate?

Incorporation by Reference

The American Institute of Architects (AIA) is an example of one division of the construction industry which has developed a series of documents for use by the various parties involved in the construction project—the owner, the architect, the general contractor, and others. The AIA General Conditions of the Contract of Construction (A201) contains an agreement between the owner and general contractor to arbitrate their disputes.[3] The contract between the general contractor and the subcontractor contains language which relates back to these General Conditions, and this language has been interpreted by the courts as incorporating by reference into the subcontractor's agreement the arbitration clause found in the contract between the owner and the general contractor, even where the subcontract contained no express arbitration provision.[4]

The language affecting the incorporation was that the subcontractor, in its agreement with the prime (general) contractor, "assumed toward the prime contractor those responsibilities and obligations which the prime contractor assumed toward the owner in the prime contract."

No Incorporation by Reference

Where the subcontract contained no arbitration clause and neither directly nor indirectly incorporated the terms of the main (or prime) contract, New York courts would not compel arbitration with the subcontractor even when the main contract obligated the prime contractor to bind the subcontractors to the terms of the main contract.[5]

In another New York case, the court found that a sub-subcontractor was not by definition a subcontractor[6] and was therefore not entitled to arbitrate with the owner and general contractor based upon the subcontractor's agreement. The court said:

> It appears that the intent and purpose of the contract was to permit a major subcontracting of part of the work specified by the main contract and by so doing create the relationship of contractor and subcontractor, but was not to apply and create such relationship where minor subcontracts or additional work of a minor nature outside of the specifications and general conditions of the major were contracted for.[7]

Arbitration on Behalf of Another, but No Assignment

Dicta in the above-mentioned case referred to the fact that the subcontractor may arbitrate a claim with the contractor on behalf of the sub-

subcontractor.[8] In those cases there is often no arbitration clause in the subcontract documents and no language incorporating by reference the arbitration provisions of the main contract. Where there is also no authorization in the main documents to assign the right to arbitrate, an attempted assignment of the right to arbitrate would be void.[9]

Incorporation by Reference as It Affects Consolidation

In one case where New York's Court of Appeals compelled arbitration demanded by the general contractor against the subcontractor and the surety, the surety had sought a stay of arbitration contending that it was not required to arbitrate its liability under the performance bond, which otherwise contained no provision for arbitration. The court found that although the surety company did not agree to participate in any arbitration, it did accept the agreement of the general contractor with the subcontractor that disputes between them would be settled by arbitration.

> An implicit corollary of that acceptance was agreement by the surety company that for purposes of later determining its liability under its performance bond, it would accept and be bound by the resolution reached in the arbitration forum of any dispute between the general contractor and the subcontractor.[10]

The surety bond in this case contained express language that, on issues covered by the performance bond, the subcontractor and the surety "bind themselves, jointly and the severally," and as to the subcontract, it "is by reference made a part thereof."[11]

While most of the cases on this issue involve the contractual arrangements between the subcontractor, the owner, the general contractor, and the surety, one consolidation case[12] involved an architect seeking to compel arbitration with a subcontractor. In denying the claim of the architect to compel the subcontractor to arbitrate, the court found that the terms of the main contract were incorporated into the subcontract. There was, however, no incorporation by reference of the architect's contract with the subcontract nor was the subcontractor a party to the contract of the architect. The subcontractor would have been bound to arbitrate the issue of the roof defects with the owner, but it was the architect and not the owner who sought to compel arbitration with the subcontractor. The architect may not stand in the shoes of the owner, the court said. The architect had contended that since all parties had agreed to arbitrate with the owner, they could be compelled to arbitrate with one another, or at least that the architect could stand in the shoes of the owner. The court disagreed. In this case the court would not compel arbitration on the basis of implication.

In another case, where a federal court described the issue as "whether a subcontractor-contractor-owner dispute must be arbitrated,"[13] the court found two provisions of significance: the first was the broad arbitration clause in the contract between the owner and contractor; and the second was the language in the subcontract that the "Subcontractor shall be bound to the contractor by the terms and provisions of all of the Contract Documents, and assumes toward the Contractor, with respect to the Subcontractor's work, all of the obligations and responsibilities which the Contractor, by the Contract Documents has assumed toward the Owner. . . ." The court concluded that these two provisions provided for consolidated arbitration of disputes involving the subcontractor, contractor, and owner.[14]

Miller Act

In one case,[15] where the subcontractor had commenced arbitration and had later filed a suit under the Miller Act,[16] the court was asked to dismiss the Miller Act suit on the ground that it was barred under the theory of election of remedies. While the Miller Act suit was stayed pending the arbitration, the court found that this congressionally mandated remedy was not barred by the subcontractor's arbitration. The court found that the subcontractor, by arbitrating and by suing under the Miller Act, was not seeking to recover twice, which would not have been allowed, but was seeking to safeguard against the possibility that the contractor might become insolvent and unable to pay an arbitration award in its favor.[17]

Broad Arbitration Clause Modified

In yet another case (*HRH Construction Corporation* v. *Bethlehem Steel Corporation*) the subcontract documents did contain a broad arbitration clause. Added to the broad clause was the language:

> Provided, however . . . that any determination reached [in court or arbitration, etc.] between the Contractor and the Owner [relating to the work herein] and hereby undertaken to be done and performed by the Subcontractor, shall, with like force and effect, be determinative and conclusive of any controversy or dispute with reference thereto between the parties to this Agreement and in the event of any such action or proceeding brought against

the Contractor by the Owner . . . the Subcontractor may, at the option of the Contractor, be brought into such action or proceeding as a third-party defendant.

The subcontractor demanded arbitration with the contractor. Thereafter, the owner sued the general contractor in court. The general contractor made two moves. It impleaded the subcontractor in the owner's court suit and moved to stay the arbitration, alleging that under the above-mentioned proviso in the subcontract arbitration clause, "because of the identity of subject matter of the two sets of claims, the institution by the owner of the legal action operated *ipso facto* to remove the claims of the subcontractor against the general contractor . . ." from arbitration.[18] The court noted that under the contractor's interpretation, arbitrability would hinge on the act of one not a party to the controversy between the contractor and the subcontractor. The court disagreed with the general contractor's interpretation of the language and held that "all disputes are to be submitted to arbitration in the normal manner except that as to disputes which are also raised in proceedings between the owner and the general contractor, the results in the latter shall also determine the outcome in arbitration between the general contractor and the subcontractor."[19]

We thus see the courts giving full meaning to the broad arbitration clause as it appeared in the subcontract documents. In the *HRH* case the issue arose from the language within the subcontract documents themselves. In those cases where several documents were examined to determine arbitrability, the courts looked for two factors: (1) a clear provision to arbitrate and (2) a clear intent to be bound by the agreement to arbitrate, either directly or indirectly.

Notes

[1] A sample broad arbitration clause is: Any controversy or claim arising out of or relating to this contract, or the breach thereof, shall be settled by arbitration in accordance with the Construction Industry Arbitration Rules of the American Arbitration Association, and judgment upon the award rendered by the Arbitrator(s) may be entered in any Court having jurisdiction thereof.
[2] Matter of American Rail & Steel Co. [India Supply Mission], 308 N.Y. 577, 127 N.E.2d 562 (1955).
[3] In A201 (1976), the agreement is found in article 7.9.
[4] J S & H Construction Co. v. Richmond County Hospital Authority, 473 F.2d 212 (5th Cir. 1973). See also Howard Hill, Inc. v. George A. Fuller Co., 473 F.2d 217 (5th Cir. 1973); Bartley, Inc. v. Jefferson Parish School Board, 302 So.2d 280 (La. 1974).
[5] Corbetta Construction Co., Inc. v. George F. Driscoll Co., 233 N.Y.S.2d 225, 17 A.D.2d 176 (1st Dept. 1962).
[6] AIA document A201 (1976), 5.1.1 describes a subcontractor as a person or entity who has a direct contract with a contractor to perform any of the work at the site and also provides that "The term Subcontractor does not include any separate contractor or his subcontractors."

[7] Application of Peele Co., 216 N.Y.S.2d 869, 874 (Kings Co. 1961).

[8] *Id.* at 875.

[9] For a discussion of this, see Old Colony Regional Vocational Technical High School District v. New England Constructors, Inc., 363 N.E.2d 260 (Mass. 1977).

[10] Fidelity and Deposit Co. of Maryland v. Parsons & Whittemore Contractors Corp., 48 N.Y.2d 127, 397 N.E.2d 380 (1979).

[11] *Id.* at p. 382; see also Powers Regulator Co. v. United States Fidelity & Guaranty Co., 388 N.E.2d 1205, 1207 (Mass. 1979). For a case where the surety was permitted to compel arbitration with the subcontractor, see J. & S. Construction Co., Inc. v. Travelers Indemnity Co., 520 F.2d 809 (1st Cir. 1975).

[12] Cumberland-Perry Area Vocational-Technical School Authority v. Bogar Bink, Pa., Super., 396 A.2d 433 (1978).

[13] Gavlik Construction Co. v. H.F. Campbell Co., 526 F.2d 777 (3d Cir. 1975).

[14] See also Uniroyal, Inc. v. A. Epstein and Sons, Inc., 428 F.2d 523 (7th Cir. 1970).

[15] United States, etc. v. Weiss Pollution Control Corp., 532 F.2d 1009 (5th Cir. 1976).

[16] 40 U.S.C.A. §270(a) *et seq.*

[17] The Miller Act was discussed in a different context in other subcontractor arbitration cases relating to the interpretation of language incorporating dispute resolution clauses by reference. See Washington Metropolitan Area Transit Authority v. Norair Engineering Corp., 553 F.2d 233 (D.C. Cir. 1977). For a discussion on mechanic's liens and other Miller Act decisions as they relate to subcontractors, see 1 *Lawyers' Arbitration Letter* 10, June 15, 1975.

[18] HRH Construction Corp. v. Bethlehem Steel Corp., 412 N.Y.S.2d 366, 367, 45 N.Y.2d 695 (1978).

[19] *Id.* at p. 369.

The Architect's Duty: Owner-Contractor Disputes Involving Allegations of Architect's Fault

ALAN H. KENT

Most standard form construction contracts between contractors and nongovernment owners contain language providing that the architect shall be the initial arbiter of all claims, disputes, and other matters in question between the contractor and the owner, and that his decisions are final subject to a timely demand for arbitration. Typical of such language, and perhaps the most widely used, are the clauses contained in the standard form of General Conditions of the Contract for Construction[1] published by the American Institute of Architects. Article 2 of such form provides, in pertinent part, as follows:

2.2.7. Claims, disputes and other matters in question between the Contractor and the Owner relating to the execution or progress of the Work or the interpretation of the Contract Documents shall be referred initially to the Architect for decision which he will render in writing within a reasonable time.

2.2.10. Any claim, dispute or other matter that has been referred to the Architect ... shall be subject to arbitration upon the written demand of either party. However, no demand for arbitration of any such claim, dispute or other matter may be made until the earlier of:

2.2.10.1. The date on which the Architect has rendered his written decision, or

2. the tenth day after the parties have presented their evidence to the Architect or have been given a reasonable opportunity to do so, if the Architect has not rendered his written decision by that date.

The question arises: What is the effect of such language when claims or disputes between the owner and the contractor involve allegations that the architect was negligent or in some other way at fault?[2] For example, a contractor's claim may be based on allegations of defective plans and specifications prepared by the architect or the delay or failure of the architect to issue certain necessary directives or drawings. Curiously, the

AIA Code of Ethics and Professional Conduct[3] fails to address itself specifically to this subject.

It is true that even if the architect renders a decision on a matter concerned with an allegation of his own fault, the decision may nevertheless be appealed to an arbitrator for a de novo evaluation of the claim or dispute. It is also true that the architect's decision in such instance is impeachable on the ground that it has the obvious appearance of bias. There lurks the possibility, however, that an arbitrator, consciously or subconsciously, may still give some weight to such a decision. For this reason, sound professional judgment may well dictate that an architect faced with this type of claim or dispute should refrain from rendering any decision. In that event the AIA General Conditions would permit the parties to bring the matter directly before an arbitrator.[4] This would avoid the possibility of a costly and time-consuming initial presentation of the dispute to an architect whose ultimate decision would be immediately challengeable as biased.

The thesis that an architect should not render a decision on matters involving the performance of his own duties is based on elementary concepts of fairness as well as prevailing law. Article 2.2.9 of the AIA General Conditions refers to the architect as acting in the capacity of interpreter and judge. In the words of one New York court, however, "Every litigant is not only entitled to present his claims to an impartial judge, but to one who by no act on his part has justified a doubt as to his impartiality."[5] In the same vein, the United States Supreme Court, in discussing the premise for rules requiring disqualification of arbitrators and judges for partiality, stated that "any tribunal permitted by law to try cases and controversies not only must be unbiased but also must avoid even the appearance of bias."[6] This rule applies by analogy to all arbiters of disputes, including architects to whom claims are submitted for initial determination. The impartiality of the architect is most assuredly in doubt when he is faced with deciding matters involving allegations of his own fault or negligence; the appearance of a conflict of interest in this situation is clear.

The few published judicial decisions on this point are quite clear in uniformly proscribing an architect from deciding matters involving a determination of the question of the architect's own fault. In a 1971 case,[7] the New York Court of Appeals affirmed the decision of a lower court denying the application by a building owner to stay arbitration brought by its contractor. The Court of Appeals held that the contractor's claim should be submitted to arbitration notwithstanding the contractor's non-compliance with article 20 of the contract, which provided that the architect should make decisions, subject to arbitration, on all claims of the owner and contractor. The court's decision was based in part on its finding that the general contractor would have been obliged to submit to the architect, for his preliminary determination, the question of the architect's own fault. The court found that:

> Considering, too, the inconsistency and, indeed, futility of a submission to the architect of a claim which would have been predicated on [the architect's] own fault . . . it is clear that article 20 rendered operative the provisions of article 40, the arbitration article, which the contractor has properly invoked.[8]

The Supreme Court of Pennsylvania likewise has ruled that the arbitration clause in a building contract does not authorize architects to decide the question of whether they themselves were at fault. In an early Pennsylvania case[9] a contractor brought an action for the balance allegedly due for the construction of a synagogue. The contract contained a provision that the architect shall, in all cases, make final and binding determinations of all questions relative to the work and construction, and that in case any question shall arise, such decision shall be a condition precedent to the right of the contractor to receive any money under the agreement. The architect determined that the delay in completing the project was chargeable to the contractor and assessed liquidated damages against him in the amount of $12,000. The lower court refused to admit into evidence an offer by the contractor to show that the delay in completing the building was chiefly chargeable to the delay of the architect in furnishing certain necessary detailed drawings. Holding this to be reversible error, the court stated:

> The agreement to abide by the decision of the architects could hardly have been intended to authorize them to pass upon the question of the performance of their own duties.[10]

Similarly, in another early case[11] a contractor brought an action for money due on a building contract. Under the terms of the contract, the architects were made the sole arbiters of disputes that might arise between the parties. At the trial, there was no showing that the matters in dispute had ever been submitted to the architects for determination as required by the contract. The Pennsylvania Supreme Court reversed the trial court's directed verdict for the building owner, holding as follows:

> If questions arise between the contracting parties not included in the arbitration clauses, or if the questions raised relate to failure or dereliction in the performance of duties by the architects themselves, the right to have these matters passed upon by a jury cannot be denied upon the ground of failure to arbitrate. Nearly all the rejected offer of testimony relates to the fault in the performance of duties imposed upon the architects by the contract, and *certainly it could not have been the intention of parties to*

deliberately enter into a convenant providing that the arbiters shoud have the right to pass upon and finally determine questions involving their own failure in the performance of duties. At this stage of the case, it is perhaps only necessary to say that the arbitration clauses only refer to the questions therein specified, and do not relate to questions concerning the performance, or failure to perform, the professional duties of the architects.[12] (Emphasis supplied.)

In a comparatively recent case[13] involving a contractor's appeal from the denial of its petition for a stay of arbitration, the Appellant Court of Illinois held that the clause of a contract between a contractor and a subcontractor allowing the architect to decide certain disputes did not give the architect the power to pass upon his own errors and omissions. The contractor contended that although paragraph 39 of the subcontract provided generally for arbitration of "all disputes arising hereunder," it excluded items "determined by the architect pursuant to paragraph 21 hereof" which, in turn, incorporated paragraph 35 of the General Conditions and took the position that certain items of dispute were to be determined by the architect and were thus excluded from the arbitration provisions. The court held as follows:

> While paragraph 35 of the General Conditions, above set out, does give the architect the power to . . . adjust and determine disputes between the contractor and other contractors, it does not in our considered opinion, give the architect the power to pass upon his own errors and omissions. . . . To permit this would be an outrageous result not contemplated by the parties, and one not compelled by the language of the contract.
>
> We therefore hold that items 1 through 5 are not matters to be decided by the architect and are thus not excluded from the general arbitration clause.[14]

In view of the foregoing it is plain that, in all propriety and under the clear mandate of judicial decisions, an architect should not render a decision on any claims or disputes that are premised, in whole or in part, upon allegations of the architect's errors, omissions, acts, or failure to act in regard to the performance of his duties.

Notes

[1] AIA document A201 (April 1970).
[2] In view of the fact that the architect is retained by the owner, it is obvious that such allegations would be raised, if at all, by the contractor.
[3] AIA document J330 (July 1, 1978).
[4] See article 2.2.10 of the AIA General Conditions, *supra.*
[5] In re Friedman, 215 A.D. 130, 135, 213 N.Y.S. 369, 374 (1929).
[6] Commonwealth Coatings Corp. v. Continental Casualty Co., 393 U.S. 145, 89 Sup. Ct. 337, 340 (1968).
[7] Methodist Church of Babylon v. Glen-Rich Construction Corp., 27 N.Y.2d 357, 318 N.Y.S.2d 297 (1971).

[8] *Id.*, 27 N.Y.2d at 362, 318 N.Y.S.2d at 300.

[9] Reilly v. Rodef Sholem Congregation, 243 Pa. 528, 90 A. 345 (1914).

[10] *Id.*, 90 A. at 346.

[11] Hunn v. Pennsylvania Institution for Instruction of the Blind, 221 Pa. 403, 70 A. 812 (1908).

[12] *Id.*, 70 A. at 815.

[13] Paschen Contractors, Inc. v. John L. Calnan Company, 13 Ill. App.3d 485, 300 N.E.2d 795 (1973).

[14] *Id.*, 13 Ill. App.3d at 490, 300 N.E.2d at 799.

The Professional Liability Shuffle

MILTON F. LUNCH

Probably the single most common concern of engineers in private practice is the growing and worsening pattern of exposure to professional liability lawsuits. It provides little solace to the engineer that he is not alone in this concern and that other professions are suffering the same trends.

Confronted with this situation, the various professions, and particularly the medical profession, have cast about for alternatives to alleviate the problem. In the engineering world a great deal has been done through the internal approach of the development of better written contract documents, workshops and seminars on office practice, publication of practice manuals, quality control guidelines, and improved training courses for design employees.

In addition to these efforts, however, attention has shifted to the possibility of remedial state legislation. Instigated largely by the medical profession, professional liability laws have been adopted in some states and many bills are pending in other states to cope with particular aspects of the problem.

The purpose of this review of the major concepts in such legislation is to report on the different ideas that have been presented and to analyze them from both a legal and practical standpoint.

Pretrial Arbitration

The most universal approach in existing professional liability laws and in pending bills is a requirement that before a claimant may bring a suit in court against a professional, the claimant must submit the case to an arbitration panel. The composition of the panel varies, but generally calls for three members: one from the profession involved, one lay member, and one attorney. The panel would hear the case and then decide if the professional is liable and, if so, the amount of the award.

If either party is dissatisfied with the decision or the amount of award, that party then may take the case to a trial court for a de novo (from the beginning) procedure under regular state legal procedures. But the findings of the panel may be offered in evidence at the trial. The theory is that the panel will more ably (better than juries) weed out cases that have no real merit and will better determine a fair award if relief is justified.

There are several major considerations in the analysis of the pretrial arbitration requirement. First, the result may be a duplicate procedure with double costs for attorneys' fees, expert witnesses, and other legal procedures. The proponents of the idea claim that in many situations the losing party will be convinced that the case has such little merit as to preclude the use of the right to start over in court. They further contend that even when the case is taken to court, the findings of the panel of highly qualified persons will have great weight with a jury. These remain conjectural points because of the relatively little experience with the concept in the states where it has been enacted.

The second major question is about the constitutionality of a mandatory nonjudicial proceeding as a condition precedent to the right to file a claim in court. Here the courts are divided in the few instances where the point has been litigated. In the first test case, involving the medical profession, the Illinois Supreme Court rejected the mandatory panel requirement. The court held that the scheme violated the state constitutional provision vesting the entire and exclusive judicial power in the state courts. It also further rejected the plan under the provisions of the constitution granting citizens the right to jury trial, even though in Illinois law an aggrieved party could take the issue to a jury trial after the panel decision was rendered.

The Florida Supreme Court reached a contrary result, but only barely. In a case arising from a medical injury the patient sought direct legal action, but the trial court dismissed the case because the patient had not first submitted the claim to an arbitration panel as required by state law. Under that statute the plaintiff has no choice as to procedure, but the defendant physician did have an option to let the case proceed to trial in court or have it first determined by the panel. Despite this lack of equal treatment, the Florida Supreme Court rationalized the point by construing it to mean that if the physician fails to participate in the panel hearing, that fact is admissible into evidence in the subsequent civil medical malpractice trial.

On the broader issue of denying the plaintiff a direct entry into the courts, the court said that the prelitigation burden on the claimant reached "the outer limits of constitutional tolerance," basing its conclusion in major part on the recognition of an "imminent danger that a drastic curtailment in the availability of health care services would occur in this state," and the subsequent recognition by the state legislature of the need to do something for the benefit of the public health. By its emphasis on the health care "crisis" in Florida which generated the law, it may be surmised that the court might reach a different constitutional result if the same procedure were applied to engineering or architectural services, or services of accountants, lawyers, or other professionals.

In still other cases, an Ohio trial court has thrown out a similar pretrial arbitration requirement for medical cases on the ground that the requirement has the effect of dissuading the filing of medical malpractice suits and places added pressure and expense on a plaintiff or defendant who loses at arbitration. It also found the procedure constitutionally objectionable because it reduced a party's ability to prove his case, since that party must persuade a jury that the panel decision was incorrect. In contrast, a New York trial court upheld such a requirement on the premise that it was justified "as part of a massive legislative effort to solve a critical health care crisis."

All that can be concluded on this point is that the pretrial mandatory arbitration panel approach will be in legal dispute for some time to come and that for nonmedical cases it is, at best, a dubious tool.

Workers' Compensation

A somewhat more promising legislative idea in some of the pending bills, particularly important to engineers and architects, is to amend the state workers' compensation laws to limit the amount paid for injury or death to the compensation award, thus barring a suit against the design professional. As it now stands, an injured worker or the estate of a worker killed in the performance of his work is entitled as a matter of right to an award without proof of negligence by the employer. As is well known in A-E circles, however, the compensation awards in construction cases are followed by independent suits against others than the employer, including the engineer or architect who was involved in construction, even if only to the extent of ascertaining that construction was in accord with plans and specifications.

While this type of change in the state law would be of major benefit to A-Es, it would run only to the extent of injury or death cases. While these claims against A-Es draw unusual attention and very large monetary claims, the fact is that of all the costs of professional liability insurance they amount to less than 20 percent of the total costs; the large majority of total costs involve property claims. It should also be noted that it will be very difficult to enact the sole remedy change in the face of anticipated opposition from unions which represent construction workers. They will argue that the compensation awards are inadequate as a basis to prevent a follow-on suit against a party who allegedly was negligent. It further may be anticipated that if legislatures could be convinced to buy the sole remedy idea, it would be likely to substantially increase the compensation award formula, necessitating an increase in workers' compensation premiums.

Statute of Limitations

Here the design professions are ahead of the medical profession, which now is pushing in some state legislatures for a cutoff period to bring suit for alleged malpractice from the date of performance of service instead of the normal statutory period running from date of discovery of the injury. One such state bill covering all professions proposes a two-year period after the act of alleged malpractice occurs. That state now has a 10-year statute of limitation for A-Es. While the shorter period sounds attractive, it may well generate a new question of constitutionality.

In one case, however, a bill written particularly for the design professions would cut the present A-E limitation period from 12 years to 4. With the present time periods for A-Es in some 40 states now averaging about 6 to 7 years, it seems unlikely that the new wave of professional liability bills will produce a significantly lower period.

Limitation on Recovery Amount

The legislation oriented toward medical practice often calls for a monetary limitation on the amount of damages. An Illinois decision rejected a $500,000 limitation in medical malpractice cases as a violation of the constitutional prohibition of special legislation because the arbitrary limit discriminated against very seriously injured medical malpractice victims. An Idaho court, on the other hand, allowed a monetary limitation on the technical basis that the legislature could amend common-law rights existing at the time the constitutional provision was adopted in 1890 to guarantee to every person a remedy for every injury.

So far the various state bills have not undertaken to specify a limitation on amount of recovery for the design professions. Some advocates of the concept have argued for a dollar limitation in the contract between the engineer and his client. This approach, which appears to have been little implemented to date, would not, however, have any application to an injured worker or anyone not a party to the engineer-owner agreement. It also raises the legal issue of whether the courts will enforce such a provision as being possibly contrary to public policy, with the decision perhaps turning on the degree of sophistication of the client agreeing to such a provision. The other and broader issue is whether the engineer wishes to say to his client, in effect, "I recognize that I may be negligent in performing my services. If so, I wish you to share in the losses suffered by you due to my negligence."

Contingent Fees

Many A-Es have expressed the view that a major source of their liability problem is the existence of a contingent fee system widely used in the legal profession. They reason that if the contingent fee system were abolished there would be fewer suits, particularly the "shotgun" suits in which A-Es are named along with everyone else involved in an accident. While the contingent fee system has no doubt been abused in some cases, with lawyers taking up to 50 percent of the amount recovered, the problem is to find a substitute whereby an injured average worker with limited resources will be able to file a claim he believes to be meritorious.

A somewhat more promising approach in some pending malpractice bills would limit the percentage of contingent fees. One bill suggests a limit of 30 percent for the first $100,000 of an award, 25 percent for the next $100,000, and 20 percent of any balance. In many states the courts have already imposed percentage limits of this type, but even the lowest percentage suggested does little to discourage any attorney from taking a case with a potential award of hundreds of thousands of dollars.

Frivolous Suits

Another popular idea is for aggrieved engineers and architects who believe themselves victims of unjustified suits, particularly in the "shotgun" situation, to retaliate with a countersuit against the lawyer who brought them into the case without good cause. The idea was mainly generated by an Illinois case in which a radiologist who had been sued filed such a countersuit and won a jury award of $8000. That decision has now been appealed.

The basis for the Illinois countersuit was, oddly enough, an old Illinois statute having nothing to do with countersuits or frivolous suits. The wording is unique:

> If any person shall wickedly and willfully excite and stir up any suits or quarrels between the people of this state, either at law or otherwise, with a view to promote strife and contention, he shall be deemed guilty of the petty offense of common barratry; and if he be an attorney or counselor at law, he shall be suspended from the practice of his profession, for any time not exceeding six months.

Under that statute the trial judge allowed the case to go to the jury on the theory that it provided the basis for a tort action, i.e., a civil wrong against another. It will not be known for some time whether that interpretation will hold up in the higher state courts. Meanwhile, however, decisions in other states have rejected the frivolous suit approaches unless there is a showing of actual malice on the part of the plaintiff's attorney. Because of the widespread interest in the concept, NSPE has commissioned a special legal study by outside attorneys to determine whether or to what extent support might be given to engineers who feel they have been victims of so-called frivolous suits.

A related aspect of this is found in some of the pending state legislation to the effect that if a claim is resolved in favor of the party who prevailed in the arbitration proceeding and who also prevailed in the subsequent court procedure, the court may award reasonable attorneys' fees in addition to court costs against the party who pressed the case to a full new hearing. Again, however, it is likely that this approach might run afoul of constitutional provisions as a deterrent to the right of citizens to have their day in court.

In another bill the related proposal is that the arbitration panel itself may award all costs incurred by the defendant if it finds that a claim was "capricious, trivial, frivolous, or unreasonable." In another state a bill containing a similar provision carries an explanation by its sponsor that the purpose is to give some relief to A-Es, contractors, and land surveyors

> who are improperly named as defendants in suits arising out of the condition of real property improvements. The practice of listing such persons as parties to lawsuits, where there is no legal basis for such a claim, merely to force a contribution toward settlement, demeans the legal process and imposes a needless expense upon the professional so named.

Aside from constitutional questions which likely will be asserted under this kind of proposed legislation, there is the broader question of it leading to a basic change in the legal system in the United States under which attorneys' fees are not usually allowed between parties. In Europe the allowance of reasonable attorneys' fees to the prevailing party is the usual rule. If such a change in the system should develop, however, it is possible that it would cut both ways, and the A-Es who lose their cases might be

required to pay the attorneys' fees of the plaintiff over and above the award
of damages.

Potpourri

These are only some of the highlights of various legislative proposals to
cope with the professional liability problem. In the laws enacted thus far,
and in the various bills to date, there are other equally controversial
provisions, such as a requirement that the professional practitioner carry
certain levels of malpractice insurance (upheld in the Idaho case). One of
the state bills covering A-Es spells out in great detail the establishment of
a state-controlled professional liability insurance association, with the
requirement that all practicing professionals in the state must carry at least
$100,000–$300,000 professional liability insurance or post a bond covering
their practice in the amount of $100,000.

It is not clear from the wording whether the insurance must be with the
state-run insurance fund or whether it might be carried by a private
insurance company. Nor is it clear how the stipulated coverage would
apply to firms, as distinguished from individual practitioners, or how it
would deal with amounts of deductibles, areas of coverage, and many other
fine points.

Other pending proposals call for the arbitration board to report to the
state licensing board for possible disciplinary action against the professional
following an adverse finding against him on the basis of either a tort or
breach of contract.

Conclusion

Only time will tell how these different concepts, if enacted, will work out
in practice, and then only after the legal challenges, certain to come, are
resolved. For the immediate future, state legislation is not a promising
answer to the growing problem.

During the interim period of trial and error, perhaps the only quick
answer is that given by an experienced attorney who has said that there are
three solutions: buy more insurance; buy more insurance; buy more
insurance. What he did not add, however, is that in doing so the practicing
professional must increase his fees accordingly.

Selection of Engineering Experts

MAX SCHWARTZ

An owner of a new office building seeks legal advice. The building is only one-year old, yet it has constantly been plagued with serious problems. The elevator functions erratically, stopping three feet below floor levels, making sudden drops, and the doors close prematurely. In addition, not only have some of the glass plates popped out from the curtain walls, but two of the floors sag so badly that the doors jammed closed and the walls cracked.

Should the attorney accept the owner's case? It is now the attorney who has the problem. How involved are the intricacies of building construction? Who should be retained to get the facts? What type of engineer is best suited to investigate and testify for litigation purposes? In other words, how is the attorney to find an expert witness for construction litigation?

Engineers Knowledgeable about Building Construction

It can be said that complaints that evolve out of a building construction are similar to complaints made about the human body. As knowledge of man's bone structure is within the expertise of the orthopedic specialist, a building frame is within the expertise of the structural engineer. Similarly, as a neurosurgeon may be called to testify on nervous disorders, an electrical engineer is the qualified expert of electrical distribution in building systems.

Beyond these simple analogies, it can be seen that the design of a building reflects the specialties of specific discipline engineers whose depth of knowledge and training are orchestrated to provide the details necessary to construct a complete facility. When litigation fever pends as a result of complaints, these specialists become essential in rendering a proper diagnosis, prognosis, and treatment of the problem.

A typical complaint regarding site work may involve grading, excavation, foundations, pavements, roadways, drainage, irrigation systems, landscaping, or fencing. In these instances, the required specialist would be the civil

Reprinted with permission of the American Arbitration Association from *The Arbitration Journal.* © 1977.

engineer. For more detailed determinations of land surface measurements, a licensed land surveyor is the qualified expert. If an investigation involves the subsurface conditions, analyzing soil borings, or making subsequent determinations of the type, strength, and faults of the underlying soil and earth structure, a soils engineer would be the specialist. The soils engineer can make recommendations as to the type of foundation, the removal of substandard soil, the methods of improving existing soil properties, and safe bearing strengths. This specialist can report on anticipated settlement and potential earth movement due to subsidence, land slides, and foundation pressures. When the subject concerns earthquake faults, potential seismic activity, and general geological investigations, an engineering geologist is critical.

Grading, excavation, compaction, and general construction of earthwork structures such as dikes, dams, and levees are specialties of the civil engineer. In addition to earthwork this specialist is concerned with storm water and sanitary waste drainage systems, roadways, parking facilities, airport runways, tunnels, and water supply and irrigation systems such as canals, reservoirs, pipelines, and pumping stations. Many civil engineers engage in structural design for building construction. There are, however, two limitations to a civil engineer's authority to design structures. The law prescribes that "high-rise" office buildings (eight stories and above) and school building structures must be designed by a structural engineer. A structural engineer is a registered civil engineer who has passed a special examination given by the State Board of Registration for Professional Engineers and is thereby authorized to use such a title.

In a typical large building, the plumbing, waste, ventilation, heating, and air conditioning systems are designed by a mechanical engineer. This engineer is also responsible for the adequacy and safety in distributing natural gas, water, and steam in the building. The mechanical engineer also designs and specifies the equipment necessary to heat, treat, filter, and control water, as well as air, throughout the building.

The electrical distribution system in the largest building can be traced back from the smallest light bulb through to the utility company's service. Such a field concerns the expertise of the electrical engineer, whose skills include the selection of switchboards, safety devices, wires, conduits, and lighting fixtures throughout the facility. Furthermore, this engineer determines the amount of light required in each area and designs accordingly and often will specify automatic controls such as time switches that operate lights and air conditioning equipment.

There are many factory-designed and fabricated components in a building, including elevators, boilers, fans, pumps, electrical switch gear, and motor control panels. Although some of these components may be specified by the architect or the mechanical or electrical engineer, these specifications are normally limited to the output or the required capabilities of the equipment. For example, an elevator may be specified to have a 6 foot by 8 foot cab, to stop at five floors, and to have a 3000 pound capacity and interior finish of wood paneling. But the selection of the power equipment, controls, cab frame, and other items making up the unit is the responsibility of the elevator manufacturer. The local laws do not require that the person designing the elevator for the manufacturer be a registered engineer. The elevator is only required to meet certain tests upon completion and installation. These tests are observed by a government inspector and a certificate is issued for that particular installation. Even though the manufacturer is usually the party responsible for the elevator, a malfunction can occur for reasons outside of the control of the elevator manufacturer or installer. For example, the building could have tilted, the machinery room could have been improperly ventilated causing overheating of the elevator controls or motors, or the power supply could have been inadequate. When such events occur, the experts who may be involved in the investigation include the elevator manufacturer, the architect, the soils engineer, the mechanical engineer, or the electrical engineer.

Registered and Nonregistered Engineers

We have seen the term "engineer" used in reference to such a large number of diverse skills and responsibilities that it is small wonder that attorneys, as well as the general public, have difficulty in recognizing a professional expert. One way of classifying engineers is to separate them as registered and nonregistered. The California State Board of Registration for Professional Engineers has recognized certain disciplines of engineering as requiring compliance with minimum educational, experience, and ethical standards. These include civil, chemical, electrical, industrial, mechanical, metallurgical, petroleum, and structural engineering. Furthermore, it should be noted that the Business and Professions Code requires practicing engineering in these fields to be registered by the state.

There are many industrial engineering disciplines for which the state board requires no registration but which fall within the body of knowledge of one of the "registered" engineering disciplines. These include hydraulic, electronic, communications, sanitary, and plant engineering.

Another group of engineers exists that does not necessarily fall within the normally accepted definition of an engineer. The American College Dictionary uses "a skillful manager" as one of the definitions of the term "engineer." This third group functions as skillful managers in such fields as sales, machinery application, time study, stationary boilers, and cost appraisal. These are respectively called sales engineers, application engineers, efficiency engineers, stationary engineers, and appraisal engineers.

One area often subject to confusion involves inconsistent sister-state registration policies. For instance, there are a number of states in this country that register certain disciplines not required in California, such as traffic, agricultural, and sanitary engineering.

There is a reason for the registration of professional engineers. The explanation, as cited in the Professional Engineers Act, is to safeguard life, property, health, and the public welfare. In considering whether an engineering discipline qualifies for registration, the State Board of Registration of Professional Engineers must determine whether the public life, safety, property, health, and welfare would be protected by policing of this discipline.

The factors that qualify an engineer for registration can also be used to guide the lawyer in selection of an expert. The lawyer should inquire into the following areas: (1) whether the individual graduated from an accredited university in the specific specialty required with a B.E., Masters, or Ph.D.; (2) the number of years of responsible work that the individual had in this specific field; (3) whether the individual had military experience in this field; (4) whether this individual has written books, articles, or papers on this specific field; (5) whether this individual has teaching experience in this specific field.

The following engineering disciplines have been recognized and accepted by California Board of Registration for Professional Engineers: industrial, aerospace, nuclear, land surveyor, chemical, petroleum, manufacturing, civil, quality, mechanical, electrical, and safety. Other states have registered the following disciplines: sanitary, mining, highway, agricultural, fuel technology, and water treatment.

According to a recent study, the preliminary findings show that of the approximately 209,000 engineers in California, only 25 percent, or 50,000, are registered with the state. This study also shows that the largest number of registered engineers have been licensed without testing by a method known as "grandfathering." This method is used when a new engineering discipline is approved for registration by the board, and all applicants deemed qualified by the board are automatically granted recognition as registered professional engineers without passing a written examination.

Guide for Selecting Engineering Experts

As a rough checklist for the attorney seeking an expert on some particular phase of construction, the following is a brief guide to the body of knowledge of each discipline involved in construction.

The architect's responsibility and expertise includes the overall planning of buildings and sitework; enclosures such as walls, floors, roofs, and ceilings; layout of room sizes; locations of exits, fenestration, and vertical transportation, including stairs, elevators, and escalators. Further, the architect is responsible for conformance with zoning, parking, and other environmental laws and must coordinate the efforts of the consulting engineers on the project.

A civil engineer's body of knowledge is one of the oldest disciplines and covers the largest field. This area of expertise includes: land surveying and fixed works, such as railroads, dams, canals, bridges, port facilities, and water distribution and sewage systems. Civil engineering also includes flood control, inland waterways, purification of water, refuse disposal, air fields, water power, structures, and buildings.

Electrical engineers, when part of public utilities, are basically involved in power generation and distribution. When connected with the private sector, they are responsible for the generation and distribution of electricity within the building or plant sites, electrical controls, lighting, and instrumentation. Some are associated with manufacturers of electrical switch gear, motors, transformers, and control panels.

Chemical engineers are generally classified according to the type of industry in which they are involved—to name a few: petroleum, detergents, soaps, dyes, plastics, and metal finishing. The special activities of chemical engineers also include the development and application of processes involving chemical changes in materials, unit physical operations, research, design production, operation, organization, and economic aspects of the above.

One of the recently recognized professional disciplines that is important to the attorney involved in product liability cases is the safety engineer. The state board defines safety engineering as

> that specialty branch of professional engineering which requires such education and experience as is necessary to understand the engineering principles essential to the identification, elimination and control of hazards to man and property, and requires the ability to apply this knowledge to the development, analysis, production, construction, testing and utilization of systems, products, procedures and standards in order to eliminate or optimally control hazards.

The body of knowledge of the mechanical engineer is also very broad. It includes machinery, tool design, heating, ventilation, air conditioning, plumbing, and piping. It is very concerned with energy use and conservation and includes the research, design, production, operation, organization, and economic aspects of these specialties.

In addition to the above-recognized professions, there are many that are not listed under the California Act of Professional Engineers. These include specialties involved in, for example, the manufacture of fabrics, shoes, and numerous other products. These people are experts having special knowledge and skill in their particular field and are recognized as authorities by their industry.

There is much controversy over when an engineer can be considered a professional. State engineering registration laws are not consistent. Most states do, however, take into account the previously discussed requirements. The National Council of State Board of Engineering Examiners has proposed to improve the professional standards by defining and utilizing nationally recognized qualifications for professional engineering registration that will be applicable to all states. At present, possessing a license in one state does not necessarily allow an individual to practice in another state. Most states will, however, either allow temporary permits or grant registration to out-of-state licensees, providing the host state's requirements are met.

There are a number of nonprofessional experts in the construction industry. These may include the general contractors, construction superintendents, deputy inspectors, and subcontractors. Other possible experts can be the craft journeymen, clerks of the works, or field engineers.

The contractor and superintendent have their greatest expertise in coordinating the many trades and materials into an orderly and efficient effort. Their principal assets are not only insight, knowledge, and experienced judgment; the experienced contractor must be fully conversant with the language of all the various engineering disciplines shown on the plans and specifications as well as the business end of the contract and general conditions. This individual must also be aware of all safety laws governing the work and abide by the various union contracts effective on the job. Some of the principal subcontractors are steel fabricators and erectors, carpenters, roofers, plumbers, electricians, sewer installers, and plasterers.

Manufacturers of building materials constitute another group of experts who are usually most familiar with the limitation of their products as well as their chemical, structural, and physical properties. When referring to the manufacturers as a group, it must be understood that this includes manufacturers of all component parts as well as the final assembler. For example, an elevator manufacturing company must purchase motors, pumps, valves, electrical switch gear, and many other components before he can assemble and install an elevator. Other experts closely related to the manufacturing and fabricating organization are stress analysts, draftsmen, detailers, specification writers, and quality-control personnel.

A recommended way for an attorney to locate a specialist in a particular field is to contact one of the professional associations, such as American Society of Civil Engineers, American Society of Mechanical Engineers,

Structural Engineers Association of California, American Institute of Chemical Engineers, Instrument Society of America, Society of Automotive Engineers, and American Society of Safety Engineers. The main objective of these organizations, while forming a worthy basis for a qualified expert witness, are to attain recognition by their peers and by the public as a responsible profession, to improve the competence of their profession, to encourage further education in their field, and to enhance their engineering discipline as a profession.

Use of Testing Laboratories

When searching for a laboratory to run specific tests, it is recommended to contact the American Council of Independent Laboratories, Inc. This nationwide organization can help the attorney locate a local laboratory staffed and equipped for specific tests. Laboratories are generally divided between physical testing and chemical testing laboratories. Most laboratories specialize in a specific area such as: soils, concrete, masonry, bacteriology, chemistry, water quality, air quality, fire resistance, electrical systems, and electronics. In cases of structural failure of buildings, machinery, or other items, laboratories can determine the extent of fatigue, creep, stress, rupture, chemical deterioration, or other causes of failure. These reports can augment the testimony of the engineer expert.

Conclusion

The world of the engineering profession is in a continuous state of change. New disciplines and specialties are constantly developing and multiplying into subgroups, while others seem to fade away. The great expansion of aerospace work created many new highly skilled disciplines, a large number of which are accepted in industry as recognized professions although universities do not include these fields in their curriculum, and the states recognize only a relatively small proportion of engineers that industry deems necessary.

It is fortunate that the construction industry mostly uses the same engineering disciplines that have been in existence for a long period of time and are recognized by the state. This simplifies the problem of the attorney in the selection of an expert witness in construction litigation. The attorney in need of an expert witness should seek an engineer from the appropriate discipline. If he is also a registered engineer in that special discipline the engineer's credits and qualifications have been already determined by the state, and the individual's value as an expert witness will be enhanced as will be his skill in investigating and testifying.

Evidence in Construction Arbitration

MAX SCHWARTZ

Most problems dealing with construction blossom into real litigation after the completion and occupation of a project. Even though some controversy arises during construction, the pressure and stress of maintaining schedules prevent the exposure of the source of the dispute and, indeed, often cover or bury the defective work.

The attorney is then short of evidence to determine such items as the nature of the soil under foundations, number and location of reinforcement bars in concrete beams, the amount of water used in plaster, the number of bolts in a beam, and other critical elements of a building or structure.

Material and Documentary Evidence

Evidence used in construction litigation is either material or documental. Material evidence can be soil samples, concrete cores, sections cut from steel beams, plugs from roofing, and other samples removed from the structure.

Documentary evidence includes the plans and related details, revisions to the plans, specifications and addenda, vendors' drawings, shop drawings, and other data that were made specifically for a particular job.

In addition to the above, there are other pertinent data generated during a construction project that constitute the written communication between parties of construction. These may include: construction status reports written by the clerk of the works or field superintendent; construction inspection report recorded by the architect, engineer, or inspector; construction observation report logged by consulting engineers; minutes of building committee meetings; addenda to original bid documents; manpower logs; schedules; bulletins from architect or engineer notifying contractor and owner of potential changes; change orders to contract documents; and proposals of contractor to original bidding documents and subsequent bulletins.

There are also many important pieces of evidence pertaining to a construction job that are general in scope; for example, the building material manufacturer's advertisement and publications for the application or installation of their material or equipment. These may contain brochures and pamphlets, ads, installation and operation manuals, quotations and proposals, vendors' drawings, and photographs.

Obtaining the documentary evidence noted above requires patience and often "dusty" work. Superseded drawings and memos often are thrown away or, at best, not filed in an orderly manner. Disinterested parties do not have the time to search old records and frequently will say that "everything has been thrown away." A quiet, unobtrusive search may, however, bring forth enough data to recreate a situation at a certain period of the project.

Dating of the documents is very important. In addition to the reports that architects, engineers, and others submit, they often keep diaries that can help provide dates of certain occurrences and their related documents.

Vendors' and contractors' drawings provide a great source of evidence in construction. Vendors' drawings cover a wide range of material and nature of work and go far beyond the information given in the architect or engineer's design drawings. Steel fabricators provide drawings dimensionally showing each separate steel member, whether it is a column, beam, or a small clip angle. Although these drawings are made primarily for the erector's own personnel, they are a very accurate representation of the work as installed. Other vendors' drawings include elevators, air conditioning equipment, process machinery, pumps, fans, and the many other items that are prefabricated before delivery to job site.

One class of vendors' drawings that is very critical is "certified drawings." These represent the final drawings submitted by the vendor for approval before beginning fabrication or delivery. Such drawings are signed by an agent of the vendor and are guaranteed to be truly representative of the material to be delivered in size, character, and material. Upon receipt of copies signed as approved by owner's agent, fabrication and delivery is commenced. If the delivered items are not in accordance with certified drawings, refusal to accept by the owner or back charges can result.

Laboratory Analysis of Construction Materials

In many cases in which there is a suspected failure or defect in material of construction, laboratory analysis is recommended. Indeed, certain portions of a building are required by authorities to be tested during construction. This is especially true with concrete, masonry, welding, as well as other structural elements. Certificates of Occupancy for completed buildings are dependent upon acceptable laboratory findings of these tests.

In addition to the tests required by the building department for individual buildings, most building material and equipment manufacturer associations police themselves by establishing minimum standards. The function of a testing laboratory can be to establish whether a suspected component of a building or machine meets the industry's standards. Analysts can also determine cause of failure, strength of material, contamination, and other characteristics.

It is useful to understand the state's viewpoint regarding recognized testing laboratories. According to the California Professional Engineers Act, reports issued from any testing laboratory must be prepared by or under the supervision of a registered civil, electrical, or mechanical engineer as appropriate and signed and sealed by him when the report goes beyond the tabulation of test data. This would include: interpretation of data to draw conclusions; expressing engineering judgment or recommendations as resulting from the test data; and performing design work in the preparation of plans, specifications, or other documents requiring registration as a civil, mechanical, or electrical engineer.

Generally laboratories are divided between physical and chemical types. Some specialize in testing of soils, concrete, masonry, metal, and other construction materials. These laboratories can provide construction inspection services as required by code. In the field of environmental and chemical analysis, many specialize in the general areas of water supply, wastewater, air and solid wastes.

For very specific analysis and testing, laboratories should be selected that have the latest sophisticated apparatus such as atomic absorption, spectrophotometry, mass spectrometry, gas chromotography, and thermogravimetric analysis.

For guidance in selection of a qualified laboratory for specific work, it is recommended to contact the American Council of Independent Laboratories, Inc., 1725 K Street, N.W., Washington, D.C. 20006 (202–887–5872).

Virtually all member laboratories perform analysis, testing, and sampling or inspection of construction materials. A majority do research and development in fields of their specialty. Most of the laboratories also provide consultation services.

Litigation over either building construction or machinery often involves defective or overstressed materials. This may result in cracks caused by tension, compression, shear, bending, or excessive wear due to physical or chemical destruction. Samples of the suspected components should be saved for testing and analysis. If the material is susceptible to additional changes due to atmospheric or other natural conditions, the samples should be preserved as well as possible. This may mean protecting the sample from excessive change of temperature or moisture content.

It is important to obtain the samples as early after the problem has occurred as possible. They should be tagged to identify the exact location of their source as well as the date obtained.

Use of Land Surveyor

Other important sources of evidence in construction are the field notes, sketches, and drawings prepared by the land surveyor. Surveyor's work includes: setting out the property lines, building lines, depth and location of underground drains and sewers, finish grades, and street improvements. Surveyors are also instrumental in keeping buildings and structures vertical and square. They check the accuracy of the alignment of a steel structure before the building is closed up with walls and floors. Throughout the surveyor's work, notes are maintained in field books. These notes are valuable in determination of the accuracy of construction during its early phases.

Previous settlement, cracking, or other defects in adjoining property can also be recorded by survey. Public agencies and engineering constructors often mark with yellow paint all cracks in pavements and walls that existed before construction started.

Written Information on Construction Jobs

Practically all large construction projects have a number of people inspecting or supervising the various phases of work. Daily and weekly reports are made by superintendents, field engineers, clerks of the works, building department inspectors, deputy inspectors, project architects and engineers, and others. In addition, there are delivery tickets on concrete, steel, and other building materials that are backed up, in turn, by manufacturer analysis and test results of concrete mixes, strength tests, and chemical analysis for each run or batch of material. Lumber is grade inspected and marked; plaster boards carry a coded production number identifying the day and shift of manufacturer. Therefore, with some effort it is possible to trace back the material to its very source.

Examples of Important Evidence in Construction Cases

In the following typical construction litigation cases, these were found to be the most important items of evidence:

Large Hospital Facility — Construction log, change-order records, payroll records, construction schedule as represented by "Critical Path Method" (CPM), and Impacted or Revised CPM as resulted by changes.

Town House Apartment Complex — Comparison between design drawings and specifications, a shower mixing valve, a sample plug of roofing, temperature readings of the hot water system, and vendors' documents on air conditioning system.

Elevators in a Hospital — Temperature reading of hydraulic fluid in elevator equipment, testing of relays in control system, maintenance records, and manufacturer manuals for components of elevator.

Tunnel Boring Machine — Manufacturer's certified drawings, operating manual, records of repair work and replacement of equipment, photographs of defective parts, soil engineer's report, data from manufacturers of components, and metallurgical analysis of broken gear.

Stiff-Legged Derrick — Sales advertisement document as compared to Crane Manufacturers Association Standards.

Rock Crushing and Screening Plant — Design drawings, steel shop drawings, and field survey to check accuracy of installed structures.

Collapsed Masonry Wall during Construction of Two-Story Commercial Building — Laboratory testing of brick and mortar.

Floor Settlement of Three-Story Office Building — Structural design notes and computer printout, concrete test results, and steel shop drawings.

Collapsed Gypsum Ceilings in Apartment Complex — Samples of gypsum board and acoustic filler, laboratory analysis of compositions of gypsum, duplication in laboratory of site conditions to determine cause of failure, manufacturers' standards for gypsum, and building department standards for gypsum.

The above-noted construction cases illustrate the broad range of evidence available to the attorney to determine the causes of failure or dispute between parties in the project.

Conclusion

In summary, the attorney should be aware that the construction of a building or mechanical facility is the result of the combined efforts of many parties. Behind the owner, designer, and builder are numerous subcontractors, material suppliers, manufacturers, government agencies, and others. There is a complexity of documentation between all of these parties as well as an interrelationship of their efforts.

Lawyers' Arbitration Letters

Arbitrators' Immunity from Civil Liability—Deposition of Arbitrators[1]

This letter concerns two areas of post-arbitration litigation affecting arbitrators: (1)arbitral immunity from civil liability, and (2) deposition and testimony of arbitrators. The first section will trace the evolution of the immunity doctrine and its application to arbitrators. The second section will explore the question of whether an arbitrator can be subpoenaed to testify or be deposed for the purpose of impeaching or clarifying the award.

Arbitral Immunity

Evolution of Doctrine of Judicial Immunity

The doctrine of judicial immunity from civil liability is founded upon considerations of public policy and is deeply rooted in the common law. *Floyd* v. *Barker* (1868), 12 Co. Rep. 23, 15 Eng. R.C. 37; *Scott* v. *Stansfield* (1868), L.R. 3 EX. 220, 15 Eng. R.C. 42. The purpose of the doctrine is to preserve the integrity and independence of the judiciary so as to insure that their actions will be based on convictions that are free from any apprehension as to possible personal consequences.

An early American court applied the doctrine in the case of *Pratt* v. *Gardner,* 2 Cushing 68, 70–71 (Mass. 1848) and concluded that "where the subject matter and the person are within the jurisdiction of the court, the judge, whether of a superior or inferior court, is justified. His judgment may be revised in an appellate court, and revised or affirmed; but he himself can be liable only to an impeachment for corruption or other misconduct, if there be any."

In *Bradley* v. *Fisher,* 80 U.S. 646, 13 Wall 335 (1871) the United States Supreme Court, applying the doctrine, ruled that judges of Courts of Records of superior or general jurisdiction are not liable in civil actions for their judicial acts. See also *Allen* v. *Biggs,* 62 F. Supp. 229 (1945) and *Hohensee* v. *Goon Squad,* 171 F. Supp. 562 (1959).

Lawyers' Arbitration Letter is a quarterly publication containing commentaries on significant arbitration issues in the law. Reprinted with permission of the American Arbitration Association.

Extension of Immunity Doctrine to Arbitrators

It has long been recognized that arbitrators are quasi-judicial officers, bound by the rules governing such officers. "An arbitrator acts in a quasi-judicial capacity, and should possess the judicial qualifications of fairness to both parties . . ." *American Eagle Fire Ins. Co.* v. *New Jersey Co.,* 240 N.Y. 398, 405, 148 N.E. 562 (1925), and while arbitrators are not "eo nomine judges, they are in fact bound by the same rules as govern such officers." *In re Friedman,* 213 N.Y.S. 369, 373 (1926).

Apparently, the first case in the United States to extend the doctrine of judicial immunity to the arbitrator was *Jones* v. *Brown,* 54 Iowa 74, 6 N.E. 106, 108 (1880). In that case the arbitrator brought suit to collect his fee of $240. The defendant answered and cross-claimed for $500 in damages alleging that the plaintiff and another arbitrator had conspired together to defraud him in the making of the award. The court dismissed the cross-complaint holding that arbitrators are "empowered to determine questions of law and fact . . . to adjudicate all questions presented to them . . . and to determine the rights of the parties . . . the fact that their award may be subject to review by the court to which it is required to be returned, does not divest them of judicial functions." Further, the court, relying on *Pratt* v. *Gardner, supra* extended the immunity doctrine to arbitrators in their capacity as judicial officers.

Similarly, in *Hoosack Tunnel, Dock, and Elevator Co.* v. *James W. O'Brien,* 137 Mass. 424, 426 (1884), the court ruled that an arbitrator, appointed under a rule of court, is not liable in a civil action by one of the parties for fraudulently inducing and conspiring in the making of an unjust award, stating that:

> An arbitrator is a quasi-judicial officer, under our laws, exercising judicial functions. There is as much reason in this case for protecting and insuring his impartiality, independence, and freedom from undue influences, as in the case of a judge or juror. The same considerations of public policy apply, and we are of the opinion that the same immunity extends to him.

In *Rubenstein* v. *Otterbourg,* 357 N.Y.S.2d 62 (Civ. Ct. N.Y. County 1973), the plaintiff alleged tortious conduct on the part of the arbitrator. The court granted the arbitrator's motion for summary judgment on the ground that he was immune from civil liability.

The doctrine has also been applied to those who are sometimes designated quasi arbitrators. See *Lundgren* v. *Freidman,* 307 F.2d 104 (1962), where the court ruled that architects were not liable to the building contractor for their actions as quasi arbitrator, in their good faith resolution of disputes between the contractor and owner. See also *Hutchins* v. *Merrill* (surveyor held to be quasi arbitrator), 109 Me. 313, 322, 84 A.412 (1913) and *Melady*

v. *St. Paul Live Stock Exchange* (Board of Directors of Live Stock Exchange held to be quasi arbitrators), 142 Minn. 194, 196 (1919).

Deposition of Arbitrators or Use of Arbitrators' Testimony

The General Rule

There is a sizable body of case law supporting the contention that an arbitrator may not be deposed for the purpose of clarifying or impeaching an award. Thus, in *Gramling* v. *Food Machinery and Chemical Corp.*, 151 F. Supp. 853 (W.D.S.C. 1957) the court, concluding that the testimony of an arbitrator tending to impeach an award is incompetent, noted that "the deliberations of arbitration board are as much a part of the judicial process as the deliberations of a jury and should be jealously protected." *Id.* at 860.

In *Gramling* the parties had entered into a settlement agreement whereby a panel of six arbitrators were to determine the amount of plaintiff's damages based on stipulated instructions approved by counsel for both sides and given by the court. The award was challenged on the ground that the panel had violated the arbitration agreement and the judge's instructions. To substantiate the charge defendant tendered the affidavits of two arbitrators and moved for an order requiring all the arbitrators to appear in court for examinations regarding the method of arriving at their award. The court denied this motion reasoning that (151 F. Supp. at p. 861):

> ... it would be most unfair to the arbitrators to order them to come into court to be subjected to grueling examinations by the attorneys for the disappointed party and to afford the disappointed party a "fishing expedition" in an attempt to set aside the award. To do this would neutralize and negate the strong judicial admonitions that a party who has accepted this form of adjudication must be content with the results.

In *Fukaya Trading Company, S.A.* v. *Eastern Marine Corp.*, 322 F. Supp. 278 (E.D. La. 1971), the court vacated an order allowing the depositions of the arbitrators, who were unanimous in their award. The court reasoned that "since only dissenting arbitrators are allowed to impeach their award, there is no basis for allowing it in this case. Nor has any objective basis been advanced, such as the engineer's bill in Continental Materials Corp. ... which could serve as a basis for allowing depositions." *Id.* at 280.

Accord *Shirley Silk Co.* v. *American Silk Mills*, 257 App. Div. 357, 13 N.Y.S.2d 309 (1st Dept. 1939), wherein the appellate court modified a lower court order that directed the arbitrators to appear before a designated referee for the purpose of making depositions upon certain items including partiality and misconduct. The court concluded that "an arbitrator who is a quasi-judicial officer should not be called upon to give reasons for his decisions." 13 N.Y.S.2d 309, 311. As there was sufficient evidence purporting to show alleged partiality of one of the arbitrators, however, the court ordered a hearing before a referee who was to take proof and report to the court on partiality. There was, however, no order of the court allowing any of the parties to compel the arbitrator to make a deposition and it is unclear whether the referee was authorized to do so. See also *Morysville Body Works Inc.* v. *United Steelworkers of America, Local Union 6622,* Civil Action No. 75-2498, E.D. Pa., order filed October 8, 1976, where the court, relying on *Gramling, supra* and *Fukaya, supra,* granted a protective order forbidding plaintiff from taking the deposition of an arbitrator.

The use of affidavits is also frowned upon by the court. Accordingly, in *Daklke* v. *X-L-O Automotive,* 337 N.Y.S.2d 86 (App. Div. 1st Dept. 1972), the arbitrator's affidavit was admitted as it was deemed surplusage since it related only to form and did not seek to enlarge or impeach the award. The court noted, however, that this was a practice not to be encouraged.

The courts have rejected the testimony of arbitrators who alleged that a mistake caused an unintended result or that the award did not reflect their intentions. In *Grudem Brothers Co.* v. *Great Western Piping Corp.,* 213 N.W.2d 920 (Minn. 1974), the Minnesota Supreme Court affirmed the district court's refusal to allow the testimony of an arbitrator to show an alleged mistake in the award that caused an unintended result. The court stated that the award should be interpreted from the language used therein rather than the testimony of one of the arbitrators as to what they meant to do by the award.

The court, in *Martin Weiner Co.* v. *Fred Freund Co.,* 155 N.Y.S.2d 802, 805 (1st Dept. 1956) *aff'd memo* 3 N.Y.2d 806, 166 N.Y.S.2d 7 (1957), vacated a lower court order directing the appointment of an official referee to hear and report as to whether the arbitrators understood the meaning and effect of the award at the time it was executed. The court held that "if any arbitrator may not be questioned as to the reasons underlying an award in order to impeach it, then by the same token he cannot be heard to impeach it upon the ground that it does not reflect his intentions."

In *Alexander* v. *Fletcher,* 175 S.W.2d 196 (Ark. 1943) the court rejected testimony of arbitrators to the effect that they did not intend to make a binding award but only to recommend a basis for the parties to settle their dispute.

The inadmissibility of arbitrators' testimony is also discussed in the following cases: *Patriotic Order Sons of America* v. *Hartford Fire Insurance Company,* 305 Pa. 107, 157 A.259, 261 (1931); *Giannopulos* v. *Pappas,* 80

Utah 442, 15 P.2d 353, 357 (1932); *Sapp* v. *Barenfeld,* 34 Cal.2d 515, 212 P.2d 233 (1949); *New York City Omnibus Corp.* v. *Quill,* 73 N.Y.S.2d 289 (1947).

The principle was summed up in *Big-W Construction Corp.* v. *Horowitz,* 192 N.Y.S.2d 721 (1959) *aff'd memo* 218 N.Y.S.2d 530 (2d Dept. 1961). In that case a motion to vacate the award was supported by the attorney's affidavit, which contained admissions alleged to have been made by the arbitrators after the rendition of the award. The court rejected the affidavit saying (192 N.Y.S.2d at pp. 733–34):

> The practice of interviewing arbitrators after an award has been made in an effort to find out from their reasoning a flaw upon which to base an attack upon their award, is to be deplored both as an unwholesome practice and because the results of such endeavors have no efficacy as a matter of law. Our public policy, as enunciated by decisional law, has made it manifest time and again that arbitrators, jurors or other persons sitting in similar capacities, may not by their own statements made *after* their determination, impeach it.

Testimony of Arbitrator Allowed under Limited Circumstances

There have been a few decisions in some jurisdictions that have admitted the testimony of arbitrators into evidence under exceptional circumstances. Thus, it has been held that a dissenting arbitrator, the award not being his or her own, may testify as to misconduct on the part of other arbitrators. *Griffith Co.* v. *San Diego College for Women,* 45 Cal.2d 501, 289 P.2d 476 (1955). The testimony of an arbitrator was held admissible where the plaintiff called an arbitrator merely for the purpose of identifying testimony that was before the arbitrator, the defendant cross-examined, and the plaintiff rebutted. *Oregon-Washington R. & Nav. Co.* v. *Spokane, P. & S. R. Co.,* 163 P. 600, 83 Or. 528, 541 (1917); *William H. Estates Co.* v. *Lederer Realty Corp.,* 35 R.I. 352, 86 A. 881 (1913). See also *Continental Materials Corp.* v. *Gaddis Mining Co.,* 306 F.2d 952, 955 (10th Cir. 1962), where there was lengthy cross-examination of one of the arbitrators. The admissibility of the arbitrators' testimony was not addressed by the court, however, as it apparently had not been challenged.

Standard Packing Corp. v. *Curwood,* 365 F. Supp. 134 (N.D. Ill. E.D. 1973) holding that patent examiners are quasi-judicial officers who may only be deposed on matters which are factual and do not invade their decision-making mental processes.

Sapp v. *Barenfeld, supra* holding that the testimony of the arbitrator, while not admissible to impeach the award, is admissible to show what matters were submitted for decision and were considered by the arbitrators. Accord, *Giannapulos* v. *Pappas, supra.*

Twin Lakes Reservoir & Canal Co. v. *Platt Rogers,* 147 P.2d 828, 836 (Colo. 1944) admitted testimony of the arbitrators as to what was the matter in controversy, what took place before them, and what matters entered into the decision. The court noted that the testimony was not intended to add or vary the terms of the award.

Arbitrator Misconduct

A major exception to the general rule involves the deposition of arbitrators in order to determine if there was arbitrator misconduct. In the case of *Carolina-Virginia Fashion Exhibitors, Inc.* v. *Gunter,* 230 S.E.2d 380, 388 (N.C. 1976) the North Carolina Supreme Court held that "where an objective basis exists for a reasonable belief that misconduct has occurred, the parties to the arbitration may depose the arbitrators relative to that misconduct, and such depositions are admissible in a proceeding . . . to vacate an award."

In *Gunter* the arbitrators had, on an ex parte basis, viewed the premises in dispute without the consent of the parties, inspected them, and utilized the information obtained in rendering their opinion. The court recognized and reaffirmed the strong policy that favors the arbitration process and protects arbitrators from any inquiry into their mental processes or the reasoning behind the award, stating (230 S.E.2d at p. 387):

> We do not by this ruling, authorize inquisition into the mental process of the arbitrators. We share the view expressed by other courts that such inquiry into the reasoning behind an award would relegate arbitration to a superfluous role in the judicial process.

The court stated that it was clear from a review of the cases on the admissibility of arbitrators' testimony for purposes of impeachment or clarification, that no consensus had emerged in the issue of admissibility for the purpose of establishing arbitrator misconduct.

In allowing the testimony the court noted that (230 S.E.2d at p. 388):

> To refuse to admit testimony of the arbitrators where there is an objective basis reasonably to believe that misconduct has occurred would deprive the aggrieved party of its most effective means of ascertaining and providing the alleged misconduct . . . Admission of the testimony will, in many instances, aid in averting substantial injustice, which is surely the first duty of any court.

Summary

The cases are unanimous in holding that arbitrators are quasi-judicial officers and as such are immune from civil liability when acting in their official capacity. This concept has been expanded by one federal court to include challenges to the authority of the arbitrators to hear the dispute.

In general the courts have held that an arbitrator may not be deposed or required to testify in order to impeach, clarify, or otherwise show that the award resulted in an unintended outcome. There have been only a few exceptions to this rule, such as the admissibility of testimony of a dissenting arbitrator or admissibility of testimony to show arbitrator misconduct. In those cases, however, the testimony was admitted primarily to show what matters were considered or to show misconduct by the arbitrators. Therefore, while a few jurisdictions have allowed the limited use of arbitrators' testimony, none have allowed it for the express purpose of impeaching the award through a general inquiry into the manner in which the award was arrived at.

●

Arbitrators' Equitable Powers[2]

Between 1958 and 1960 the New York Court of Appeals reaffirmed in three landmark cases the well-established rule that, in making an award, arbitrators have authority to grant equitable relief instead of, or in addition to, money damages or other legal remedies. These cases were memorable not only because of the relief they granted—enjoining a slowdown by employees under their collective bargaining agreement (*Matter of Ruppert [Egelhofer]*, 3 N.Y.2d 576, 170 N.Y.S.2d 785 [1958]); granting specific performance of (1) a contract to continue an officer in the employ of a corporation (*Matter of Staklinski [Pyramid Elec. Co.]*, 6 N.Y.2d 159, 188 N.Y.S.2d 541 [1959]), and (2) a contract to construct a retail department store (*Matter of Grayson-Robinson Stores, Inc. [Iris Constr. Corp.]*, 8 N.Y. 2d 303 [1960])—but also because of their insistence that judicial enforcement could not be withheld simply because a court, faced with the same issues, would not or could not have reached the same result.

This letter deals with a number of situations since that time—outside the labor field—in which the courts have upheld the exercise of equitable or "remedial" powers by arbitrators.

Employment Ordered

In the first of these cases, *Matter of Exercycle (Maratta)*, 9 N.Y.2d 329, 214 N.Y.S.2d 353 (1961), the Court of Appeals upheld a right of arbitration against a claim that the relief sought—to require a corporation to continue the employment of a vice president for life—was not within the arbitrator's

power. Pointing to the broad arbitration clause in the contract of employment, the court declared that "a court is not justified in staying the
arbitration even if the claim would not be enforceable at law" (9 N.Y.2d
at p. 337). See also on arbitral award of mandatory injunction *Matter of
De Vitre (Bohn),* 22 A.D.2d 856, 254 N.Y.S.2d 235 (1st Dept. 1964).

Consequential Damages

Soon after *Exercycle,* the court, in *Matter of De Laurentiis (Cinemato-
grafica),* 9 N.Y.2d 503, 215 N.Y.S.2d 60 (1961), strongly intimated that an
arbitrator might grant the equitable relief of an award of "consequential
damages," despite the rule to the contrary in *De Lillo Constr. Co.* v. *Lizza
& Sons,* 7 N.Y.2d 102, 195 N.Y.S.2d 825 (1959) and in *Matter of Marchant*
v. *Mead-Morrison Mfg. Co.,* 252 N.Y. 284, 303, 169 N.E. 386 (1929).
Pointing to the incorporation of AAA rules into the arbitration clause and,
specifically, to the provision in rule 43 that the arbitrator "may grant any
remedy or relief which seems just and equitable and within the scope of the
agreement of the parties," the court wrote (9 N.Y.2d at p. 510):

> When we incorporate Rule 42 [now 43] into that [arbitration] clause we
> have a grant of power to the arbitrators so broad that it would be
> inappropriate to determine in advance of an arbitration that there must be
> eliminated from any award any items of damage which the arbitrators might
> consider "just and equitable" under the facts as developed before the
> arbitrators.

For another case permitting an arbitrator to award "consequential damages," see *United Buying* v. *United Buying Northeast,* 38 A.D.2d 75, 327
N.Y.S.2d 7, 12 (1st Dept. 1971).

Option Ordered Exercised

Some years later, the courts of New York upheld the authority of an
arbitrator to "command" the president of a close corporation to exercise
an option to purchase a warehouse. See *Matter of Vogel (Lewis),* 19 N.Y.2d
589 (1967), *affg* 25 A.D.2d 212, 268 N.Y.S.2d 237. In this case, petitioner
president and respondent secretary-treasurer had taken over the corporation as sole stockholders for the purpose of carrying on a moving and
storage business. Their undertaking was embodied in an agreement that
provided for arbitration of any dispute "in the course of their transaction
with each other" (268 N.Y.S.2d at p. 239).

The warehouse, which they had leased for five years with an option to purchase, was necessary to the continuance of their business. The respondent, alleging that petitioner president was acting in bad faith in refusing to exercise the option to buy at the end of the lease term, sought arbitration. The New York courts refused to grant the petitioner a stay of arbitration, holding it within the authority of the arbitrator to decide whether or not the option should be exercised, characterizing the relationship of the parties to the property as "that of a fiduciary," and rejecting the argument of the president that the arbitrator's decision would involve merely a question of business judgment (268 N.Y.S.2d at p. 240). See also *Morris* v. *Zuckerman,* 72 Cal. Rptr. 880, 446 P.2d 1000 (1968), involving an attempt by one joint venturer to force the second to join in the sale of property in which they each had a half interest, to a corporation controlled by the first. In the arbitration proceeding brought to resolve the controversy, the arbitrator, pointing to the "fiduciary relationship" of the two joint venturers, authorized the proposed sale but only on the condition that the second joint venturer be permitted to share as buyer therein.

Unconscionability

Matter of Granite Worsted Mills (Aaronson Cowen, Ltd.), 25 N.Y.2d 451, 306 N.Y.S.2d 934 (1939), the petitioner buyer of allegedly damaged merchandise sought arbitration under a contract that contained a damage limitation clause specifically excluding consequential damages by reason of defective goods. The arbitrator awarded the buyer an amount in excess of that permitted in the damage limitation clause.

The Court of Appeals reversed the decision of the appellate division upholding the award and remitted the matter to the arbitrator, the majority rejecting as "pure speculation" the buyer's contention that the arbitrator might properly have refused to apply the damage limitation clause because he found it "unconscionable." The dissenters were of the view that the facts warranted the inference that was, in fact, the basis of the arbitrator's award. Both the majority opinion and the strongly worded dissent, however (pp. 457-60), were unanimous in recognizing that an arbitrator has equitable power "to refuse to enforce a damage limitation clause on the ground of unconscionability" (p. 457).

Unjust Result

More recently, in *Lentine* v. *Fundaro,* 29 N.Y.2d 382, 328 N.Y.S.2d 418 (1972), the high court of New York declared that the arbitrators had the authority to direct an *unequal* distribution of partnership assets, despite the provision in the partnership agreement for an *equal* distribution. Applying the rule that, "short of complete irrationality," the arbitrators "may fashion the law to fit the facts before them (*Matter of Exercycle [Maratta],* 9 N.Y.2d 329, 336)" to prevent an "unjust" result, the court held that the "arbitrator, in an attempt to find a just solution to the controversy, might consider the inequality of the capital contributions, especially if the inequality were contrary to the partnership understanding, despite lack of ambiguity in the partnership agreement" (29 N.Y.2d at pp. 385-86).

Dissolution of Partnership

More recently still, in *Matter of Steinberg (Steinberg),* 32 N.Y.2d 671 (1972), *affg* 32 A.D.2d 57, 327 N.Y.S.2d 245, appellate division, Justice Eager, writing for an unanimous First Department, aptly described the arbitrator's power to dissolve a partnership (327 N.Y.S.2d at p. 247):

> Certainly, if breaches of a partnership agreement or misconduct and wrongdoing in partnership affairs are submitted for determination by an arbitrator and are within the scope of the arbitration clause contained in the agreement, then the arbitrator, in a settlement of the partnership disputes, would generally have the power to direct dissolution and fix the terms thereof. . . . Particularly, this is so where, as here, the parties have agreed to conduct the arbitration under the Rules of the American Arbitration Association which provide, *inter alia,* that the arbitrator in his award may grant any remedy or relief he deems just and equitable and within the scope of the agreement of the parties.

An interesting sidelight of this opinion is the court's holding that an arbitration clause should not be construed to cover a claim for damages for the wrongful institution of a prior arbitration proceeding thereunder, "in the absence of language expressly embracing [such] a claim." As the court puts it, "Actually, the use of an arbitration proceeding to challenge the bringing of a prior arbitration proceeding is incompatible with the purpose of an arbitration clause and would undermine the effectiveness of this valuable remedy" (327 N.Y.S.2d at p. 248).

Injunction

Finally, even though the case of *Matter of Girvan, Inc. (Robilotto),* 33 N.Y.2d 425, 353 N.Y.S.2d 958 (1974) is a labor arbitration matter, it is of some interest here in that the Court of Appeals upheld an arbitrator's exercise of the power to award a mandatory injunction. Acting under a "very broad" arbitration clause, the arbitrator directed the reinstatement of two employees accused of theft on the ground that the evidence before him did not justify their discharge on the only issue before him, namely, whether or not it had been for "just cause" (353 N.Y.S.2d at p. 960).

Other Examples of an Arbitrator's Equitable Powers

In addition to the cases discussed in this section, there have been a number of other decisions, chiefly in New York, that have approved the exercise of a variety of equitable powers by arbitrators. See, e.g., *Matter of Coler (G.C.A. Corp.),* 31 N.Y.2d 775, *affg* 39 A.D.2d 656, 331 N.Y.S.2d 938 (1st Dept. 1972) (court permitted an arbitrator to decide whether a contract should be *rescinded* on the ground of fraud in the inducement; to same effect *Matter of Amphenol Corp. [Microlab],* 49 Misc.2d 46, 266 N.Y.S.2d 768 [Sup. Ct. N.Y. County 1965]); *Matter of All State Tax Serv. of Area 5 (Kerekes Bros., Inc.),* 34 A.D.2d 935, 312 N.Y.S.2d 166 (1st Dept. 1970) (court held that it was for the arbitrator to decide whether or not a *restrictive covenant* would be enforced); *Bradigan* v. *Bishop Homes, Inc.,* 20 A.D.2d 966, 249 N.Y.S.2d 1018 (4th Dept. 1964) (court ruled arbitrators had power to direct *specific performance* of unfinished work); *Suffolk Develop. Corp.* v. *Pat-Plaza Amuse. Corp.,* 236 N.Y.S.2d 71 (Sup. Ct. Suffolk County 1962) (arbitrators empowered to require *specific performance* of contract to provide parking facilities); *Matter of Agora Development Corp. (Low),* 19 A.D.2d 126, 241 N.Y.S.2d 126 (1st Dept. 1963) (where relief sought was *reformation of a contract* to conform to the original agreement of parties, and court, though only in dictum, held such decision within the powers of arbitrator; see also *American Home Insurance Co.* v. *American Fidelity & Casualty Co.,* 356 F.2d 690, 692 [2d Cir. 1966]); but cf. *Matter of Vincent J. Smith, Inc. [B.N. Laurie Trucking, Inc.],* 19 A.D.2d 763, 241 N.Y.S.2d 507 [3rd Dept. 1963]; *Television Programs Inter., Inc.* v. *U.S. Commun. of Phila.,* 336 F. Supp. 405 (E.D. Pa. 1972) (arbitration permitted of a dispute in which the plaintiff sought *to enjoin* the defendant from exhibiting or advertising animated films under a licensing agreement); *Matter of Meda Internatl., Inc. [Salzman],* 24 A.D.2d 710, 263 N.Y.S.2d 12 (1st Dept. 1965) (arbitration allowed of controversy in which plaintiffs sought an *injunction* restraining defendants from using their name, representing them, or competing with them); *Register* v. *Herrin,* 110 Ga. App. 736, 140 S.E.2d 82 (1964) (court, *inter alia,* held that arbitrators had authority to establish a *disputed boundary* line).

Summary

Since 1960 the Court of Appeals of the State of New York has continued to uphold the exercise of broad equitable powers by arbitrators in a number of areas. It has given its approval of arbitral awards granting the relief of specific performance, consequential damages, and a mandatory injunction enforcing an obligation of a fiduciary character—and, in this, California has joined New York. It has also approved awards reflecting the spirit rather than the letter of a contract in dispute in order to carry out the understanding of the parties.

Similarly, in the lower courts arbitral awards granting equitable relief cover such areas as rescission and reformation of contracts; enforcement, or refusal to enforce, restrictive covenants; establishment of boundary lines for real property. In addition, these lower court cases include further examples of specific performance and injunction.

Disqualification of Arbitrators—Arbitrators' Duty to Disclose[3]

Arbitrators exercise broad discretion in determining the parties' controversies. The grounds for vacating an arbitrator's award are very limited. Therefore, in order to insure the viability of the process it is essential that controversies that are submitted to arbitration are determined by an impartial arbitrator. One of the grounds for vacating the award is the partiality of the arbitrator. This letter will discuss standards by which the court measures relationships that affect an arbitrator's impartiality, give the appearance of bias, or may prove partiality.

Arbitration laws in the United States do not contain specific language calling for the arbitrator to disclose any prior relationship that he had had with the parties. An award may, however, be vacated "where there was evident partiality or corruption in the arbitrators or either of them." 9 U.S.C. §10(b). See also New York C.P.L.R. §7511(b) and the Uniform Arbitration Act §12.

In the leading case on the subject the United States Supreme Court in *Commonwealth Coatings Corp.* v. *Continental Casualty Company,* 393 U.S. 145 (1968) held that under 9 U.S.C. §10 an award may be vacated if the arbitrator fails to disclose a meaningful relationship with a party. In *Commonwealth* the neutral arbitrator had failed to disclose his prior business relationship with one of the parties to a construction dispute. Except for this undisclosed business relationship, there was no allegation that the arbitrator had been guilty of fraud or bias in deciding the case.

In vacating the award, the court noted that Congress, in enacting §10 of the U.S. Arbitration Act, showed a desire to provide not merely for any arbitration but for an impartial one. The court further noted that the American Arbitration Association's commercial rule 19, while not controlling, was highly significant. Under that rule the arbitrator is requested to disclose any circumstances likely to create a presumption of bias or which the arbitrator believes might disqualify him or her as an impartial arbitrator. The court also referred to canon 33 of the Judicial Ethics entitled *Social Relations,* which provides that a judge should avoid "such action as may reasonably tend to awaken the suspicion that his social or business relations or friendship constitutes an element in influencing his judicial conduct." 393 U.S. at 149.

The court concluded with the often cited statement that "this rule of arbitration and this canon of judicial ethics rest on the premise that any tribunal permitted by law to try cases and controversies must not only be unbiased but must avoid even the appearance of bias." *Id.* at 149.

The avoidance of an appearance of bias is the standard that is presently applied in those cases wherein the parties seek to vacate an award due to the arbitrator's failure to disclose.

Cases vary as to how significant the undisclosed relationship must be before an award will be vacated. It is clear, however, that a mere business relationship does not disqualify an arbitrator to serve. *Texas Eastern Transmission Corp.* v. *Barnard,* 177 F. Supp. 123 (E.D. Ky. 1959) and *Kentucky River Mills* v. *Jackson,* 206 F.2d 111 (6th Cir. 1953). *Davy's Executors* v. *Faw,* 7 Cranch 171, 3 L.Ed. 305 (1812).

In *Hodges International Inc.* v. *Rembrandt Fabrics Ltd.,* 353 N.Y.S.2d 462 (App. Div. 1st Dept. 1974), the arbitrator's disclosure that he was acquainted with one of the witnesses for about 15 years and in his opinion he "talked too much" did not establish bias.

Weinrott v. *Carp,* 32 N.Y.2d 190, 344 N.Y.S.2d 848 (1973) held that where the facts established only a weak link of indirect relationship purporting to tie the arbitrator to the claimant through a third party who was known only casually by both parties, this was too remote and speculative to provide a basis for the vacatur of the award.

In *St. Paul Ins. Companies* v. *Lusis,* 492 P.2d 575 (Wash. 1971), the award was upheld where it was disclosed that the arbitrator and the counsel for one of the insured were both members of the same bar association.

Glatzer v. *Diamond,* 187 N.Y.S.2d 524 (Sup. Ct. N.Y. County 1959) *aff'd memo* 192 N.Y.S.2d 489 (1959). In that case, involving the dissolution of a partnership, respondent agreed to the arbitrator with full knowledge that the arbitrator was counsel to the firm, that his son was employed by the firm, and that he was to become a partner in the new firm. The court held that based on this knowledge the respondent could not seek disqualification of the arbitrator.

In *Perl* v. *General Tire & Casualty Co.*, 310 N.Y.S.2d 196 (App. Div. 2d Dept. 1970), the court denied a motion to vacate an award holding that an attorney arbitrator's failure to disclose that his practice was in the field of insurance and that he had an investigatory service for insurance companies did not vitiate the award.

Koenig v. *Department of Taxation and Finance of the State of New York*, N.Y.L.J. June 28, 1976, page 8, column 2 (Sup. Ct. N.Y. County) *aff'd* 392 N.Y.S.2d 376 (1977). The court upheld the award where there was no showing that the arbitrator's failure to disclose that he had, on occasion, been paid as an independent contractor by the New York State Public Employees Relation Board was prejudicial to the petitioner.

Where the arbitrator is unaware of the disqualifying relationship until after the award has been rendered, one court declined to vacate the award. Such was the case in *Overseas Private Investment Corporation* v. *Anaconda Co.*, 418 F. Supp. 107 (D.C.D.C. 1976), where after the rendering of an interim award it was disclosed that an arbitrator was negotiating an affiliation with a law firm that performed limited services related to the arbitration for the respondent. The court held that this was an insufficient basis on which to vacate the award under 9 U.S.C. §10 because the arbitrator was unaware of the relationship at the time the award was rendered. In this case, the law firm in question had been requested by respondent's counsel to provide a back-up translation of a document previously translated by Anaconda's house counsel and to obtain an affidavit by a member of the Chilean bar on a narrow issue of Chilean law. The arbitrator was not aware of this relationship until after the interim award, which decided the issue of liability but left the question of damages undecided, had been rendered. When the arbitrator discoverd that the firm he was about to join had given limited assistance to respondent's counsel, he disclosed this information and stated that he would be unable to serve as an arbitrator when the panel reconvened to determine the issue of damages.

In holding that the arbitrator's disclosure was an insufficient basis on which to vacate an award, the court relied on *Commonwealth Coatings Corp.*, *supra* and concluded that *Commonwealth* did not establish a per se rule requiring vacation whenever anyone believed that certain facts created an appearance of bias. Rather, each case must be reviewed on its own facts and the award should be set aside where the panel might reasonably be thought biased. The court also rejected petitioner's argument that the failure of counsel for Anaconda to disclose its knowledge of relationship between the arbitrator and the law firm was a ground for vacatur. The court stated that where the existence of a potentially prejudicial relationship is not known to an arbitrator, there is no possible way in which the relationship can affect his or her decision and thus disclosure would serve no purpose. As the arbitrator did not become aware of any potentially prejudicial relationship until after the award was rendered, the decision of the arbitrator was affirmed.

In the following cases courts have found that the relationship was significant enough to justify vacating the award.

The court in *J. P. Stevens & Co., Inc.* v. *Rytex Corp.*, 356 N.Y.S.2d 278, 34 N.Y.2d 123, 312 N.E.2d 466 (1974), vacated the award where the arbitrator failed to disclose a substantial business relationship. Prior to the hearings, the arbitrators disclosed the names of their employers. At that time no objections were raised. Subsequent to the award, Rytex moved to vacate on the grounds that the arbitrators could not be impartial because their employers did a substantial amount of business with Stevens. The evidence revealed that the two employers did some $2.5 million in business with Stevens annually. Also, one of the arbitrators was sales manager for his employer. The court concluded that the extent of this business relationship could not be readily ascertainable from the limited disclosure made by the arbitrators.

In *Johnston* v. *Security Insurance Co. of Hartford*, 80 Cal. Rptr. 133 (1970), the court held that a neutral umpire's failure to disclose his acquaintanceship with insured's appointed appraiser and insured's counsel and his business dealing with insured's appraiser was sufficient ground to vacate the award in favor of the insured even though no actual fraud or bias was charged or proven. See also *In re Santee Print Works, Inc. (Imptex Int. Corp.)*, N.Y.L.J. Nov. 24, 1976, page 11, column 1 (Sup. Ct. N.Y. County).

In *McKinney Drilling Co.* v. *Mach I Limited Partnership*, 359 A.2d 100 (Md. 1976), the court vacated an award where the arbitrator failed to disclose that his construction company bought concrete from one of the suppliers of McKinney. This relationship was ongoing at the time of the arbitration.

In re Kappa Frocks, Inc. (Entre Knits, Inc.), N.Y.L.J. April 8, 1976, page 6, column 5 (Sup. Ct. N.Y. County). An award was vacated when it was disclosed that one of the arbitrators, selected as a neutral, was an officer of a bank of which the respondent was a customer and which at one time acted as a factor for respondent

In *Mount Sinai Hospital of Hartford, Conn.* v. *Walter Kidde Constructors, Inc.*, N.Y.L.J. Nov. 17, 1975, page 7, column 2 (Sup. Ct. N.Y. County), disclosure by one of three arbitrators of a connection with a previously undisclosed real party in interest at the initial stage of the proceeding led the court to remove him and substitute another arbitrator.

This issue has also arisen in the labor area. In *Colony Liquor Distributors*

v. *Local 669 I.B.T.C., W & H,* 312 N.Y.S.2d 403 (App. Div. 3d Dept. 1970), *aff'd* 28 N.Y.2d 596, 319 N.Y.S.2d 849 (1971), the award was vacated where the evidence revealed that the arbitrator had failed to disclose that he had recently been employed as an attorney by two union locals belonging to the same international union as the local involved in the arbitration, that less than six months prior to the hearing he had listed his address as that of those locals, that he had received substantial compensation for his services, and that at the time of the hearing he had a close relative still employed by the union.

In *Labor Relations Sec. of Northern New York Building Exchange, Inc.* v. *Gordon,* 335 N.Y.S.2d 624 (Sup. Ct. Onondaga County 1972), the award was vacated where the arbitrator failed to disclose that he was a member of the Civil Service Employees Association.

It should be noted that there are a number of cases decided prior to *Commonwealth* in which the courts have vacated an award because of a failure to disclose a prior business relationship. See *Application of Siegel,* 153 N.Y.S.2d 673 (Sup. Ct. N.Y. County 1956). *In re Friedman,* 213 N.Y.S. 369 (1st Dept. 1926); *Petroleum Cargo Carriers Ltd.* v. *Unitas Inc.,* 220 N.Y.S.2d 724, *aff'd* 224 N.Y.S.2d 654 (1st Dept. 1962); *Knickerbocker Textiles Corp.* v. *Sheila-Lynn Inc.,* 16 N.Y.S.2d 435 (1939) *aff'd* 20 N.Y.S.2d 985 (1st Dept. 1940); *Sweet* v. *Morrison,* 116 N.Y. 19 (1889); *Milliken Woolens, Inc.* v. *Weber Knit Sportswear, Inc.,* 202 N.Y.S.2d 431 (App. Div. 1st Dept. 1960) *aff'd* without opinion 9 N.Y.2d 878, 216 N.Y.S.2d 696 (1961); *Dukraft Mfg. Co.* v. *Bear Mill Mfg. Co.,* 151 N.Y.S.2d 318 (Sup. Ct. N.Y. County 1956); and *Shirley Silk Co.* v. *American Silk Mills,* 23 N.Y.S.2d 254 (App. Div. 1st Dept. 1950).

An award was vacated where the method of appointment was not followed and the arbitrator had a business relationship with one of the parties. *American Guaranty Co.* v. *Caldwell,* 72 F.2d 209 (9th Cir. 1934). One court disqualified the sole arbitrator who was an office associate of the petitioner. *In re Albert (Spiegelberg),* 262 N.Y.S.2d 795 (Sup. Ct. N.Y. County 1932).

There are a few instances, however, where the undisclosed relationship was held not to be sufficient to vitiate the award. See *Ilios Shipping & Trading Corp.* v. *American Anthracite & Bituminous Coal Corp.,* 148 F. Supp. 698 (S.D.N.Y. 1957) *aff'd* per curiam 245 F.2d 873 (2d Cir. 1957), *Cross Properties, Inc.* v. *Gimbel Brothers, Inc.,* 225 N.Y.S.2d 1014 (App. Div. 1st Dept. 1962), *Knickerbocker Textiles* v. *Leifer Mfg. Corp.,* 105 N.Y.S.2d 200 (App. Div. 1st Dept. 105), *Dulien Steel Products Inc. of Washington* v. *M/S The Ogeka,* 147 F. Supp. 167 (W.D. Wash. N.D. 1956).

At least one court has ruled that such challenges may not be raised prior to the award. See *San Carlo Opera Co.* v. *Conley,* 72 F. Supp. 825

(S.D.N.Y. 1947). The court held that where there is an allegation of partiality due to undisclosed facts, the court under 9 U.S.C. §1 *et seq.* does not, prior to an award, have the power to order substitution of arbitrators.

Waiver

If disclosure is made during or prior to the hearing and the parties continue with the arbitration, the courts have held that the party has waived the objection and have declined to vacate the award. In *Knickerbocker Textiles Corp.* v. *Donath,* 205 N.Y.S.2d 408 (1953), where the prior business dealings of the arbitrator were disclosed to the petitioner's attorney at the beginning of the hearing and the latter chose not to investigate the circumstances further, the grounds for disqualifying the arbitrator and vacating the award were held not sufficient. See also *Cook Industries* v. *C. Itoh & Co. (America) Inc.,* 449 F.2d 106 (2d Cir. 1971).

In *Garfield & Co.* v. *Wiest,* 432 F.2d 849 (2d Cir. 1970), *cert. denied* 401 U.S. 940 (1971), the court refused to vacate an award pursuant to 9 U.S.C. §10 on the ground of partiality, notwithstanding the arbitrator's failure to disclose. The case involved a dispute between a member firm of the New York Stock Exchange and one of its former general partners. The dispute was submitted to the Board of Arbitrators as was required by the Exchange's constitution and rules. On the motion to vacate, it was agreed that the arbitrators may have had some business dealings with the former chairman of the Exchange's Board of Governors, who was a member of one of the party's firms.

In upholding the award, the court differentiated this case from *Commonwealth Coatings, supra* and noted that when petitioner became a member of the Stock Exchange he agreed to arbitrate the dispute before a panel of arbitrators who almost necessarily would have had dealings in the ordinary course of Exchange business with any potential opposing party who was also a member of the Exchange. Although the petitioner prior to the hearing had sufficient information in which to base a challenge, it did not do so.

The court emphasized that it was not holding

> ... that Exchange arbitrations are exempt from the holdings in *Commonwealth Coatings* insofar as an arbitrator is required to disclose any dealings he may have had with a party, which was *not* in the ordinary course of business ... (but) we are only holding that, when parties have agreed to arbitration with full awareness that there will have been certain, almost necessary dealings between a potential arbitrator and one of the opposing parties, disclosure of these dealings is not required by *Commonwealth Coatings*

inasmuch as the parties are deemed to have waived any objections based on these dealings. 432 F.2d 854 (Emphasis in text.)

Accord, *Ilios Shipping & Trading Co.* v. *American Anthracite & Bituminous Coal Corp., supra; Johnson* v. *Korn,* 117 S.W.2d 574 (Texas 1938), *Glatzer* v. *Diamond, infra.*

In *Baar & Beards, Inc.* v. *Oleg Cassini, Inc.,* 30 N.Y.2d 649, 331 N.Y.S.2d 670 (1972) *rev'g* 322 N.Y.S.2d 462 (App. Div. 1st Dept. 1971), the court held that a party knowingly waived objection to an arbitrator who disclosed that six years previously he had had an attorney-client relationship with the other party where the objecting party explicitly stated in writing that the arbitrator was acceptable.

In *Avalon Fabrics, Inc.* v. *Raymill Fabrics Corp.,* 89 N.Y.S.2d 166 (Sup. Ct. N.Y. County 1949), the court denied respondent's motion to vacate the award where there was no disclosure that the arbitrator designated by petitioner was associated with a firm represented by petitioner's counsel. The court held that while there had not been any disclosure of this situation, it was convinced that respondent was aware of it and consequently had waived the right to any objection.

See also *In re Amtorg Trading Corp.,* 100 N.Y.S.2d 747 (App. Div. 1st Dept. 1950) *aff'd* 304 N.Y. 519 (1952). The court held that when a buyer agreed to do business with a corporation which was in fact a trading agent for a foreign country, it waived the right to assert that the arbitrators could not be impartial because they were controlled by said foreign country.

Actual partiality may not, however, be waived. See *In re Miller,* 23 N.Y.S.2d 120 (App. Div. 1st Dept. 1940), wherein the court vacated an award where the arbitrator passed judgment on his own claim, even though the opposing party refrained from making a timely objection to the arbitrator.

Close Relationships

Challenges are sometimes made to arbitrators who have had close relationships with one of the parties. See *Siegel* v. *Lewis,* 40 N.Y.2d 687, 389 N.Y.S.2d 800 (1976) holding that where an arbitrator has been named in a contract and one party had knowledge at the time of the contract of a relationship between the arbitrator and the other side, there was a waiver of the right to seek advance disqualification of the arbitrator.

It is clear that a party may not serve as an arbitrator on his own case. See *Cross & Brown Co.* v. *Nelson,* 167 N.Y.S.2d 573 (App. Div. 1st Dept. 1957) holding that no party to a dispute or someone so identified to a party as to be considered a party can serve as an arbitrator to decide the dispute. Accord *In re Miller, supra.* An attorney-client relationship with one of the parties is not per se grounds for disqualification. *Karpinecz v. Marshall,* 218 N.Y.S.2d 88, 90 (App. Div. 2d Dept. 1961). A debtor-creditor relationship is highly likely to result in a disqualification. *In re Friedman, supra.* If the issue is solely one of appraisal, however, the arbitrator may not be disqualified due to a debtor-creditor relationship. See *Giddens v. Board of Education of City of Chicago,* 75 N.E.2d 286 (Ill. 1947) holding that an appraiser, who was a creditor or possible creditor of one of the parties, was not disqualified. *First National Bank in Cedar Falls v. Clay,* 2 N.W.2d 85 (Iowa 1942) and *McQuaid Market House v. Home Insurance Co.,* 180 N.W. 97 (Minn. 1921).

Removal of a party-appointed arbitrator is generally refused. See *Astoria Medical Group v. Health Ins. Plans of Greater New York,* 11 N.Y.2d 128, 227 N.Y.S.2d 401 (1962) holding that where there is a tripartite arbitration there can be no objection to the "partisan" arbitrator's relationship with his designee. Accord *Cecil v. Bank of American Nat. Trust & Savings Association,* 236 P.2d 408 (Cal. 1951) holding that on a tripartite panel a party may appoint his attorney as arbitrator. See also *Goodrich v. Hulbert,* 123 Mass. 190 (1887), *Riccomini v. Pierucci,* 202 P. 244 (Cal. 1921).

Close family relationships will be closely scrutinized, but where the family relationship is deemed distant, one court declined to disturb the award. Thus, in *Bell v. Campbell,* 143 S.W. 953 (Tex. 1912), where the arbitrator's nephew had married a sister of one of the parties, the court held this was not a sufficient basis to set aside the award.

Summary

The arbitrator's duty to disclose is a continuing obligation. Each case must, in large measure, be governed by its own facts. In recognition of the importance of disclosure the AAA, in its form notifying the arbitrator of appointment, contains the following clause:

> It is most important that the parties have complete confidence in the Arbitrator's impartiality. Therefore, please disclose any past or present relationship with the parties or their counsel, direct or indirect, whether financial, professional, social, or other kind. Any doubt should be resolved in favor of disclosure. If you are aware of such relationship, please describe it on the back of this form. The AAA will call the facts to the attention of the parties' counsel.

Evidence in Arbitration[4]

In arbitration, as in any other adjudicative process, there is a fundamental requirement that propositions are proven by the presentation of evidence.

While the strict rules of evidence with regard to form and admissibility are relaxed, the court decisions indicate that the requirements of a fair hearing, even when coupled with the generally broad authority of the arbitrator, produce some outlines of a specialized law of arbitration evidence.

The Collection of Evidence

Pretrial Discovery

It is considered a relatively inflexible rule that parties to an arbitration do not have recourse to standard discovery devices under court aegis. See 98 A.L.R.2d 1247 (1969); 74 Harv. L. Rev. 940 (1961). In New York, the courts have uniformly applied the rule of *Katz* v. *Burkin,* 3 App. Div.2d 238, 160 N.Y.S.2d 159 (1st Dept. 1957) that "necessity rather than convenience should be the test." The rule has been widely followed: *MVAIC* v. *McCabe,* 19 App. Div.2d 349, 243 N.Y.S.2d 495 (1st Dept. 1963); *Penn Tanker Co.* v. *CHZ,* 199 F. Supp. 716 (S.D.N.Y. 1961); *Foremost Yarn Mills, Inc.* v. *Rose Mills, Inc.,* 25 F.R.D. 9 (E.D. Pa. 1960); *Commercial Solvents Corp.* v. *Louisiana Liquid Fertilizer Co.,* 20 F.R.D. 359 (S.D.N.Y. 1957).

It should be noted that the comparative unavailability of discovery is a judge-made rule rather than a statutory limitation. For example, while N.Y.C.P.L.R. §3102(c) permits discovery "in aid of arbitration," the courts have adopted a rule of virtual noninterference.

Similarly, compare Pennsylvania Arbitration Act §6 permitting arbitrators to request a court to direct depositions with *Harleysville Mutual Casualty Co.* v. *Adair,* 218 A.2d 791 (1966) (discovery surrendered in arbitration). Discovery was deemed "incongruous" with arbitration in *Cavanaugh* v. *McDonnell & Co.,* 258 N.E.2d 561 (Mass. 1970). In both *McRae* v. *Superior Court,* 221 Cal. App.2d 166, 34 Cal. Rptr. 346 (1963) and *Atlas Floor Covering* v. *Crescent House & Garden, Inc.,* 166 Cal. App.2d 211, 333 P.2d 194 (1958) discovery was declined by the court, but see California Code Civ. Prac. §1283 which grants arbitrators the power to order discovery procedures.

Where the parties have agreed to make discovery available, the court will enforce the agreement. *Local 99, I.L.G.W.U.* v. *Corise Sportswear Co.,* 44 Misc.2d 913, 255 N.Y.S.2d 282 (Sup. Ct. N.Y. County 1964). On the other hand, the early resort to discovery has, in one case, been held a waiver of the arbitration clause. *Unicon Management Corp.* v. *Pavcrete Const. Corp.,* 23 App. Div.2d 837, 259 N.Y.S.2d 598 (1st Dept. 1965).

Discovery may be ordered by a court in connection with an application before it as, for example, when there is an issue as to existence of an agreement to arbitrate. *RLC Electronics, Inc.* v. *American Electronics Laboratories, Inc.,* 39 App. Div.2d 757, 332 N.Y.S.2d 119 (2d Dept. 1972). See also Weinstein-Korn-Miller, *New York Civil Practice* ¶7502.06. The unavailability of discovery is not a grounds for a stay of arbitration. *Siegel* v. *Ribak,* 43 Misc.2d 7, 249 N.Y.S.2d 903 (Sup. Ct. Kings County 1964).

Subpoena and Subpoena Duces Tecum

The power of an arbitrator to issue a subpoena is a right conferred by statute and not one that is naturally a part of that function. In states that have adopted the Uniform Arbitration Act see §7, under the Federal Arbitration Act see 9 U.S.C. §7. Under New York law, subpoenas may be issued by an attorney of record, N.Y.C.P.L.R. §7505. Where no subpoena power is granted to the arbitrator or attorney of record, a party may frequently be able to apply to a local court for an enforceable subpoena. See, e.g., Mich. Ct. rule 769.

The subpoena power of an arbitrator is coextensive with judicial process and is intended to be enforceable against nonparties as well as parties to the agreement. Enforcement may be sought by the party seeking the witness or evidence and not necessarily by the arbitrator as "issuer." *Nelson* v. *Biderman,* 43 Misc.2d 132, 249 N.Y.S.2d 971 (Sup. Ct. N.Y. County 1964). Subpoenas may be quashed or enforcement denied if the evidence sought is not proven to be material to the arbitration. In this sense, there is an interlocutory appeal from subpoenas issued in arbitration. See *Ocean Transport Corp.* v. *Alcoa Steamship Co.,* 129 F. Supp. 160 (S.D.N.Y. 1954); *In re Landegger,* 54 N.Y.S.2d 76 (Sup. Ct. N.Y. County) *modified* 269 App. Div. 737, 54 N.Y.S.2d 701 (1st Dept. 1945); *In re Sun Ray Cloak Co.,* 256 App. Div. 620, 11 N.Y.S.2d 202 (1st Dept. 1939).

On the other hand, it has been indicated that issuance or denial of subpoenas should be a matter for the arbitrator's discretion and refusal of arbitrators to issue subpoenas was tantamount to a ruling on materiality and hence not reviewable on an interlocutory basis. *L.C.L. Corporation* v. *New York Central R.R.,* N.Y.L.J. May 23, 1968, page 2 (Sup. Ct. N.Y. County 1968) (N/O/R). In that case, where it was alleged that the material sought contained trade secrets, the court enforced a subpoena *duces tecum* and appointed a referee to protect the movant's interests.

On review of an award, failure to issue a subpoena has similarly been held to be a matter of discretion neither judicially reviewable nor grounds for vacatur. *Atlas Floor Covering* v. *Crescent House & Garden, Inc., supra;*

Knickerbocker Textiles Corp. v. *Kingsley Fashions Inc.,* 80 N.Y.S.2d 425 (Sup. Ct. N.Y. County 1948).

It has been persuasively argued that the combination of subpoena power and comparative freedom from the formal rules of evidence eliminates the necessity for standard discovery devices but may not, on the other hand, authorize the use of discovery devices under the arbitrator's aegis. *Duberstein Iron & Metal Co.* v. *Bache & Co.,* N.Y.L.J. June 4, 1951, page 2054, column 6 (N/O/R).

The Presentation of Evidence in the Hearing

The principles of limited judicial review of arbitration awards, both statutory and common law, create a basic premise that errors in applying evidentiary rules are not a basis for judicial interference with an award. 5 Am. Jur.2d §122 ("Arbitration and Award"); 29 Am. Jur.2d §5 ("Evidence"). Evidentiary rulings are questions of law and thus not reviewable. *Burchell* v. *Marsh,* 58 U.S. (17 How.) 344 (1855). A transcript need not and generally is not kept; close technical review of rulings is impossible as a practical matter and hence the use of arbitration has been held a waiver of the exclusionary rules of evidence. *Lauria* v. *Soriano,* 180 Cal. App.2d 163, 4 Cal. Rptr. 764 (1960). The parties may, however, agree to apply the rules of evidence that would apply in court. *Housing Authority* v. *Henry Ericson Co.,* 2 So.2d 195 (La. 1941).

A federal court in a labor case ruled that the general understanding of the nature of arbitration prevents the arbitrator from invoking the formal rules of evidence without notice. *Harvey Aluminum, Inc.* v. *United Steelworkers of America,* 263 F. Supp. 488 (D.C. Calif. 1967). The particular problems of proof in labor arbitrations are thoroughly discussed in *Proceedings of the 19th Annual Meeting of the National Academy of Arbitrators* (BNA 1966).

An arbitration award is not reviewable if against the weight of the evidence or even ". . . if . . . there is no evidence in the record to support it. . . ."*Everett* v. *Brown,* 120 Misc. 349, 198 N.Y.S. 462 (Sup. Ct. Onondaga County 1923). This is based, in part, on the expertise concept. The rationale is that the parties expect arbitrators to draw upon their common sense and knowledge of affairs generally, but an award cannot be based wholly upon evidence not before the arbitrators. *Stef Shipping Corp.* v. *Norris Grain Co.,* 209 F. Supp. 299 (S.D.N.Y. 1962).

On the other hand, arbitrators may not make independent examinations or investigations without notice to the parties. *Berizzi Co.* v. *Krausz,* 238 N.Y. 315, 146 N.E. 436 (1924); *Horowitz* v. *Kaplan,* 248 N.Y. 547, 162

N.E. 519 (1927); *290 Park Avenue* v. *Fergus Motors,* 275 App. Div. 565, 90 N.Y.S. 613 (1st Dept. 1949). The rule is not inflexible; it was held that an ex parte objective test of material by the arbitrators that confirmed evidence already adduced at the hearing did not vitiate an award. *E. Gerli & Co., Inc.* v. *Oscar Heineman Corp.,* 258 N.Y. 484, 180 N.E. 243 (1929). See also *Robins Silk Mfg. Co.* v. *Consolidated Piece Dye Works,* 224 App. Div. 83, 229 N.Y.S. 500 (1st Dept. 1928).

From an evidentiary point of view, the expertise or special knowledge of the arbitrator expands the areas that are subject to a form of judicial notice but does not abrogate the requirement that all evidence placed before the arbitrators as proof of a claim or a proposition in the case be done in the presence of both parties. This, of course, includes taking testimony. *Katz* v. *Uvegi,* 18 Misc.2d 576, 187 N.Y.S.2d 511 *aff'd* 11 App. Div.2d 773, 205 N.Y.S.2d 972 (2d Dept. 1960).

Matters of witness competency and expert qualification are subjects for the arbitrator's determination and involve the basic issues of credibility and relevancy. Arbitrators may, for example, exercise control by means of limiting subpoenas, a refusal to issue a subpoena being considered a ruling on relevancy. See *L.C.L. Corp., supra.* Denial of a subpoena, by analogy, may also go to the issue of competency.

Admissibility (Generally)

It is common for parties to an arbitration to present their evidence in the generally accepted manner. Witnesses may be called, documents placed into evidence, and real evidence produced. In these instances it may be assumed that few objections will be made. The fact that hearsay evidence may be admitted eliminates a number of technical objections but this has been criticized. B. Aaron, *Some Procedural Problems in Arbitration,* 10 V. and L. Rev. 733 (1957).

Perhaps the most extreme case involving admissibility sought to draw a distinction between evidence as incompetent or irrelevant and evidence that is unfair or prejudicial. While the lower court indicated that such a distinction could and should be drawn, an appellate court reversed an order vacating the award. The court refused to vacate an award, notwithstanding that the arbitrator had admitted in evidence the report of a detective, which consisted of matters that were hearsay, defamatory, and irrelevant. That such evidence would not have been accepted in a civil action, the court held, was not controlling. To admit the report was neither misconduct by the arbitrators nor "undue means," within the meaning of statutory provisions for vacatur. *Brill* v. *Muller Brothers Inc.,* 17 App.

Div.2d 804, 232 N.Y.S.2d 806 (1st Dept. 1962) *aff'd* 13 N.Y.2d 776, 242
N.Y.S.2d 69, 192 N.E.2d 34 (1963), *cert. denied* 376 U.S. 927 *rehearing
denied* 376 U.S. 974. Similarly, the fact that a deposition was not executed
in accordance with the state statutory provisions did not render it inad-
missible and an award was not subject to vacatur on that grounds. *Frantz
v. Inter-Insurance Exchange* 40 Cal. Rptr. 218 (Ct. App. 1963).

Admissibility (Privilege)

Questions of privilege do not frequently arise in arbitration, in part
because the arbitrator does not have the power to compel testimony. The
privilege against self-incrimination has been sustained before arbitrators,
Langemyr v. *Campbell,* 21 N.Y.2d 796, 288 N.Y.S.2d 629, 235 N.E.2d 770
(1968), though invoking the privilege is not a grounds for adjournment. In
Dick v. *Supreme Body of the International Congress,* 138 Mich. 372, 101
N.W. 564 (1904) a common-law award was vacated where the arbitrator
admitted testimony by a doctor which had been acquired in the course of
attending a patient. In that case, the privilege existed by statute. It may be
assumed that arbitrators will be held to similar statutory privileges where
they exist. This is particularly important since the privilege belongs to the
source or subject of the statements and not to the declarant. Hence, the
ability to have the award vacated is the only form of judicial protection.

Admissibility (Parol Evidence)

While the parol evidence rule is not in reality a rule of evidence at all,
the fact that arbitrators can admit evidence otherwise barred by its
application can be an extremely important facet of arbitration practice. See
Lentine v. *Fundaro,* 29 N.Y.2d 382, 328 N.Y.S.2d 418, 278 N.E.2d 633
(1972); *DeCicco* v. *Viviano,* C.B. App. Div.2d 541, 299 N.Y.S.2d 769 (2d
Dept. 1969); *In re Bay Iron Works,* 17 App. Div.2d 809 (1st Dept. 1962).
See also *United Furniture Workers* v. *Virgo Manufacturing Corp.,* 257 F.
Supp. 138 (E.D. Ark. 1966). There are, however, limitations as, for
example, in *Albert* v. *Goor,* 218 P.2d 736 (Ariz. 1950), where it was held
that arbitrators were bound by the Statute of Frauds requirement of a
writing in order to grant an award of real estate brokerage commissions.

Cross-Examination

The right to cross-examine witnesses is generally secured by statute [see
Uniform Arbitration Act §5(b); N.Y.C.P.L.R. §7506(c); but see 9 U.S.C.

§1-14, where a failure to permit cross-examination must be couched in terms of a §10(c) "misbehavior" of the arbitrators]. The right to cross-examine, however, is not unlimited and arbitrators may exclude cross-examination as to matters outside the scope of direct testimony. *In re Colasante,* 16 Misc.2d 923, 185 N.Y.S.2d 203 (Sup. Ct. Queens County 1959).

Exclusion (Generally)

It has also been held that an arbitrator has the same freedom as a court to exclude evidence where the risk of confusion or the time expended would outweigh the relevancy. *Sizer* v. *Bunt,* 4 Denio 426 (N.Y. 1846); cf. *In re Compu Dyne Corp.,* 255 F. Supp. 1004 (E.D. Pa. 1966). Exclusion of evidence, however, may raise issues that have the effect of undermining the award. Since a ruling may not be attacked on the basis of its correctness, the issues will arise on a motion to vacate as an "abuse of discretion," "misconduct," or an excess of powers. There are numerous decisions vacating an award where there has been a refusal to hear evidence, such as in *Gervant* v. *New England Fire Ins. Co.,* 306 N.Y. 393, 118 N.E.2d 574 (1954), where the court said that arbitrators:

> ... are not free to disregard, arbitrarily, pertinent evidence presented by [one party], and ... a flat refusal ... is condemned ... as legal misconduct for which the award will be set aside.

See also *Universal Metal Products Co., Inc.* v. *United Electrical Radio & Machine Workers of America,* 179 Misc. 1044, 40 N.Y.S.2d 265 (Sup. Ct. Kings County 1943) (exclusion termed imperfect execution of powers); *Smaglio* v. *Fireman's Fund Ins. Co.,* 247 A.2d 577 (Pa. 1968) (denial of full and fair hearing).

On the other hand, there are courts that deem an exclusion to be a "mere refusal" and not grounds for vacatur; for example, *John Post Construction Corporation* v. *Good Humor Corporation,* 9 Misc.2d 392, 170 N.Y.S.2d 383 (Sup. Ct. N.Y. County 1957), where the court stated: "The arbitrator's decision not to admit the proffered evidence is one of law and ... not reviewable by the courts." See also *Messina & Briante, Inc.* v. *Blitman Construction,* 32 Misc.2d 21, 223 N.Y.S.2d 533 (Sup. Ct. West County 1961) (refusal to receive two photographs termed "error of judgment which, in general, may not be the subject of attack ..."); *Newark Stereotyper's Union No. 18* v. *Newark Morning Ledger Co.,* 261 F. Supp. 832 (D.N.J. 1966) (refusal to accept evidence not a deprivation of due process).

If these cases are to be usefully compared, it would appear that the courts will not reweigh an issue of admissibility but will be much more critical of exclusion. Similarly, on a claim of exclusion, the court will be unable to resist ruling upon the pertinent or material characteristics of the evidence but appear to base confirmation or vacatur on the issue of prejudice. The rule, if any is in fact possible, would seem to be that if a party is permitted to give evidence on an issue, elemental fairness requires that the adverse party be permitted to give proof of any sort on the *same* issue.

Posthearing Evidence

The propriety of a posthearing brief in arbitration has not been seriously questioned, since copies are served upon the adverse party and the arbitrator must give an adequate time for reply before issuing an award. *Greenwood Cemetery* v. *Cemetery Workers,* Misc.2d (Sup. Ct. N.Y. County 1973) (N.Y.L.J. Feb. 2, 1973, page 18, column 3). In *Korein* v. *Rabin,* 29 App. Div.2d 351, 287 N.Y.S.2d 975 (1st Dept. 1968), the court reversed a trial court determination that acceptance of posthearing documents was "misconduct." The appellate court reasoned that absent a showing of prejudice, the submission would not vitiate the award. The adverse party, however, was given an opportunity to comment, in writing, on the material admitted. The evidence in question was not "newly discovered" nor offered after the award was rendered. The rule in such cases is not clear. There may be judicial power to remand a case in extreme circumstances, *Balton* v. *General Accidents Fire & Life Assurance Corp.,* 295 N.Y. 734, 51 N.Y.S.2d 762, 65 N.E.2d 563 (1946), but the burden upon the party seeking to open an award or a judgment on an award may be almost impossible to sustain. See *Mole* v. *Queen Insurance Co.,* 14 App. Div.2d 1, 217 N.Y.S.2d 330 (4th Dept. 1961).

Provisional Remedies, Disclosure, and Arbitration[5]

A provisional remedy has been defined as "preliminary judicial relief granted by a court in a civil action to secure a plaintiff against loss, injury, or the dispersion or waste of the matter in dispute while the action is pending." Seide, *Dictionary of Arbitration* (1970), p. 189. Disclosure is a method of obtaining evidence the purpose of which "is to advance the function of a trial to ascertain truth and to accelerate the disposition of suits." *Rios* v. *Donovan,* 21 A.D.2d 409, 411, 250 N.Y.S.2d 818, 820 (1st Dept. 1964). Included are such devices as examinations before trial, interrogatories, discovery, and inspection of documents or property. Although these remedies and devices have evolved in the setting of court actions, it is obvious that, where the dispute is one that the parties have agreed to resolve by arbitration rather than by litigation, the same need may arise to safeguard a plaintiff or claimant against loss or waste, or to assist both parties in their search for evidence. This letter deals with cases in which certain provisional remedies—attachments, mechanic's liens, injunction, and replevin—as well as various disclosure devices have been granted (or refused) in connection with an arbitration proceeding.

In resorting to the court for such preliminary relief pending arbitration, parties are sometimes faced with the risk that such action will be taken as a waiver of the right to arbitrate. They would, therefore, be well advised to preserve that right by an express reservation thereof in any preliminary application that might be made to the court. As a matter of fact, explicit provision is made for the preservation of such right by section 47(a) of the Commercial Arbitration Rules of the AAA, which recites:

> No judicial proceedings by a party relating to the subject matter of the arbitration shall be deemed a waiver of the party's right to arbitrate.

A provision for arbitration pursuant to AAA rules contained in an arbitration clause has been held to incorporate such rules into the agreement. See *People ex rel Delisi Const. Co., Inc.*.v. *Board of Ed.*, 326 N.E.2d 55, 58 (Ill. 1975); *Matter of Wenger & Co.* v. *Proper S. H. Mills*, 239 N.Y. 199, 202 (1924); *Bradford Woolen Corp.* v. *Freedman*, 189 Misc. 242, 71 N.Y.S.2d 257 (N.Y. County 1947)—AAA rules "are by references made a part of the contract" (p. 259). See also *Matter of Staklinski (Pyramid Elec. Co.)*, 6 N.Y.2d 159, 163 (1959). The quoted section would, therefore, in the absence of countervailing considerations, protect a party invoking court process in aid of an arbitration from a charge of waiver.

Attachments

Arbitration statutes, as a rule, make no special reference to provisional remedies. But see 9 Utah Code §78-31-12; see also United States Arbitration Act §8, which permits a type of attachment of property.[6]

Section 8 of the U.S. Arbitration Act makes provision for the libel and seizure of the vessel or other property involved in order to give an "aggrieved" party the "benefit of the security provided by jurisdiction *in rem* while preserving the right to arbitrate." *Diana Co. Maritima, S.A. of P.* v. *Subfreights of S.S. Adm. F.*, 280 F. Supp. 607, 615 (S.D.N.Y. 1968).

In upholding an order directing arbitration following the institution of such an action, the Supreme Court declared in *Marine Transit Corp.* v.

Dreyfus, 284 U.S. 263 (1932) that, by the "express terms of §8, the libel and seizure are authorized as an initial step in a proceeding to enforce the agreement for arbitration" (p. 275). See also *The Anaconda* v. *Amer. Sugar Co.,* 322 U.S. 42 (1944), where the Supreme Court held that parties to an arbitration agreement in an admiralty matter could not decide to make §8 inapplicable, saying that "traditional admiralty procedure with its concomitant security should be available to the aggrieved party without in any way lessening his obligations to arbitrate his grievance rather than litigate the merits in court" (p. 46); *Greenwich Marine, Inc.* v. *S.S. Alexandra,* 339 F.2d 901 (2d Cir. 1965)—upholding the right of libel and seizure in aid of arbitration in principle though not in the circumstances presented.

In *Ships & Freights, Inc.* v. *Farr, Whitlock & Co.,* 188 F. Supp. 438 (E.D.N.Y. 1960), an attachment obtained by a libelant—of bank accounts in connection with the arbitration of disputes arising out of the charter of libelant's vessel—was vacated because the banks were not located, even though the vessel was, within the jurisdiction of the court.

In a federal case involving an attachment outside the admiralty field, *McCreary Tire & Rubber Co.* v. *CEAT,* 501 F.2d 1032 (3d Cir. 1974), the court vacated an order granting such relief. The American plaintiff had sued an Italian corporation in a Pennsylvania court for breach of contract, although the contract provided for arbitration. Following Pennsylvania procedures, the plaintiff attached the defendant's property in that state, by filing a Praecipe and Complaint in Foreign Attachment. Upon removal of the case to the federal district court, the defendant moved to dissolve the foreign attachment and to stay the action pending arbitration. The district court denied the motion. Reversing, the Court of Appeals granted the stay, vacated the attachment, and referred the disputed claims to arbitration, declaring that the 1958 United Nations Convention—to which the United States is a party—obligated our courts to recognize and enforce the agreement to arbitrate. Noting that the plaintiff had had no intention of submitting to arbitration when it sought the attachment, the court wrote (p. 1038):

> Quite possibly foreign attachment may be available for the enforcement of an arbitration award. This complaint does not seek to enforce an arbitration award by foreign attachment. It seeks to bypass the agreed upon method of settling disputes. Such a bypass is prohibited by the Convention if one party to the agreement objects. Unlike §3 of the federal Act, article II(3) of the Convention provides that the court of a contracting state shall "refer the parties to arbitration" rather than "stay the trial of the action." The Convention forbids the courts of a contracting state from entertaining a suit which violates an agreement to arbitrate. Thus the contention that arbitration is merely another method of trial, to which state provisional remedies should equally apply, is unavailable.

The Pennsylvania court apparently felt that under the convention "state provisional remedies" are ordinarily unavailable in arbitration proceedings. It added (p. 1038):

> The obvious purpose of the enactment of Pub. L. 91-368 [9. U.S.C. §§201-208 which implements the U.N. Convention], permitting removal of all cases falling within the terms of the treaty, was to prevent the vagaries of state law from impeding its full implementation. Permitting a continued resort to foreign attachment in breach of the agreement is inconsistent with that purpose. The relief requested, a release of all property from the attachment, should have been granted.

In New York the courts have upheld attachments—usually sought in connection with court actions—and have stayed such actions "pending [the] arbitration" provided for in the contract. Since the defendants were almost always desirous of arbitration, the issue of the plaintiff's waiver by institution of a court action did not arise.

In *Compania Panamena* v. *International Union Lines,* 17 Misc.2d 969, 188 N.Y.S.2d 708 (N.Y. County 1959), the plaintiff asserted, in papers in support of the application for a warrant of attachment, that it was commencing an action, although it had previously demanded arbitration. After the warrant had been obtained, the defendant moved to vacate it on the ground that the parties were committed to arbitration. The court denied the defendant's motion, saying that the warrant would not be vacated but that the action would be stayed pending arbitration. The court further observed that a "warrant to secure the collection of an award is as much an enforcement of the award as a judgment to be entered upon any award made" (17 Misc.2d at p. 970). See also *Matter of Loutex Corp. (Star Pipe Line Co.),* 22 Misc.2d 709, 194 N.Y.S.2d 983 (N.Y. County 1959), where the court declared in dictum that a "valid attachment is not vacatable merely because the attaching party has submitted to judicial determination a matter embraced in an agreement to arbitrate, although the attachment action will be stayed pending arbitration" (p. 711).

A leading case on attachment is *American Reserve Ins. Co.* v. *Chinese Ins. Co.,* 297 N.Y. 322, 78 N.E.2d 425 (1948), in which an American plaintiff brought suit for the balance of the sum due under a reinsurance contract, procuring an ex parte warrant of attachment against the property of the Chinese corporate defendant in New York. The defendant sought vactur of the attachment by reason of the arbitration clause in the contract. The court declared (p. 327):

> [I]t cannot be said that a plaintiff fails to state a prima facie cause of action merely because the contract upon which suit is brought contains an agreement to arbitrate. Defendant's sole remedy is to apply for a stay of plaintiff's action until the arbitration has been had.

In answer to the defendant's complaint that the plaintiff might delay arbitration in order to pressure the defendant into making concessions while its property was attached, the court added (p. 327):

If defendant does obtain a stay pending arbitration, and if plaintiff does refuse to arbitrate, that may be ground for Special Term, *in its discretion*, to vacate the warrant of attachment. (Emphasis in text.)

Mechanic's Lien

Somewhat related to the use of the attachment is the filing of a mechanic's lien by a contractor or other supplier of labor and materials upon property under construction or repair. Here the chief problem has been whether the filing of such a lien constitutes a waiver and abandonment of the right to arbitrate. Thus, in the early leading case of *Matter of Young* v. *Crescent Development Co.*, 240 N.Y. 244 (1925), the New York Court of Appeals held that it did. A few years later, the legislature nullified the effect of *Young* by enacting section 35 of the Lien Law, which recites in part that the "filing of a notice of lien shall not be a waiver of any right of arbitration of a contractor, subcontractor, material man or laborer secured to him by his contract to furnish labor or materials."

In *Matter of Modular Technics Corp* v. *Graverne Contr. Corp.*, 32 N.Y.2d 673 (1973), the court held that the filing of a mechanic's lien was not a waiver of the right to arbitrate despite a contract provision that the contractor waived such right. See to same effect *Sommer* v. *Quarant Contr.*, 40 A.D.2d 95 (1st Dept. 1972); see also *A. Burgart, Inc.* v. *Foster-Lipkins Corp.*, 30 N.Y.2d 901, 335 N.Y.S.2d 562 (1972), where the court ruled that a subcontractor had not waived its right to arbitrate where it had not only filed a lien but had commenced an action to foreclose; to same effect *A. Sangivanni & Sons* v. *F. M. Floryan & Co.*, 158 Conn. 467, 262 A.2d 159 (1969); and see *Matter of Oxer* v. *Stewart*, 36 Misc.2d 314 (Nassau County 1962), in which the court declared that the institution of an arbitration proceeding was not a condition sufficient for the continuance of a lien where the lienor had failed to commence an action to foreclose within the statutory period.

In *Frederick Contractors, Inc.* v. *Bel Pre-Medical Center, Inc.*, 334 A.2d 526 (Md. 1975), a somewhat different problem is presented. The Maryland high court, treating the contractor's lien as in the nature of an attachment, held that a demand for arbitration would have the effect of staying the foreclosure proceeding, pursuant to statutes going back to 1698 (9 & 10 William III, chap. 15) and that any award in the contractor's favor might be enforced by a proceeding to enforce the lien. Said the court (p. 531):

While the parties may have bound themselves by the general conditions of the contract to accept the resolution of disputes by arbitration, they in no way limited themselves in the manner by which payment of an award may be enforced.

Miller Act

Similar problems arise under the Miller Act (40 U.S.C. §270b) which, instead of the mechanic's lien procedure, requires persons awarded contracts by the federal government for the construction of public works and buildings to furnish a payment bond, with surety, for the protection of laborers and materialmen and authorizes the latter to *sue* upon such bond for nonpayment in any federal district court in which the work is being performed. Despite this statute, an arbitration clause in the contract calling for arbitration in a different locale will be enforced. See, e.g., *United States v. American Employers Ins. Co. of Mass.*, 290 F. Supp. 139 (U.S.D.C. S. Car. 1968); *Warren Brothers Co. v. Cardi Corp.*, 471 F.2d 1304 (1st Cir. 1973); see also *Electronic & Missile Facilities, Inc. v. United States*, 306 F.2d 554 (5th Cir. 1962), *revd* on other grounds 374 U.S. 167; *United States v. Electronic & Missile Facilities, Inc.*, 364 F.2d 705 (2d Cir. 1966), in which the court stated that "the United States Arbitration Act . . . when it is applicable, quite clearly is broad enough to include Miller Act suits within its scope, and, with equal clarity, it gives the parties an enforceable right to agree to refer to arbitration differences arising under their contract" (p. 708); see also *Matter of Unicon Management Corp. (Pavcrete Constr. Corp.)*, 23 A.D.2d 837, 259 N.Y.S.2d 598 (1st Dept. 1965), where the appellate division wrote that the initiation of a Miller Act suit after arbitration had been commenced might well result in the waiver of the right to arbitrate but, since the opposing party had joined in the arbitration, it was disqualified from seeking to stay it.

Injunctions

Courts are not inclined to grant injunctive relief when parties have chosen to resolve their disputes by arbitration. Thus, in *Matter of New England Petroleum Corp. (Asiatic Petroleum Corp.)*, N.Y.L.J. Feb. 27, 1975, page 2, column 4 (New York County), in refusing to grant the petitioner a preliminary injunction against termination of a long-term contract for the sale of oil in the absence of a showing of irreparable injury, the judge observed that courts "may be understandably reluctant to grant preliminary injunctive relief, where the parties have agreed to submit their disputes to arbitration, for not only do the courts not wish to interfere with the jurisdiction of the arbitrators, but the courts lack the control which they normally exercise over litigated matters, arbitration proceeding as it does in another forum" (p. 14). See *Meda Int.* v. *Salzman,* 24 A.D.2d 710, 263 N.Y.S.2d 12 (1st Dept. 1965), where a temporary injunction to restrain the defendants, among other things, from using plaintiffs' business name or competing with them was denied, the court stating that the arbitrators could "adequately dispose of all the issues posed in the action" (p. 711). See also *E. F. Hutton & Co.* v. *Bokelmann,* 56 Misc.2d 910 (New York County 1968), where the court granted an order compelling arbitration of a restrictive convenant in an employment contract but denied temporary injunctive relief. It did, however, contemplate that such relief might be granted thereafter.

Courts have, on occasion, granted injunctive relief pending arbitration for the same reasons such relief is afforded pending a court trial: namely, to preserve the status quo and to prevent irreparable injury. Such injury should, however, be clearly demonstrable. Thus, in *American Eutectic Weldings Alloys Sales Co.* v. *Flynn,* 399 Pa. 617, 161 A.2d 364 (1960), plaintiff contending that defendant, a former employer, had breached a restrictive covenant in his contract of employment not to compete in plaintiff's business, sought to enjoin the defendant from continuing in such competition pending arbitration. The injunction was granted to "prevent the possibility of further perpetration of wrong which might materially and irreparably damage the plaintiff's rights." The court further remarked that "unless the status quo be preserved, there may well be nothing left to arbitrate with any real effect" (pp. 365, 367).

Finally, in a case that is truly *sui generis—Matter of Auto Mechanics Lodge No. 1053, Int. Assn. of Machinists (Houdaille Constr. Materials),* 23 A.D.2d 953, 259 N.Y.S.2d 510 (4th Dept. 1965), the court held that "an arbitrator should not be mandated by a court to pass upon a framed issue that a party *in futuro* shall comply with the terms of a contract." In this case, the union sought arbitration of its dispute with the company over whether or not the latter's discharge of two employees was permitted under the terms of the collective bargaining agreement. The court at Special Term granted the union's motion as well as its further request that the employer be compelled to abide by the terms of the agreement for its duration. In rejecting the second part of Special Term's directive, the appellate division declared, "Absent some reason therefor that may occur to the arbitrator, it is a transparent device (if implemented) to remove future disputes from arbitration and place them in courts by use of a contempt proceeding for failure to comply with the mandatory injunction in the award of the arbitrator" (pp. 953–54).

Disclosure

The United States Arbitration Act and many state statutes in general give arbitrators broad discretionary powers to require the production of documents and to compel the testimony of witnesses. See, e.g., U.S.A.A. §7; N.Y.C.P.L.R. 7505; Calif. C.C.P. §§1282, 1283; Ill. Ann. Stats., ch. 10, §107; Mass. Gen'l Laws, ch. 251, §7; Pa. Stats., tit. 5, ch. 4, §§166–167. When parties to an arbitration have invoked the aid of courts to obtain such disclosures, however, the courts have not been consistent in their response. Thus, in several cases, the federal courts refused to order discovery, usually in a pending arbitration proceeding, holding that the discovery provisions of the Federal Rules of Civil Procedure were not applicable to arbitration proceedings. See *Commercial Solvents* v. *Louisiana Liquid Fertilizer Co.,* 20 F.R.D. 359 (S.D.N.Y. 1957)—ex parte order sought, with no action pending; *Foremost Yarn Mills, Inc.* v. *Rose Mills, Inc.,* 25 F.R.D. 9 (E.D. Pa. 1960)—discovery available only in court proceedings under Arbitration Act, not in arbitration proceeding proper; *Penn Tanker Co. of Delaware* v. *C.H.Z. Rolimpez, Warszawa,* 199 F. Supp. 716 (S.D.N.Y. 1961)—court had ordered arbitration and after arbitrators were selected, respondent sought court order for discovery. The court denied the request, saying that it might be permitted "upon a showing of true necessity because of an exceptional situation, which this case does not appear to be" (p. 718).

There has been no lack of exceptional cases, however. Thus, in *International Assn. of H. & F. I. & A. W., L. 66* v. *Leona Lee Corp.,* 434 F.2d 192 (5th Cir. 1970), the union filed a complaint in the federal district court contending that the company had breached a settlement agreement between them to which the arbitration clause of their collective bargaining agreement applied. The court directed the parties to submit to arbitration and, among other things, provided for discovery under the Federal Rules of Civil Procedure. In affirming, the Court of Appeals declared that the district court had not erred in making "available to the parties federal discovery proceedings 'to the extent necessary for the presentation of matters submitted' " to arbitration since such order "effectuates the policy aiding arbitration" (p. 194).

In *Bigge Crane and Rigging Co.* v. *Docutel Corp.,* 371 F. Supp. 240 (E.D.N.Y. 1973), plaintiff subcontractor sued the general contractor, among others, to recover payment of monies remaining due for its work on a baggage-handling system for defendant Pan American World Airways. Defendant general contractor moved to stay the suit pending arbitration, and the plaintiff thereupon moved to depose various officials of defendant and to inspect defendant's correspondence, records, and other documents. The court directed arbitration and granted a stay of the trial in the meantime, "without prejudice" to the rights of the parties "to utilize the pretrial discovery proceedings of the Federal Rules of Civil Procedure in a manner which does not delay the course of arbitration" (p. 246). The court noted that federal courts had taken different positions on this issue citing, in addition to some of the cases discussed above, *Steamship Co. of 1949, Inc.* v. *China Union Lines*, 123 F. Supp. 802 (S.D.N.Y. 1954)—parties ordered to arbitration and taking of deposition directed under threat of contempt order; *Dickstein* v. *DuPont*, 320 F. Supp. 150 (D. Mass. 1970), *affd* on other grounds, 443 F.2d 783 (1st Cir. 1971)—court stayed all proceedings pending arbitration, including a motion for discovery; *International U. of E. R. & M. W.* v. *Westinghouse Elec. Corp.*, 48 F.R.D. 298 (S.D.N.Y. 1969)—discovery permitted on issue of arbitrability, not on merits; *H.K. Porter Co., Connors Div. W. Va. W.* v. *Local 37, United Steel*, 400 F.2d 691 (4th Cir. 1968)—not an abuse of discretion to quash notice of deposition relating to merits; *Ferro Union Corp.* v. *S.S. Ionic Coast*, 43 F.R.D. 11 (S.D. Tex. 1967)—discovery permitted in the exceptional circumstance that the ship was about to leave port, so that facts might be made available to inspectors. See also *Chevron Transp. Corp.* v. *Astro Vencedor Compania Naviera*, 300 F. Supp. 179 (S.D.N.Y. 1969), where the court disapproved of the *arbitrators'* failure to allow sufficient disclosure. It denied a motion to vacate an award without prejudice to petitioner's right to move to reargue on that issue alone. The court wrote (p. 181):

> The absence of statutory provision for discovery techniques in arbitration proceedings does not negate the affirmative duty of arbitrators to insure that relevant documentary evidence in the hands of one party is fully and timely made available to the other side before the hearing is closed.

In one instance, participation in pretrial discovery proceedings resulted in the waiver of the right to arbitrate, even where the right was sought to be reserved. Since the party seeking arbitration had participated in the trial as well, however—*Demsey & Associates* v. *S. S. Sea Star*, 461 F.2d 1009 (2d Cir. 1972)—a finding of waiver is readily understandable. No waiver of the right to arbitrate was found in *Hilti* v. *Oldach*, 392 F.2d 368 (1st Cir. 1968)—discovery held not "inconsistent with continued assertion of the right to arbitration" (p. 371)—or in *Carcich* v. *Rederi A/B Nordie*, 389 F.2d 692 (2d Cir. 1968)—where the party desirous of arbitration participated only in the pretrial proceedings; the court took the position that a finding of waiver depended on whether or not the participation prejudiced the other party.

In New York, section 3102(c) of the C.P.L.R. provides that "disclosure to aid in arbitration may be obtained, but only by court order." However, as the commentator in 8 Weinstein-Korn-Miller ¶7505.06 observes, it is "contemplated that disclosure devices will be sparingly used in arbitration procedures." See *Matter of MVAIC (McCabe),* 19 A.D.2d 349, 243 N.Y.S.2d 495 (1st Dept. 1963)—"Where a party agrees to the settlement of disputes by arbitration, he is deemed to have consented to a limitation of his rights and remedies to the extent necessary to give full effect to such agreement . . . Court action . . . is not justified except where shown to be absolutely necessary for the protection of the rights of a party" (p. 353); motion for stay of arbitration pending examination of victim denied; *Matter of Katz (Burkin),* 3 A.D.2d 238 (1st Dept. 1957)—motion for "examination before trial in arbitration proceeding" denied; not to be granted "except under extraordinary circumstances" (pp. 233–39); see also *Matter of First Natl. Oil Corp. (Arrieta),* 4 A.D.2d 782, 165 N.Y.S.2d 132 (2d Dept. 1957); cf. *North Amer. Rayon Corp.* v. *Putnam Mills Corp.,* 276 App. Div. 832, 93 N.Y.S.2d 728 (1st Dept. 1949), *affg* without opinion N.Y.L.J. Oct. 13, 1949, page 819, column 6 (N.Y. County)—pretrial examination "incompatible with whole purpose and methods of procedure in arbitration"; *Matter of Hooper (MVAIC,)* 42 Misc.2d 446, 248 N.Y.S.2d 255 (N.Y. County 1963)—" 'necessity rather than convenience should be the test' " for ordering disclosure; but see *RLC Electronics, Inc.* v. *American Electronics Laboratories, Inc.,* 39 A.D.2d 757, 332 N.Y.S.2d 119 (2d Dept. 1972)—where the court reversed orders denying discovery and inspection of documents and further examination of respondent and granted the relief sought; the court declared that "in order to fully protect rights of all parties and in order to narrow the issues and expedite a hearing thereof (if arbitration be warranted), a large degree of liberality should be accorded opposing parties to disclose all matters material and necessary" (p. 758); and cf. *Matter of Mins. Corp. (Panamer. Com.),* 15 A.D.2d 432, 224 N.Y.S.2d 763 (1st Dept. 1962), lv. to app. den. 12 N.Y.2d 672, *cert. denied* 372 U.S. 910—where documents called for upon the arbitration are possibly of a privileged and confidential nature, party is entitled to a judicial determination as to confidentiality "without advance disclosure to the arbitrators" (p. 434).

The courts of a number of jurisdictions other than New York have been unsympathetic to the use of discovery in connection with arbitration. See *McRae* v. *Superior Ct.,* 221 Cal. App.2d 166, 34 Cal. Rptr. 346 (Ct. App. 2d Dist., Div. 2, 1963)—where arbitration of a dispute over profits from the dissolution of a partnership had already been ordered when petitioner

sought, and was granted, an order prohibiting the taking of his deposition
for discovery purposes. The court wrote: "it would be wholly incompatible
with established policies for the law to permit the court to . . . intervene in,
and unnecessarily interfere with, the arbitration" by ordering the taking of
a deposition (p. 171); *Cavanaugh* v. *McDonnell & Co.*, 357 Mass. 452, 258
N.E.2d 561 (1970), in which plaintiff security salesman sought discovery of
defendant employer's records prior to arbitration, alleging the latter had
falsely represented the character of plaintiff's employment. The court,
indicating that it was for the arbitrators to decide the need for defendant's
records, declared that "arbitration once undertaken should continue freely
without being subjected to judicial restraint which would tend to render
the proceedings neither one thing nor the other, but transform them into
a hybrid, part judicial and part arbitrational" (p. 564); *Harleysville Mutual
Casualty Co.* v. *Adair*, 421 Pa. 141, 218 A.2d 791 (1966) in which, after
insured, injured in an automobile accident, had requested arbitration,
insurer submitted certain interrogatories to be answered by the victim.
Arbitrator ruled that interrogatories need not be answered. Insurer sought
to stay arbitration and his complaint was dismissed. The Supreme Court
stated, "When appellant [insurer], by its own contract, agreed to abide by
the rules of the American Arbitration Association, it voluntarily surrendered the right to invoke any of the procedural devices which would be
available in an action at law" (p. 794); *Lutz Eng. Co., Inc.* v. *Sterling Eng.
& Const. Co., Inc.*, 314 A.2d 8 (R.I. 1974), in which the court declared that
a complaint by a subcontractor in a suit against a general contractor for
unpaid balance on construction work seeking discovery in aid of arbitration
will not lie. But compare *Frieder* v. *Lee Myles Associates Corp.*, Case No.
75–4417 (Cir. Ct. 11th Jud. Cir. Dade County, Fla. 1975), where court
denied defendant's motion to vacate arbitrator's order requiring witness to
appear at deposition on condition that plaintiff advance costs to witness
for his appearance.

For a more exhaustive outline of the cases, authorities, and treatment of
the subject, see Page, *Pretrial Discovery and Arbitration,* N.Y.L.J. Jan. 15,
1975, page 1, columns 1, 2; Note 98 A.L.R.2d 1247.

Replevin

Lease Plan Fleet v. *Johnson Transp.*, 67 Misc.2d 822, 324 N.Y.S.2d 928
(Monroe County 1971) involved a right to replevin leased motor vehicles,
as provided in the lease, prior to and apart from the arbitration. The court,
stating that the right to retake was not a matter as to which the parties had
agreed to arbitrate, ruled that the right to retake should precede arbitration,

but the right to arbitrate would not be destroyed by the retaking of the vehicles, the lessor being liable, if found in the wrong by the arbitrator, for all damages caused by the retaking. Once the vehicles were replevied, the court said, the replevin action would be stayed pending the determination of the arbitrator. See also *Benmar Knitwear Corp.* v. *Comet Knitting Mills, Inc.,* N.Y.L.J. May 18, 1973, page 18, column 5, where the court, in a replevin action, granted the plaintiff's motion for an order of seizure, at the same time granting defendant's cross-motion for a stay of the replevin action pending arbitration. Said the court: "replevin of a chattel and arbitration are not inconsistent remedies."

Notes

[1] Vol. 1, No. 20—December 1977.
[2] Vol. 1, No. 6—June 15, 1974.
[3] Vol. 2, No. 21—March 1978.
[4] Vol. 1, No. 1—March 15, 1973.
[5] Vol. 1, No. 10—June 15, 1975.
[6] Section 78-31-12 of the Utah Code, entitled "Conservation of property pendente lite," reads: "At any time before final determination of the arbitration the court may, upon application of a party to the submission, make such order or decree or take such proceedings as it may deem necessary for the preservation of the property or for securing satisfaction of the award."
Section 8 of the U.S.A.A., insofar as pertinent, recites: "If the basis of jurisdiction be a cause of action otherwise justifiable in admiralty, then . . . the party claiming to be aggrieved may begin his [arbitration] proceeding hereunder by libel and seizure of the vessel or other property of the other party according to the usual course of admiralty proceedings, and the court shall then have jurisdiction to direct the parties to proceed with the arbitration. . ."

Construction Industry Arbitration Rules

Effective January 1, 1981

Section 1. AGREEMENT OF PARTIES—The parties shall be deemed to have made these Rules a part of their arbitration agreement whenever they have provided for arbitration under the Construction Industry Arbitration Rules. These Rules and any amendment thereof shall apply in the form obtaining at the time the arbitration is initiated.

Section 2. NAME OF TRIBUNAL—Any Tribunal constituted by the parties for the settlement of their dispute under these Rules shall be called the Construction Industry Arbitration Tribunal, hereinafter called the Tribunal.

Section 3. ADMINISTRATOR—When parties agree to arbitrate under these Rules, or when they provide for arbitration by the American Arbitration Association, hereinafter called AAA, and an arbitration is initiated hereunder, they thereby constitute AAA the administrator of the arbitration. The authority and duties of the administrator are prescribed in the agreement of the parties and in these Rules.

Section 4. DELEGATION OF DUTIES—The duties of the AAA under these Rules may be carried out through Tribunal Administrators, or such other officers or committees as the AAA may direct.

Section 5. NATIONAL PANEL OF ARBITRATORS—In cooperation with the Construction Industry Arbitration Committee, the AAA shall establish and maintain a National Panel of Construction Arbitrators, hereinafter called the Panel, and shall appoint an arbitrator or arbitrators therefrom as hereinafter provided. A neutral arbitrator selected by mutual choice of both parties or their appointees, or appointed by the AAA, is hereinafter called the arbitrator, whereas an arbitrator selected unilaterally by one party is hereinafter called the party-appointed arbitrator. The term arbitrator may hereinafter be used to refer to one arbitrator or to a Tribunal of multiple arbitrators.

Section 6. OFFICE OF TRIBUNAL—The general office of a Tribunal is the headquarters of the AAA, which may, however, assign the administration of an arbitration to any of its Regional Offices.

Section 7. INITIATION UNDER AN ARBITRATION PROVISION IN A CONTRACT—Arbitration under an arbitration provision in a contract shall be initiated in the following manner:

The initiating party shall, within the time specified by the contract, if any, file with the other party a notice of an intention to arbitrate (Demand), which notice shall contain a statement setting forth the nature of the dispute, the amount involved, and the remedy sought; and shall file two copies of said notice with any Regional Office of the AAA, together with two copies of the arbitration provisions of the contract and the appropriate filing fee as provided in Section 48 hereunder.

The AAA shall give notice of such filing to the other party. A party upon whom the demand for arbitration is made may file an answering statement in duplicate with the AAA within seven days after notice from the AAA, simultaneously sending a copy to the other party. If a monetary claim is made in the answer the appropriate administrative fee provided in the Fee Schedule shall be forwarded to the AAA with the answer. If no answer is filed within the stated time, it will be treated as a

199

denial of the claim. Failure to file an answer shall not operate to delay the arbitration.

Section 8. CHANGE OF CLAIM OR COUNTERCLAIM—After filing of the claim or counterclaim, if either party desires to make any new or different claim or counterclaim, same shall be made in writing and filed with the AAA, and a copy thereof shall be mailed to the other party who shall have a period of seven days from the date of such mailing within which to file an answer with the AAA. However, after the arbitrator is appointed no new or different claim or counterclaim may be submitted without the arbitrator's consent.

Section 9. INITIATION UNDER A SUBMISSION—Parties to any existing dispute may commence an arbitration under these Rules by filing at any Regional Office two (2) copies of a written agreement to arbitrate under these Rules (Submission), signed by the parties. It shall contain a statement of the matter in dispute, the amount of money involved, and the remedy sought, together with the appropriate filing fee as provided in the Fee Schedule.

Section 10. PRE-HEARING CONFERENCE—At the request of the parties or at the discretion of the AAA a pre-hearing conference with the administrator and the parties or their counsel will be scheduled in appropriate cases to arrange for an exchange of information and the stipulation of uncontested facts so as to expedite the arbitration proceedings.

Section 11. FIXING OF LOCALE—The parties may mutually agree on the locale where the arbitration is to be held. If any party requests that the hearing be held in a specific locale and the other party files no objection thereto within seven days after notice of the request is mailed to such party, the locale shall be the one requested. If a party objects to the locale requested by the other party, the AAA shall have power to determine the locale and its decision shall be final and binding.

Section 12. QUALIFICATIONS OF ARBITRATOR—Any arbitrator appointed pursuant to Section 13 or Section 15 shall be neutral, subject to disqualification for the reasons specified in Section 19. If the agreement of the parties names an arbitrator or specifies any other method of appointing an arbitrator, or if the parties specifically agree in writing, such arbitrator shall not be subject to disqualification for said reasons.

Section 13. APPOINTMENT FROM PANEL—If the parties have not appointed an arbitrator and have not provided any other method of appointment, the arbitrator shall be appointed in the following manner: Immediately after the filing of the Demand or Submission, the AAA shall submit simultaneously to each party to the dispute an identical list of names of persons chosen from the Panel. Each party to the dispute shall have seven days from the mailing date in which to cross off any names to which it objects, number the remaining names to indicate the order of preference, and return the list to the AAA. If a party does not return the list within the time specified, all persons named therein shall be deemed acceptable. From among the persons who have been approved on both lists, and in accordance with the designated order of mutual preference, the AAA shall invite the acceptance of an arbitrator to serve. If the parties fail to agree upon any of the persons named, or if acceptable arbitrators are unable to act, or if for any other reason the appointment cannot be made from the submitted lists, the AAA shall have the power to make the appointment from other members of the Panel without the submission of any additional lists.

Section 14. DIRECT APPOINTMENT BY PARTIES—If the agreement of the parties names an arbitrator or specifies a method of appointing an arbitrator, that designation or method shall be followed. The notice of appointment, with name and address of such arbitrator, shall be filed with the AAA by the appointing party. Upon the request of any such appointing party, the AAA shall submit a list of members of the Panel from which the party may make the appointment.

If the agreement specifies a period of time within which an arbitrator shall be appointed, and any party fails to make such appointment within that period, the AAA shall make the appointment.

If no period of time is specified in the agreement, the AAA shall notify the parties to make the appointment, and if within seven days after mailing of such notice such arbitrator has not been so appointed, the AAA shall make the appointment.

Section 15. APPOINTMENT OF ARBITRATOR BY PARTY-APPOINTED ARBITRATORS—If the parties have appointed their party-appointed arbitrators or if either or both of them have been appointed as provided in Section 14, and have authorized such arbitrator to appoint an arbitrator within a specified time and no appointment is made within such time or any agreed extension thereof, the AAA shall appoint an arbitrator who shall act as Chairperson.

If no period of time is specified for appointment of the third arbitrator and the party-appointed arbitrators do not make the appointment within seven days from the date of the appointment of the last party-appointed arbitrator, the AAA shall appoint the arbitrator who shall act as Chairperson.

If the parties have agreed that their party-appointed arbitrators shall appoint the arbitrator from the Panel, the AAA shall furnish to the party-appointed arbitrators, in the manner prescribed in Section 13, a list selected from the Panel, and the appointment of the arbitrator shall be made as prescribed in such Section.

Section 16. NATIONALITY OF ARBITRATOR IN INTERNATIONAL ARBITRATION—If one of the parties is a national or resident of a country other than the United States, the arbitrator shall, upon the request of either party, be appointed from among the nationals of a country other than that of any of the parties.

Section 17. NUMBER OF ARBITRATORS—If the arbitration agreement does not specify or the parties are unable to agree as to the number of arbitrators, the dispute shall be heard and determined by three arbitrators, unless the AAA, in its discretion, directs that a single arbitrator or a greater number of arbitrators be appointed.

Section 18. NOTICE TO ARBITRATOR OF APPOINTMENT—Notice of the appointment of the arbitrator, whether mutually apppointed by the parties or appointed by the AAA, shall be mailed to the arbitrator by the AAA, together with a copy of these Rules, and the signed acceptance of the arbitrator shall be filed prior to the opening of the first hearing.

Section 19. DISCLOSURE AND CHALLENGE PROCEDURE—A person appointed as neutral arbitrator shall disclose to the AAA any circumstances likely to affect his or her impartiality, including any bias or any financial or personal interest in the result of the arbitration or any past or present relationship with the parties or their counsel. Upon receipt of such information from such arbitrator or other source, the AAA shall communicate such information to the parties, and, if it deems it appropriate to do so, to the arbitrator and others. Thereafter, the AAA shall determine whether the arbitrator should be disqualified and shall inform the parties of its decision, which shall be conclusive.

Section 20. VACANCIES—If any arbitrator should resign, die, withdraw, refuse, be disqualified or be unable to perform the duties of office, the AAA shall, on proof satisfactory to it, declare the office vacant. Vacancies shall be filled in accordance with the applicable provision of these Rules. In the event of a vacancy in a panel of neutral arbitrators, the remaining arbitrator or arbitrators may continue with the hearing and determination of the controversy, unless the parties agree otherwise.

Section 21. TIME AND PLACE—The arbitrator shall fix the time and place for each hearing. The AAA shall mail to each party notice thereof at least five days in advance, unless the parties by mutual agreement waive such notice or modify the terms thereof.

Section 22. REPRESENTATION BY COUNSEL—Any party may be represented by counsel. A party intending to be so represented shall notify the other party and the AAA of the name and address of counsel at least three days prior to the date set for the hearing at which counsel is first to appear. When an arbitration is initiated by counsel, or where an attorney replies for the other party, such notice is deemed to have been given.

Section 23. STENOGRAPHIC RECORD—The AAA shall make the necessary arrangements for the taking of a stenographic record whenever such record is requested by a party. The requesting party or parties shall pay the cost of such record as provided in Section 50.

Section 24. INTERPRETER—The AAA shall make the necessary arrangements for the services of an interpreter upon the request of one or both parties, who shall assume the cost of such services.

Section 25. ATTENDANCE AT HEARINGS—Persons having a direct interest in the arbitration are entitled to attend hearings. The arbitrator shall otherwise have the power to require the retirement of any witness or witnesses during the testimony of other witnesses. It shall be discretionary with the arbitrator to determine the propriety of the attendance of any other persons.

Section 26. ADJOURNMENTS—The arbitrator may adjourn the hearing, and must take such adjournment when all of the parties agree thereto.

Section 27. OATHS—Before proceeding with the first hearing or with the examination of the file, each arbitrator may take an oath of office, and if required by law, shall do so. The arbitrator may require witnesses to testify under oath administered by any duly qualified person or, if required by law or demanded by either party, shall do so.

Section 28. MAJORITY DECISION—Whenever there is more than one arbitrator, all decisions of the arbitrators must be by at least a majority. The award must also be made by at least a majority unless the concurrence of all is expressly required by the arbitration agreement or by law.

Section 29. ORDER OF PROCEEDINGS—A hearing shall be opened by the filing of the oath of the arbitrator, where required, and by the recording of the place, time and date of the hearing, the presence of the arbitrator and parties, and counsel, if any, and by the receipt by the arbitrator of the statement of the claim and answer, if any.

The arbitrator may, at the beginning of the hearing, ask for statements clarifying the issues involved.

The complaining party shall then present its claims, proofs and witnesses, who shall submit to questions or other examination. The defending party shall then present its defenses, proofs and witnesses, who shall submit to questions or other examination. The arbitrator may vary this procedure but shall afford full and equal opportunity to the parties for the presentation of any material or relevant proofs.

Exhibits, when offered by either party, may be received in evidence by the arbitrator.

The names and addresses of all witnesses and exhibits in order received shall be made a part of the record.

Section 30. ARBITRATION IN THE ABSENCE OF A PARTY—Unless the law provides to the contrary, the arbitration may proceed in the absence of any party, who, after due notice, fails to be present or fails to obtain an adjournment. An award shall not be made solely on the default of a party. The arbitrator shall require the party who is present to submit such evidence as deemed necessary for the making of an award.

Section 31. EVIDENCE—The parties may offer such evidence as they desire and shall produce such additional evidence as the arbitrator may deem necessary to an understanding and determination of the dispute. An arbitrator authorized by law to subpoena witnesses or documents may do so upon the request of any party, or independently. The arbitrator shall be the judge of the admissibility of the evidence offered and conformity to legal rules of evidence shall not be necessary. All evidence shall be taken in the presence of all of the arbitrators and all of the parties, except where any of the parties is absent in default or has waived his or her right to be present.

Section 32. EVIDENCE BY AFFIDAVIT AND FILING OF DOCUMENTS— The arbitrator may receive and consider the evidence of witnesses by affidavit, giving it such weight as seems appropriate after consideration of any objections made to its admission.

All documents not filed with the arbitrator at the hearing, but arranged for at the hearing or subsequently by agreement of the parties, shall be filed with the AAA for transmission to the arbitrator. All parties shall be afforded opportunity to examine such documents.

Section 33. INSPECTION OR INVESTIGATION—An arbitrator finding it necessary to make an inspection or investigation in connection with the arbitration shall direct the AAA to so advise the parties. The arbitrator shall set the time and the AAA shall notify the parties thereof. Any party who so desires may be present at such inspection or investigation. In the event that one or both parties are not present at the inspection or investigation, the arbitrator shall make a verbal or written report to the parties and afford them an opportunity to comment.

Section 34. CONSERVATION OF PROPERTY—The arbitrator may issue such orders as may be deemed necessary to safeguard the property which is the subject matter of the arbitration without prejudice to the rights of the parties or to the final determination of the dispute.

Section 35. CLOSING OF HEARINGS—The arbitrator shall specifically inquire of the parties whether they have any further proofs to offer or witnesses to be heard. Upon receiving negative replies, the arbitrator shall declare the hearings closed and a minute thereof shall be recorded. If briefs are to be filed, the hearings shall be declared closed as of the final date set by the arbitrator for the receipt of briefs. If documents are to be filed as provided for in Section 32 and the date set for their receipt is later than that set for the receipt of briefs, the later date shall be the date of closing the hearing. The time limit within which the arbitrator is required to make an award shall commence to run, in the absence of other agreements by the parties, upon the closing of the hearings.

Section 36. REOPENING OF HEARINGS—The hearings may be reopened by the arbitrator at will, or upon application of a party at any time before the award is made. If the reopening of the hearing would prevent the making of the award within the specific time agreed upon by the parties in the contract out of which the controversy has arisen, the matter may not be reopened, unless the parties agree upon the extension of such time limit. When no specific date is fixed in the contract, the arbitrator may reopen the hearings, and the arbitrator shall have thirty days from the closing of the reopened hearings within which to make an award.

Section 37. WAIVER OF ORAL HEARINGS—The parties may provide, by written agreement, for the waiver of oral hearings. If the parties are unable to agree as to the procedure, the AAA shall specify a fair and equitable procedure.

Section 38. WAIVER OF RULES—Any party who proceeds with the arbitration after knowledge that any provision or requirement of these Rules has not been complied with and who fails to state an objection thereto in writing, shall be deemed to have waived the right to object.

Section 39. EXTENSIONS OF TIME—The parties may modify any period of time by mutual agreement. The AAA for good cause may extend any period of time established by these Rules, except the time for making the award. The AAA shall notify the parties of any such extension of time and its reason therefor.

Section 40. COMMUNICATION WITH ARBITRATOR AND SERVING OF NOTICES—There shall be no communication between the parties and an arbitrator other than at oral hearings. Any other oral or written communications from the parties to the arbitrator shall be directed to the AAA for transmittal to the arbitrator.

Each party to an agreement which provides for arbitration under these Rules shall be deemed to have consented that any papers, notices or process necessary or proper for the initiation or continuation of an arbitration under these Rules and for any court action in connection therewith or for the entry of judgment on any award made thereunder may be served upon such party by mail addressed to such party or its attorney at the last known address or by personal service, within or without the state wherein the arbitration is to be held (whether such party be within or without the United States of America), provided that reasonable opportunity to be heard with regard thereto has been granted such party.

Section 41. TIME OF AWARD—The award shall be made promptly by the arbitrator and, unless otherwise agreed by the parties, or specified by law, not later than thirty days from the date of closing the hearings, or if oral hearings have been waived, from the date of transmitting the final statements and proofs to the arbitrator.

Section 42. FORM OF AWARD—The award shall be in writing and shall be signed either by the sole arbitrator or by at least a majority if there be more than one. It shall be executed in the manner required by law.

Section 43. SCOPE OF AWARD—The arbitrator may grant any remedy or relief which is just and equitable and within the terms of the agreement of the parties. The arbitrator, in the award, shall assess arbitration fees and expenses as provided in Sections 48 and 50 equally or in favor of any party and, in the event any administrative fees or expenses are due the AAA, in favor of the AAA.

Section 44. AWARD UPON SETTLEMENT—If the parties settle their dispute during the course of the arbitration, the arbitrator, upon their request, may set forth the terms of the agreed settlement in an award.

Section 45. DELIVERY OF AWARD TO PARTIES—Parties shall accept as legal delivery of the award the placing of the award or a true copy thereof in the mail by the AAA, addressed to such party or its attorney at the last known address or by personal service, within or without the state wherein the arbitration is to be held (whether such party be within or without the United States of America), provided that reasonable opportunity to be heard with regard thereto has been granted such party.

Section 46. RELEASE OF DOCUMENTS FOR JUDICIAL PROCEEDINGS—The AAA shall, upon the written request of a party, furnish to such party, at its expense, certified facsimiles of any papers in the AAA's possession that may be required in judicial proceedings relating to the arbitration.

Section 47. APPLICATIONS TO COURT—No judicial proceedings by a party relating to the subject matter of the arbitration shall be deemed a waiver of the party's right to arbitrate.

The AAA is not a necessary party in judicial proceedings relating to the arbitration.

Parties to these Rules shall be deemed to have consented that judgment upon the award rendered by the arbitrator(s) may be entered in any Federal or State Court having jurisdiction thereof.

Section 48. ADMINISTRATIVE FEES—As a nonprofit organization, the AAA shall prescribe an administrative fee schedule and a refund schedule to compensate it for the cost of providing administrative services. The schedule in effect at the time of filing or the time of refund shall be applicable.

The administrative fees shall be advanced by the initiating party or parties in accordance with the administrative fee schedule, subject to final apportionment by the arbitrator in the award.

When a matter is withdrawn or settled, the refund shall be made in accordance with the refund schedule.

The AAA, in the event of extreme hardship on the part of any party, may defer or reduce the administrative fee.

Section 49. FEE WHEN ORAL HEARINGS ARE WAIVED—Where all oral hearings are waived under Section 37 the Administrative Fee Schedule shall apply.

Section 50. EXPENSES—The expenses of witnesses for either side shall be paid by the party producing such witnesses.

The cost of the stenographic record, if any is made, and all transcripts thereof, shall be prorated equally between the parties ordering copies unless they shall otherwise agree and shall be paid for by the responsible parties directly to the reporting agency.

All other expenses of the arbitration, including required traveling and other expenses of the arbitrator and of AAA representatives, and the expenses of any witness or the cost of any proofs produced at the direct request of the arbitrator, shall be borne equally by the parties, unless they agree otherwise, or unless the arbitrator in the award assesses such expenses or any part thereof against any specified party or parties.

Section 51. ARBITRATOR'S FEE—Unless the parties agree to terms of compensation, members of the National Panel of Construction Arbitrators will serve without compensation for the first two days of service.

Thereafter, compensation shall be based upon the amount of service involved and the number of hearings. An appropriate daily rate and other arrangements will be discussed by the administrator with the parties and the arbitrator(s). If the parties fail to agree to the terms of compensation, an appropriate rate shall be established by the AAA, and communicated in writing to the parties.

Any arrangement for the compensation of an arbitrator shall be made through the AAA and not directly by the arbitrator with the parties. The terms of compensation of neutral arbitrators on a Tribunal shall be identical.

Section 52. DEPOSITS—The AAA may require the parties to deposit in advance such sums of money as it deems necessary to defray the expense of the arbitration, including the arbitrator's fee if any, and shall render an accounting to the parties and return any unexpended balance.

Section 53. INTERPRETATION AND APPLICATION OF RULES—The arbitrator shall interpret and apply these Rules insofar as they relate to the arbitrator's powers and duties. When there is more than one arbitrator and a difference arises among them concerning the meaning or application of any such Rules, it shall be decided by a majority vote. If that is unobtainable, either an arbitrator or a party may refer the question to the AAA for final decision. All other Rules shall be interpreted and applied by the AAA.

Construction Industry Mediation Rules

Effective February 1, 1980

1. AGREEMENT OF PARTIES—The parties shall be deemed to have made these rules a part of their agreement whenever, by stipulation or in their contract, they have provided for mediation of existing or future disputes under AAA auspices or under these rules.

2. INITIATION OF MEDIATION—Any party or parties to a dispute may initiate mediation by filing a written request for mediation pursuant to these rules.

3. REQUEST FOR MEDIATION—A request for mediation shall contain a brief statement of the nature of the dispute and the names and addresses of all parties to the dispute. The initiating party shall simultaneously file two (2) copies of the request with the AAA and one copy with every other party to the dispute and every other person reasonably expected to have a direct financial interest in the outcome of the dispute.

4. RESPONSE TO REQUEST FOR MEDIATION—Each person who receives a request for mediation shall advise the AAA of his willingness to mediate within twenty (20) days after the date of mailing of the mediation request and the AAA shall so advise all of the other parties.

5. APPOINTMENT OF MEDIATOR—Based upon the nature of the issues in dispute and the preferences of the parties, the AAA shall appoint one or more qualified mediators to serve. In all instances, a single mediator will be appointed unless the parties agree otherwise, or the nature of the issues requires the appointment of a larger number. If the agreement of the parties names a mediator or specifies a method of appointing a mediator, that designation or method shall be followed.

6. QUALIFICATIONS OF A MEDIATOR—Any mediator appointed shall be a member of the AAA's Construction Mediation Panel, with expertise in the area of the dispute and knowledgeable in the mediation process.

No person shall serve as a mediator in any dispute in which that person has any financial or personal interest in the result of the mediation, except by consent of the parties. Prior to accepting an appointment, the prospective mediator shall disclose any circumstances likely to create a presumption of bias or prevent prompt meetings with the parties. Upon receipt of such information, the AAA shall either replace the mediator or immediately communicate the information to the parties for their comments. If the appointed mediator is unable to serve promptly, the AAA is authorized to appoint another mediator.

7. TIME AND PLACE OF MEDIATION—The mediator, with the agreement of the parties or at his own initiative, shall fix the time of each mediation session. The mediation will be held at the construction site, or at the nearest regional office of the AAA, or at any other convenient location agreeable to the mediator and the parties.

8. AUTHORITY OF MEDIATOR—The mediator is authorized to conduct joint and separate meetings with the parties and to make oral recommendations for settlement. Whenever necessary, the mediator may also obtain expert advice concerning technical aspects of the dispute, provided the parties agree and assume the expense of obtaining such advice. Arrangements for such advice shall be made by the AAA.

The mediator is authorized to end the mediation whenever, in his judgment, further efforts at mediation would not contribute to a solution of the dispute between the parties.

Normally, mediators do not write reports of the mediation process, unless the parties agree otherwise.

9. PRIVACY—The mediator shall maintain the privacy of the mediation effort. Nothing that transpires during the mediation proceeding is intended in any way to affect the rights or prejudice the position of any of the parties to the dispute in any later arbitration, litigation, or proceeding.

10. NO STENOGRAPHIC RECORD—There shall be no stenographic record of the mediation process.

11. EXPENSES—The expenses of witnesses for either side shall be paid by the party producing such witnesses. All other expenses of the mediation, including required travelling and other expenses of the mediator and representatives of the AAA, and the expenses of any witness, or the cost of any proofs or expert advice produced at the direct request of the mediator, shall be borne equally by the parties unless they agree otherwise.

American Arbitration Association
Regional Offices

ATLANTA (30303), India Johnson
100 Peachtree Street, N.W.

BOSTON (02108), Richard M. Reilly
294 Washington Street

CHARLOTTE (28218), John A. Ramsey
3235 Eastway Drive

CHICAGO (60601), Anne L. Draznin
180 N. LaSalle Street

CINCINNATI (45202), Philip S. Thompson
2308 Carew Tower

CLEVELAND (44114), Earle C. Brown
215 Euclid Avenue

DALLAS (75201), Helmut O. Wolff
1607 Main Street

DETROIT (48226), Mary A. Bedikian
1234 City National Bank Building

GARDEN CITY, N.Y. (11530), Mark A. Resnick
585 Stewart Avenue

HARTFORD (06103), J. Robert Haskell
37 Lewis Street

LOS ANGELES (90020), Jerrold L. Murase
443 Shatto Place

MIAMI (33129), René Grafals
2250 S.W. 3rd Avenue

MINNEAPOLIS (55402), James R. Deye
510 Foshay Tower

NEW JERSEY (Somerset 08873), Richard Naimark
1 Executive Drive

NEW YORK (10020), George H. Friedman
140 West 51st Street

PHILADELPHIA (19102), Arthur R. Mehr
1520 Locust Street

PHOENIX (85004), John M. Rice
222 North Central Avenue

PITTSBURGH (15222), John F. Schano
221 Gateway Four

SAN DIEGO (92101), John E. Scrivner
530 Broadway

SAN FRANCISCO (94108), Charles A. Cooper
445 Bush Street

SEATTLE (98104), Neal M. Blacker
811 First Avenue

SYRACUSE (13202), Deborah A. Brown
720 State Tower Building

WASHINGTON, D.C. (20036), Garylee Cox
1730 Rhode Island Avenue, N.W.

WHITE PLAINS, N.Y. (10601), Marion J. Zinman
34 South Broadway

INDEX

AAA CONSTRUCTION FILM

REMEMBER THE MAIN:
An Introduction to
Construction Arbitration

Animation is combined with an actual arbitration hearing in this construction training film from the AAA. Designed to introduce the viewer to arbitration, the film also explores in detail questions arising out of a typical hearing.

"Herman," a small animated figure, discovers, through his discussions with the film's announcer and the arbitration panel itself, how simple it is to submit a case to arbitration and how the American Arbitration Association expedites cases through such procedures as the prehearing conference. Along the way, he sees an arbitration panel handling a challenge raised at the hearing about one of its members' impartiality and learns about arbitral authority both at the hearing and in the rendering of an award.

This film will be of special interest to owners, contractors, design professionals, and subcontractors—all those who now participate or plan to participate in arbitration as advocates or as arbitrators.

16mm SOUND/COLOR, 22 minutes, purchase price $450, rental charge $75 per showing. $50 dicount on purchase for AAA dues-paying members. DISCUSSION GUIDE.

ABOUT THE DISCUSSION GUIDE

Key points introduced in *Remember the Main,* such as the scope of arbitrators' authority, rules of evidence in arbitration, and the form and content of an award, are further developed in the accompanying Discussion Guide. Used in combination, the film and guide serve as an introductory training program on the procedures of construction arbitration.